POLITICAL REFORMISM IN MEXICO

AN OVERVIEW OF CONTEMPORARY MEXICAN POLITICS

STEPHEN D. MORRIS

LYNNE
RIENNER
PUBLISHERS

BOULDER
LONDON

Published in the United States of America in 1995 by
Lynne Rienner Publishers, Inc.
1800 30th Street, Boulder, Colorado 80301

and in the United Kingdom by
Lynne Rienner Publishers, Inc.
3 Henrietta Street, Covent Garden, London WC2E 8LU

Library of Congress Cataloging-in-Publication Data
Morris, Stephen D., 1957–
   Political reformism in Mexico : an overview of contemporary
Mexican politics / Stephen D. Morris.
      p. cm.
   Includes bibliographical references and index.
   ISBN 1-55587-572-6 (alk. paper)
   ISBN 1-55587-594-7 (pbk. : alk. paper)
   1. Mexico—Politics and government—1970–1988. 2. Mexico—
Politics and government—1988–   I. Title.
JL1281.M67   1995
320.972'09'048—dc20   95-3472
                                                         CIP

British Cataloguing in Publication Data
A Cataloguing in Publication record for this book
is available from the British Library.

Printed and bound in the United States of America

The paper used in this publication meets the requirements
of the American National Standard for Permanence of
Paper for Printed Library Materials Z39.48-1984.

5 4 3 2 1

To my parents,
Gaye and James,
in honor of their golden wedding anniversary

Contents

Tables and Figures

Tables

Figures

Preface

As an observer of Mexican politics, I, like so many others, was swept away by the political hysteria of 1988. Exciting things were happening in the country both before and after the presidential election. Cuauhtémoc Cárdenas, with his noncharismatic charisma, seemed to excite the nation like never before. Opposition to the PRI-led regime seemed strong, united, and determined. Mexico, in short, seemed poised on the brink of change. Even the incoming president, Carlos Salinas, touted the beginning of the end of the Mexican political system as we knew it. Most agreed. But we were wrong, or at least not totally right: rather than disintegrate, collapse, suffer, or enjoy fundamental change, the old system survived—and even recovered a dose of its pre-1988 vitality.

If we critically explored the possible source of the error, we could learn more from our misses than our hits. For me, the failed forecast indicated wide gaps in my understanding of Mexican politics and the nature of political change. This pushed me to examine in greater detail not only the events and suppositions underlying the prediction, but also the erroneous forecasts of political change littering Mexican history and the remarkable processes of change taking place at that time in other parts of the world. Meanwhile, events in Mexico continued to enthrall as the possibility that change could take place at any time haunted the search for answers.

Research on this project consumed a number of years. During this time, I benefited from the help of a variety of institutions and a score of individuals. An internal research grant from the Graduate School of the University of South Alabama in 1990, a Fulbright Lecturing Award during the 1991–1992 academic year, and summer grants from the Institute of Economic and Regional Studies (INESER) of the University of Guadalajara in 1993 and 1994 greatly facilitated research in Mexico. The Fulbright grant, especially, allowed me the opportunity to link myself to INESER and lecture on global changes of the times while conducting my research. I am grateful to the people behind these institutional supports.

Many friends and colleagues also facilitated the research. Thanks go to Jesús Arroyo, Javier Hurtado, Javier Medina, César Morones, Sergio González, Alma Martínez, and Jaime Sánchez of the University of Guadalajara. I also appreciate the kind help of Lillie Anderson, my sister-in-law Verónica Díaz Solórzano, Samuel Fisher, Kenny Williams, and Anne Walton, all of the University of South Alabama. A thank you to Roderic Camp at Tulane, Joseph Klesner at Kenyon College, and John T Passé-Smith at the University of Central Arkansas for providing data, listening to ideas, and commenting on the project. My friend and colleague Richmond Brown at South Alabama diligently read and provided comments on various drafts of the chapters. Both his friendship and help are very much appreciated. Finally, as in whatever I do, I wish to thank my wife, Celina, and my children, David and Tania, for their help, patience, and love. Despite the help of these people, I alone am responsible for the contents and translations . . . and any predictions the study makes regarding the future of Mexican politics.

Introduction

Political Reform
and Political Change

The 1980s wrought crisis and transformation throughout Eastern Europe and Latin America. Ravaged by debt, structural inefficiencies, bloated state sectors, rampant corruption, and a hostile global environment, national economies deteriorated as the pillars of long-standing authoritarian rule weakened. The scope of change rivaled the depths of the crisis. The Berlin Wall crumbled, communist and military rule evaporated, entrenched dictators like Ceauşescu, Honecker, Jakes, Krasner, Pinochet, and Stroessner stepped down, and the Soviet state disintegrated. Yet, despite similar pressures, Mexico's authoritarian regime survived with its basic components—corporatism, limited pluralism, one-party hegemony, and presidentialism—largely intact. Why did such profound transformations occur in such dissimilar settings? Why the decade of the 1980s? Why were hardliners like Ceauşescu and Pinochet as well as soft-line reformists like Gorbachev unable to weather the storm? And what enabled Mexico's regime to withstand the intense pressures and forestall breakdown? Or will the Mexican regime soon succumb to the fate of other authoritarian regimes?

Research Questions

This study explores the nature of political reformism in Mexico and focuses on one overriding theoretical question: Do political reforms unleash the forces driving fundamental political change or, instead, alleviate the pressures for change? Is it true, as Alexis de Tocqueville once suggested, that "the most perilous moment for a bad government is one when it seeks to mend its ways"?[1]

This issue, to be sure, is hardly novel, echoing loudly in the practitioner's debate over the appropriate means to bring about political change. Is it more productive to push for change from within the system in a pragmatic manner or to struggle for change from outside the system by confronting it? Confrontationalists decry gradualists as unwittingly coopted by the existing system and thereby as contributors to its staying power;

gradualists label the confrontationalists as extremists and opportunists who block constructive change. Hence, the two agree not only that change is needed, but also that "the other" actually does more to prevent than foster it.

Despite the historic and practical debate, this Machiavellian dilemma has drawn little empirical attention. An inclination toward the polarities of stability and revolution has prevented mainstream comparative analysis from offering much to help account for the dynamic processes of reformism or identify the conditions under which the difficult process might be tamed. Samuel Huntington and Albert Hirschman provided critical insights into the dilemmas shaping political and economic reformism more than a generation ago, but few pursued their early cues.[2] Contemporary studies of democratization by Terry Lynn Karl, Guillermo O'Donnell, Adam Przeworski, Philip Schmitter, and many others explore key dimensions of the process but leave open a wide range of questions.[3] O'Donnell and Schmitter, for instance, while recognizing the possibility of liberalizing an authoritarian regime without undergoing democratization, as Mexico has apparently done, provide little insight into such cases or identify the decisive factors involved. Almost by definition studies of democratization tend to exclude those cases where reformism has successfully staved off democratic change.

As with mainstream work, regional studies also fall short in providing many answers. Theories born during Latin America's staunchly authoritarian 1970s fail to provide even a useful framework for interpreting the "new democracies" of the 1980s. The democratizing trends thus have contributed to a break in the analysis, forcing a renaissance of older theories like modernization.[4] Previous work on Eastern European politics also provides few cues and has been similarly cast aside. As Peter Zwick notes, the old model of Soviet politics "did not predict . . . the 'collapse of communism' . . . tell us why the changes . . . are occurring now [or] help us to anticipate the shape of the system to come."[5]

The paucity of analysis on reformism as a process may reflect the rarity of cases. Huntington stated categorically years back that due to the practical, political difficulties involved in controlling the process, "reform is rare," even rarer than revolution.[6] But surely that is no longer the case. During the last quarter of the twentieth century, reformism has replaced "revolution in most regions of the world as the preferred mode of political activists for effecting change."[7] The incredible changes of the 1980s were basically nonviolent, featuring a string of politicians actually "reforming themselves out of power."

To shed some light on this broad theoretical issue, this book concentrates on three questions relating to Mexico. Each reflects on Mexico's seeming political uniqueness vis-à-vis other countries. The first ponders the historic ability of Mexico's authoritarian regime to surmount periodic political crises: Mexico's so-called historic exceptionalism. Political crisis, as we will see, has often wracked Mexico's political system, threatening the regime's survival while producing endless predictions of its demise. Yet the regime has proved sufficiently capable to surmount the challenges. What accounts for this adaptive capacity or, when viewed from a different angle, this proven ability to use reforms to escape the pressures driving fundamental changes in the nature of the regime and/or the configuration of the state?

The second question centers on Mexico's exceptional reformist record marking the contemporary period: the ability of the regime to surmount the multiple challenges posed during the 1980s and early 1990s. As noted, in most authoritarian regimes of Latin America and Eastern Europe, crisis and reform unleashed the forces of fundamental regime change. Despite significant and important differences, most countries walked the liberalization/democratization plank, plunging headlong into new waters. But by 1994 Mexico's political system, though tattered, bruised, and mildly altered, remained virtually intact. Uncovering how or why reforms in other countries generated a process of fundamental political breakdown, whereas those in Mexico forestalled such change, is critical in understanding the nature of reformism.

The third and final question pivots on Mexico's possible future exceptionalism. It asks whether the regime will undergo basic alteration in the wake of recent political and economic reforms adopted by Presidents Miguel de la Madrid Hurtado (1982–1988) and Carlos Salinas de Gortari (1988–1994), or continue to use reform successfully in "adaptive authoritarian" fashion to prevent fundamental change. This query, of course, requires speculation rooted in an understanding of Mexico's historic adaptive capacity and the mechanics and determinants of reformism itself.

The Study of Reformism

Political reformism refers here to a dynamic process of change in authoritarian regimes. In mapping out an analytical framework, I locate reformism within a broader conceptual scheme of change, explore the major concepts and forces at play, and set out some working assumptions. This section briefly and schematically provides the theoretical context that envelops the subsequent analysis of Mexico.

Along a continuum of political change, political reformism stands at an intermediate point between the extremes of the normal functioning of a political system (dynamic equilibrium) and its complete overhaul (revolution). On the one hand, change under normal governmental operations is limited, bound, and defined by the institutional setting and existing rules of the game. Under a process of reformism, however, the rules and the institutional setting themselves become the objects of change. Reformist leaders not only support such measures to try to forestall more radical threats to the system, but also garner legitimacy by promising it. Thus, while the normal functioning of a political system introduces changes within the systemic framework, reformism contemplates piecemeal changes of the system itself.

Reformism differs from revolution, on the other hand, by the degree and speed of these institutional changes. Revolution refers to a rupture and a rapid and complete change in the political and social systems. Reformism, by contrast, contains a larger degree of continuity in the system's political direction, institutions, rules, and leadership. Huntington, for example, defines reforms as "changes limited in scope and moderate in speed in leadership, policy and political institutions."[8] Oksenberg and Dickson similarly define it as an alteration in "the basis of legitimacy of the political system [and] a [redistribution of] power and authority in the constituent elements of the state."[9] Of course, the degree of continuity marking a reformist process varies considerably. In the democratization literature, for instance, a distinction is drawn between those cases in which the regime controls the process (transition through reform), where the rules break down but leadership remains (transition through extrication), and where the regime totally collapses (transition through rupture).[10]

The process of reformism itself centers on the interplay of crisis and reform. These represent the two main conceptual components of reformism. Crisis, according to Miguel Basañez, can be defined as "a process that provokes a state of *trastorno* that extends and affects various aspects of society, the politics, the economy and the culture to impede normal developments."[11] More specifically, a crisis can be considered an untenable and unstable linkage between the objective imperatives of restoring or maintaining capital accumulation or economic growth, on the one hand, and the existing domestic institutions and structures of the state, on the other. This incongruence manifests itself in a number of ways, from undermining the historic legitimizing formula of the state and weakening the mediating mechanisms of the state and society, to ripping the threads of the ruling coalition. A crisis, furthermore, reflects the dissipation of legitimacy and popular support for the regime and the system, the erosion of the efficiency of traditional modes of orchestrating consensus, and even a questioning of the regime's ideological foundations. This weakening of the regime's pillars decreases the risks inherent in opposing it and thus enhances the demands and the mobilization of key segments of society. By so doing, it significantly heightens the degree of political uncertainty.[12] Crisis, in sum, complicates political continuity and forces the regime to respond to survive.

Not all crises are equal, of course; some are easier to overcome than others. As a general guide, crisis can be differentiated by its phase, depth, and nature. Phase distinguishes primarily between the precipitating and transitional pressures for change. A precipitating crisis involves the pressures for the initial changes in the configuration of the state; a transitional crisis refers to the pressures unleashed by those initial reforms. Economic changes designed to restore growth, for instance, may enliven pressures for political change and vice versa, which fosters problems unrelated to the initial reasons for the economic changes. With what then seems to be a dynamic all its own, the transitional crisis may rapidly come to overshadow the precipitating crisis, leaving the regime struggling to survive and to chart a new course and yet unable to return to the patterns of the past.

Beyond phase, the depth of crisis refers to the degree a given problem impacts on the functioning of the system: its reach or scope. This may refer to either the initial or transitional phases of the crisis. For instance, it is common under an authoritarian regime for an economic crisis to reach deep into the nation's political pocket—depending on the level of regime legitimacy—and force the leaders to embrace change as an ally. This is not necessarily the case in more democratic regimes or authoritarian regimes with a solid historical foundation. Though voters may "throw the rascals out" in a democracy, they rarely challenge the entire system. Generally, then, the greater the depth of a crisis, the greater the degree of change needed to respond.

Finally, the nature of crisis reflects the range of options available to surmount it. This will vary not only by regime type and domestic political and economic structures, but by key international factors as well. It can generally be assumed that prosystemic reforms or perfective reforms will be adopted to respond to a given crisis. However, when such options are not available, are limited, or are ineffective, the political leaders are forced to embrace other more dangerous and potentially destabilizing reforms (prompting a serious transitional crisis). Latin America's adoption of neoliberal economic reforms in the 1980s and 1990s, for instance, was less a positive embrace of the model than a pragmatic recognition that no other options really existed. This factor of "available responses" not only differentiates the recent economic crisis from past crises, but also goes a long way in accounting for the unique policy reactions in the region.

[The antithesis of crisis is reform.] Reform refers here to any political move or change designed to temper a crisis and restore some semblance of stability and predictability to the system. Though a variety of specific political reforms will be identified and their impact traced in this book, certain characteristics of this central variable should be made clear at the outset. First, attention here centers on political reform and political change rather than economic reform. Though much attention will be given to economic crisis and reforms taking place in Mexico and beyond during the period of analysis, the central concern is on the political impact of these economic variables and how they inform and alter the political crisis. In other words, economic crisis and economic reform are treated as independent rather than dependent variables.

Second, though Huntington defines reforms in a progressive sense as change in the direction of "greater social, economic or political equality, a broadening of participation in society and polity," the term is used here simply to refer to any political adaptation to crisis.[13] A distinction between "positive" and "negative" reform measures, however, is often made. Positive reforms refer to any moves that enhance the legitimacy of the regime or the reformer's credibility, or that broaden or strengthen the regime's supporting coalition. Negative reforms, by contrast, refer to measures targeted mainly at securing or maintaining political control, or what Huntington refers to as "consolidation." Exemplified by corruption, electoral fraud, and repression, negative reforms reduce the reformer's credibility and the system's legitimacy, thereby making the reformist task even more difficult. Negative reforms have the tendency to encourage opponents to adopt a more confrontational line and can hence polarize the opposition. Still, negative reforms can be strategically critical in alleviating crisis by offsetting conjunctural pressures on the regime, or enabling the regime to buy time while other more positive measures bear fruit.

Third, reforms may assume both tangible and nontangible form. Rhetoric and promises of change, the nontangible, play a critical and prominent role in the process of reformism, since the reformist leader's ability to gain, maintain, and nurture credibility as a reformer is a key variable shaping the outcome of the process. This stems from the fact that reformist credibility tends to weaken the "confrontational" approach within society, thereby alleviating pressures for change and permitting reformers to proceed at a pace deemed appropriate to their own interests and hence less threatening to the system. Rhetoric in and of itself may at times be sufficient to overcome a crisis if it gives the impression that change is imminent, a product of the political leader's goodwill, and that such longed-for change does not require dangerous confrontation. Like magic, politics is more image than substance.

Fourth, emphasis here on political reform focuses crucially on tactics and strategy. This implies not only the type and timing of the reforms adopted, but also the means by which they are packaged and sold, the concessions needed to gain their acceptance, and the way reformers mobilize their allies and demobilize their opponents.[14] Though it is assumed that the adoption of a specific reform indicates that the perceived cost of the targeted problem outweighs the costs of the reforms (at least in the eyes of the decisionmakers), this does not mean that all reforms work out as expected. Efforts to counter declining regime legitimacy by revitalizing the political party with democratic changes or attacking corruption, for example, often have unintended consequences, making the reforms cost more than they are worth. These unexpected developments, shaped in part by the reaction of allies and opponents, lead to a retrenchment of reforms, littering the reformist process with a myriad of stop-and-go measures, unimplemented projects, and policy reversals.

Finally, the idea of reform employed here acknowledges that reforms do not necessarily resolve underlying problems; instead, they may merely assuage them, ease tensions, or buy time for the regime. Papering over a problem, in fact, may be sufficient to counteract a crisis if during the interim the pressures for change diminish. By the same token, of course, merely papering over one crisis can eventually generate another, deeper crisis situation, as Basañez aptly demonstrates in the case of Mexico.

Like crisis, reforms can be differentiated by scope and sequence. Scope (like the depth of a crisis) refers to the degree a given reform measure impacts on the functioning of the overall system: its direct and indirect, intended and unintended consequences. Some reforms may have a limited scope, affecting just a small segment of the population while alleviating the pressures for change. Other reforms, by contrast, may have an expansive scope, tending to create more pressures than they ease. The political reforms under glasnost in the Soviet Union, for example, while designed to relieve intellectual and elite pressures on the regime and pave the way for the economic reforms under perestroika, unintentionally ignited nationalist sentiments that deepened the transitional crisis.

The sequence of reforms refers, in turn, to the pattern, pace, and direction of the multiple reforms characterizing a process of reformism. The issue of sequence encompasses, for example: (1) the relative order and weight of economic versus political reforms—whether the two are pursued simultaneously, as in Latin America, or whether one dominates over another, as in Eastern Europe; (2) the path of reforms, whether they are continuous or perfunctory; and (3) the selectivity of the reforms—where and when they are applied. Sequence can be a critical variable in the success or failure of reformism. Huntington, for example, associates the reformist success of Kemal in Turkey to his ability to deal with each reform separately.[15] Similarly, the failure of the Soviet Union to tame the reformist process may have stemmed from its inability to tackle economic reforms without engaging in political change.

The dynamic process of reformism centers on the countervailing pressures and a potentially dangerous clash between continuity and change. Crisis, encapsuling the pressures for change, jeopardizes political continuity. And yet the reforms demanded by the situation collide against the entrenched interests and the inherent danger that any changes will unleash uncontrollable or unmanageable forces of disintegration. Variably referred to in the literature as the political "realities," institutional rigidities, the lurking dangers of "ungovernability," or even what Mancur Olson describes more subtly as the "distributional coalitions," these built-in rigidities make reform just as problematic as continuity.[16] Hence the reformist dilemma: Both continuity and change are inherently risky, but no other options exist.[17]

Within this volatile setting, the existing structures and institutions of the state paradoxically become both the targets of reform (and hence obstacles to survival) while remaining the pillars of political control (the means of survival). In Mexico and the Soviet Union, for example, Salinas and Gorbachev lashed out at the entrenched bureaucratic networks within the state and the party, blaming these for the nation's problems. Yet they both continued to rely on these mechanisms to maintain power and to implement reforms designed to adapt to changing internal and external conditions.

Brokering this reformist dilemma is clearly no easy task. Reformers, as Huntington cautions, "fight a two-front war against both conservative and revolutionary" factions, struggling to protect the middle ground and prevent polarization.[18] Among other pieces of advice, reformers must enlist new allies based on the reforms without (or before) losing the trust of the old; they must garner credibility as reformers without undermining the supports provided by the old and discredited system; and they must strategically outflank their opponents and keep them divided.[19] Reformers, moreover, must time the announcement and implementation of reforms to catch their opponents off guard, steamroll certain changes, or capitalize on one successful move to plot the next. Reformist leaders, in a sense then, must labor as political carpenters attempting to partially reconstruct a house while continuing to reside there. The critical question is what conditions make this feat possible? What shapes the reformist outcome?

Generally, the pushing of the crisis and the pulling of the restraints work to fashion a seemingly unpredictable and chaotic process of political change. Eventually though, the reforms either stabilize the situation or unleash further reforms and eventually more change. The outcome is shaped by the nature and scope of the crisis, the scope and sequence of the reforms, and the nature of the institutionally determined restraints. The weight of all these factors is relative, of course. In other words, the lower the pressures for change, the easier it is for even minor restraints to thwart the reforms. Limited public pressures for campaign finance reform, for example, can easily be overcome by the weight of distributional coalitions or institutional rigidities blocking change. But as popular pressure for such change intensifies, the relative weight of these rigidities diminishes, thereby making them the targets of reform. Much of the analysis of reformism thus concentrates on exploring the weight and determinants of the pressures and restraints on change, and evaluating their interaction and development.

It is assumed here that the political change taking place during a process of reformism is a product of the countervailing pressures for and the restraints on change, the nature of the system, and international forces. This implies above all that the outcome is not the product of the goodwill, intentions, or skills of the governmental leadership.[20] I assume further that political leaders seek to broker the degree of change necessary to save the system without undermining it—what Jorge Castañeda terms the "neorealist" assumption and John Bailey calls the "survival axiom."[21] Reformist leaders, in other words, seek "to change the system just enough to save it": to bend it without breaking it.

This distinction is emphasized because the personalism of reformist leaders often captures the most attention in the literature.[22] Though the decisionmaking, strategic role is critical in the study of reformism, interest here centers more on the forces determining the reformer's course of action (that which shapes his or her political will) and the intended and unintended impact of the reformist measures adopted. Reformers, after all, not only are unable to control all the critical variables shaping the process, but also seem to react to outside forces almost as often as they initiate them.

Within this context, reformism is considered successful according to the degree of continuity achieved when the crisis is alleviated. If we take this to the level of democratization, just one possible outcome of a process of reformism, this perspective views such change generally as a reformist failure or what Przeworski calls the failure of liberalization.[23] This does not mean, however, that everything changes during democratization. Even within the area of democratization, the range of continuity may be extremely large. Still, two caveats flow from the basic assumption that "you don't change unless forced to do so." The first holds that change within an authoritarian system usually comes, in a sense, at the most inopportune time: when the pressures and the risks of such change peak. Arguably the ideal moment to democratize or modernize an authoritarian regime might be during prosperous and stable times, when a reserve of legitimacy and support exists; yet history suggests the opposite. Changes in authoritarian settings, particularly Eastern Europe and Latin America, emerge during treacherous, crisis-ridden times, when the difficulties of managing the process seem the greatest. Hard times prompt hard choices.[24]

The second caveat avers that stability within an authoritarian regime will be sought at the lowest possible cost to the system itself (and, perhaps even more important, to the reformist leaders): the reformist assumption of opting for the course of least resistance. Assuming that leaders want to enforce stability, enhance predictability, and maximize continuity, even amidst change, it follows that easy options for change will prevail over other less certain or riskier ones. This basic axiom of political behavior, in turn, influences the selection, course, and pace of the reform measures.]

To briefly recap, the conceptual framework set out here to study reformism in Mexico depicts an authoritarian political system struggling to change itself in order to survive the onslaught of internal and external pressures. The path of change is a product of the interaction of those forces pushing for change and those restraining change, set within a given institutional setting and shaped by the strategic choices of the political actors. I assume that government leaders seek the course of least resistance as they attempt to balance their contradictory desires to change the system without destroying it. Yet in this process, reformers find that the dangers of not changing the system are often as great or even greater than the dangers of changing it.[Through the use of both positive and negative, tangible and intangible measures, the reformist leadership strives to alleviate the pressures while maximizing the degree of continuity. In exploring this process, I focus on the nature of the political dilemmas, the institutional or contextual factors that shape the process, and the conditions that determine the level of continuity or change.)

Methodology and Organization

The book is divided into three parts. Part 1 presents the case study of reformism in Mexico during the period 1982–1994. Chapter 1 sets out the underlying causes of Mexico's political crisis, positing a blend of secular, conjunctural, and programmatic changes that made tenuous a continuation of Mexico's authoritarian regime. Chapter 2 then looks more closely at the dilemmas within the crisis. Using a strategic choice perspective, I examine Mexico's major political actors and the risks and opportunities they faced. Chapters 3 through 6 then explore the primary efforts of the two Mexican presidents of the period to manage Mexico's political crisis and tame the reforms. Chapter 3 examines the efforts of President Miguel de la Madrid Hurtado to surmount the political repercussions of Mexico's deep economic plunge, while Chapter 4 provides a similar analysis of reformism under his successor, Carlos Salinas de Gortari. Offering a "case within a case," Chapter 5 discusses the PRI's fortunes under Salinas in the western state of Jalisco. Chapter 6 then compares the two presidential terms to yield some preliminary conclusions on the contemporary period.

Part 2 moves beyond the case to offer three complementary comparative approaches. Chapter 7 takes a regional perspective, concentrating on trends in state and local elections and the dynamic interaction of national/

subnational actors. The regional view provides greater specificity in exploring certain factors shaping reformism in Mexico, offers a means to test some hypotheses taken from the analysis at the national level, and helps highlight the role of regional factors in shaping the national reformist agenda. As we will see, it also helps broach the question of Mexico's political future.

Chapter 8 presents a comparative historical approach; contrasting Mexico's contemporary crisis/reform period with those of the past. As such, it not only provides a foundation for interpreting the regime's historic ability to withstand crisis, but also places in perspective the recent reforms and possible political futures. The historical comparison surfaces from the simple assumption that, if indeed the crisis of the contemporary period or the accompanying reforms bodes an outcome different from those of the past, then such an outcome must be shaped by basic historical differences in the nature of the current crisis or the dynamics of the reforms.

Aiming to place the case of Mexico within a broader context, Chapter 9's cross-national, comparative perspective explores Mexico's exceptionalism and hence the broader nature of reformism. The first section of the chapter explores the common international ingredients that produced a crisis not only for Mexico's authoritarian regime, but for many other regimes as well during the period.[25] The second section then contrasts Mexico's handling of the crisis with the Eastern European and Latin American patterns.

Chapter 10 Part 3, finally, draws the preceding parts of the study together and addresses some of the questions discussed in this chapter. Taking Mexico's exceptionalism as its point of departure, it draws out the general factors influencing the reformist process. Though recognizing the limitations incumbent in a case study, this concluding chapter tries to provide at least some answers that might help us in understanding both the enigmatic case of Mexico and the unique and largely unexplored political dynamic that has made the 1980s a politically historic decade. Chapter 10 concludes by looking briefly at the first one hundred days of the administration of President Ernesto Zedillo and the emergence of new political and economic crises.

Notes

1. de Tocqueville, *The Old Regime and the French Revolution*, p. 177. Huntington, *Political Order in Changing Societies*, pp. 344–396, sets out and discusses this theoretical question at some length.

2. While Huntington, *Political Order*, focuses on political reforms in the Third World, Hirschman, *Journeys Toward Progress*, explores the delicate task of promoting economic reforms in Latin America (what he coined "reformmongering").

3. Karl, "Dilemmas of Democratization"; O'Donnell and Schmitter, *Transitions from Authoritarian Rule*; and Przeworski, *Democracy and the Market*. For a good review of the democratization literature see Munck, "Democratic Transitions in Comparative Perspective."

4. For an overview on this problem, see Morris, "Regime Cycles in Latin America"; and Pye, "Political Science and the Crisis of Authoritarianism."

5. Zwick, "The Perestroika of Soviet Studies," p. 461.

6. According to Huntington, *Political Order*, p. 345, reform is rare because of "the political talents necessary to make it a reality." If we accept the fact that reformism is more common today than in the past, then we must question either whether there is indeed more political talent today or Huntington's explanation for the rarity of successful reform.

7. Oksenberg and Dickson, "The Origins, Processes and Outcomes of Great Political Reform," p. 236.

8. Huntington, *Political Order*, p. 344.

9. Oksenberg and Dickson, "Origins, Processes and Outcomes," p. 238.

10. See Munck, "Democratic Transitions."

11. Basañez, *El pulso de los sexenios*, pp. 9–10. The term "crisis" is used here in a manner similar to the one used by Camou, *Gobernabilidad y democracia*, who underscores the fluidity, unpredictability, and transitionary nature of Mexican politics since the 1980s.

12. Collier and Norden, "Strategic Choice Models of Political Change in Latin America," p. 231.

13. Huntington, *Political Order*, p. 344.

14. Both Ascher, *Scheming for the Poor*, and Hirschman, *Journeys Toward Progress*, raise this point in their strategic analyses of economic reforms in Latin America.

15. Huntington, *Political Order*, p. 348.

16. Olson, *The Rise and Decline of Nations*.

17. Many such dilemmas have been identified in the literature on Mexico. Molinar Horcasitas, *El tiempo de la legitimidad*, highlights the countervailing demands of legitimacy versus control; Bailey, *Governing Mexico*, posits the dual exigencies of preservation versus control; and Basañez, *El pulso de los sexenios*, underscores the contradictory struggle between populism and capitalism.

18. Huntington, *Political Order*, p. 344.

19. Hirschman, *Journeys Toward Progress*, p. 272.

20. This view parallels Skocpol's, *State and Social Revolution*, treatment of the outcome of revolution as unrelated to the intentions and desires of the revolutionaries and a product of broader structural and international factors.

21. Castañeda, "Cartas marcadas"; and Bailey, *Governing Mexico*, pp. 182–183.

22. Both Huntington, *Political Order*, and Oksenberg and Dickson, "Origins, Processes, and Outcomes," focus on the "political talents" and skills of the reformer in accounting for the success or failure of reformism. Though few would deny the importance of leadership, it is difficult to truly assess the role of voluntarism in any systematic way. The most prudent course, therefore, is to treat voluntarism as a residual with perhaps explanatory power only after other factors have been examined and/or discounted.

23. Przeworski, *Democracy and the Market*, pp. 59–60.

24. The pressures for political change in many Asian countries do not necessarily follow this pattern. The Asian model depicts political pressures arising more

out of economic success than economic crisis. See, for instance, Baer, "Mexico's Second Revolution: Pathways to Liberalization."

25. The global juncture also affected the United States and Europe, where new conservatives erased the residues of Keynesian welfare or New Deal politics. On the impact on these countries see, for instance, Gourevitch, *Politics in Hard Times*; Katzenstein, *Between Power and Plenty*; and Olson, *The Rise and Decline of Nations*.

1

Political Reformism
in Contemporary Mexico

1

Mexico's Political Crisis

Political crisis haunted Mexico throughout most of the 1980s and chased it into the 1990s. During this time domestic and international pressures for political change mounted, electoral opposition from the right and left waxed, scission and instability within the official party erupted, and political violence and human rights abuses escalated. Capping a pattern of electoral decline, the Partido Revolucionario Institucional (PRI) suffered its worst performance in 1988, barely gaining a majority of the national vote in elections popularly perceived as rigged. At the time, many, including the "victor," touted the "beginning of the end" of the one-party-dominant authoritarian system.

Mexico's contemporary political crisis sprang from a series of interrelated factors. In exploring the primary causal agents, this chapter posits a tripartite web of secular, conjunctural, and programmatic changes that worked to undermine the regime's basic foundations. The weakening of the regime challenged the nation's political leaders to forge a new consensus and recast the supporting structures without losing control. Discussion here centers on the three causal ingredients of the crisis and the dilemmas they fashioned.

The Secular Component

The first and deepest component of Mexico's political crisis hinged on secular changes in its society, changes that over time had eaten away at the foundations and efficiency of the political regime. By the 1980s, Mexican society was a distant cry from the one that had given birth to the modern Mexican state.

The modern Mexican state rose gradually from the ashes of Mexico's violent social revolution of 1910–1917.[1] Struggling to overcome intense competition among rival factions, the revolutionary elite had crafted by the early 1940s a pragmatic, fluid, and inclusive system.[2] Pragmatism flowed from the centralization of power in the federal executive as the president used extensive governmental and party patronage to broker competing interests and guarantee stability. No-reelection, in turn, provided the system with fluidity by preventing one set of elites from dominating others and by ensuring that competing elites would await their opportunity to shape policy and partake in the spoils of power rather than try to overthrow the system. The prohibition on reelection further bolstered the power of the presidency by weakening the capacity of competing elites to forge strong ties with a given social constituency.[3]

[While political power rested foremost with the presidency, the "official party"—originally known as the Partido Nacional Revolucionario (PNR) and then the Partido de la Revolución Mexicana (PMR) before becoming the PRI—served as the system's primary pillar, providing the regime with its inclusive framework. Formed in 1929 by former president (though de facto ruler) Plutarco Elías Calles to stabilize and prolong the power of the "revolutionary family" (and of Calles himself), the party brokered deals with military and regional revolutionary strongmen to ease the intense rivalries.[4] Later, under President Lázaro Cárdenas (1934–1940), the party broadened its reach by shaping and incorporating the nation's major peasant and labor organizations, converting these into the "official" and privileged sectors of the party.]

The government-party link was strong and mutually supportive. The government was generally biased toward the PRI and vice versa. The government aided efforts to establish party hegemony, supporting legally and otherwise the labor and peasant organizations tied to it. The government also structured the nation's political/electoral institutions in such a way as to ensure the party's dominance over the process and hence its unfettered control over the government. The state even helped shape and define the "symbolic capital" of the revolution, thereby lavishing the party with strong nationalistic appeal and ensuring its ideological hegemony.

While the president dominated both the state and the party, this state-party network dominated society. Through corporatist controls and patron-client networks, the party/government machine reached into the factory, the peasant community, the neighborhoods, the schools, and the bureaucratic offices, absorbing "institutions that should have belonged within civil society."[5] Corporate controls allowed the regime to attend to the needs of key constituencies while at the same time controlling their potential for mobilization. The government even forged a working semicorporate alliance with the nation's bourgeoisie—a group officially excluded from the party structure—guaranteeing social stability and profits in exchange for their political acquiescence.

[The corporate-based curbs on the autonomy of social organizations coupled with noncompetitive elections appropriately earned the system an authoritarian label. Yet Mexico sported what many considered a unique brand of authoritarianism, one resting more on its structured inclusiveness and revolution-inspired consensus than on repression. Even a level of pluralism flourished. Those wishing to challenge the system from outside the dominant PRI-sanctioned channels of interest articulation not only could do so, but also enjoyed legal and even financial support from the state. Opposition parties enjoyed reserved seats in the Chamber of Deputies through proportional representation. Yet the role of opposition parties and even "nonofficial" organizations like independent labor unions remained limited, seemingly strung to the condition that such participation should pose no serious challenge to the system. Even so, placed alongside the dominant corporate-based system, this complementary layer of inclusionism gave the system a needed yet minimal degree of democratic legitimacy, a channel of communication, and a critical outlet for discontent.

Time, however, gradually eroded the system's ability to incorporate society and represent their interests, exposing severe strains and wild contradictions. Advances in communications, the spread of education, the growth of industrialization, and broadening urbanization all seemed to take their toll on the political system. Development nurtured a more procedural view of political participation and democracy while weakening the appeal of the corporatist model.[6] It forged new social organizations that stood increasingly outside the existing corporate-institutional pacts, particularly among the burgeoning urban middle class, which supported the rise and proliferation of a range of nongovernmental organizations (NGOs) by the 1980s.[7]

Economic development also fed the growing demands for autonomy among once tame social forces. Business, for instance, once a minor political player operating under the clear tutelage and financial cushion of the government, by the 1970s attained a level of organizational maturity that lessened its inclination to abide its subordinate role to the government, prompting it to push for ever broader degrees of autonomy. The establishment in 1975 of the independent Consejo Coordinator Empresarial (CCE) by northern business interests as an interest organization for business separate from its corporate-structured organizations offered a clear sign that the business-government "pact" had outlived its usefulness. Even in the countryside the agricultural bourgeoisie adopted a posture that effectively ended the state's ability to direct agrarian policy based on its alliance with peasants.[8] With time, dissident currents within PRI-dominated labor unions also began to push for a stronger say, questioning labor's dependence on and subordination to the government and the party.

These structural changes produced by the process of development "overwhelmed the system's organizational capacity" and accelerated the growing gap between the system's authoritarian-corporatist framework and civil society.[9] As a result, it became increasingly difficult for the government to effectively mediate social interests through the one-party device or attend to the contradictory demands. As Pereyra argued, there emerged "a separation between what takes place on the legal institutional sphere . . . and that which occurs at the social base where diverse forces tend to organize, creating an ever more complex civil society."[10]

These secular trends thus fed the outbreak of periodic political conflict. Crises took on a variety of forms—from dissident presidential candidates within the ranks of the official party in 1940, 1946, and 1952; to labor strife in the 1940s, late 1950s, and mid-1970s; to student protests in 1968 and 1971; to capital flight in 1976. The 1968 student movement and the government's repressive response at Tlatelolco stood as a crowning monument to modernization's toll on the corporate system.[11] Even after that watershed event, the strains in state-society relations continued to wrench, leading to "a change in the balance of social forces . . . [that made] the challenge to clientelism . . . more open now than in the past."[12]

The growing gap separating the PRI's capacity to orchestrate consensus and Mexican social reality also informed electoral trends. Though the PRI continued to dominate the process and the polls and remained the only party to cover the entire nation, the party was gradually losing its grip, as shown in Figure 1.1. Increasingly, the level of abstentionism mounted as more educated voters leaned toward the opposition, and the PRI began to rely more and more on its support among rural areas and the lower socioeconomic sectors—and, when necessary, fraud—to win.[13] This nagging "crisis of representation" pointed to growing electoral difficulties for the party by the 1980s.[14]

As the secular trends fed the rise of periodic crises and chipped away at the PRI's foundations of support, Mexican presidents responded with a host of reform measures. As we will see, the responses ranged from repression, electoral fraud, and administrative changes to anticorruption campaigns, strategic political openings and liberalization, experiments with party primaries, and new government programs designed to respond to the people's economic and social needs. And though the reforms allowed the regime to muddle through, it seemed to be pushed ever closer toward a state of virtual permanent crisis management.

In sum, the secular- and structural-based decline in the PRI's capacity to orchestrate consensus suggested that development, while paradoxically a product of the stability provided by the PRI, promised to consume the party-government system and undermine that stability. The party continued to "win" elections but was really never able to arrest its structural decline or the growing import of elections, being compelled periodically to cede governmental posts and political space to opposition parties. Similarly, the system maintained its basic corporatist structure but still had to contend with the rise of independent popular movements, new civil organizations, and novel challenges from within the official labor unions, as well as an array of maturing business groups. And though it employed a range of

Figure 1.1 PRI Vote, 1946–1982

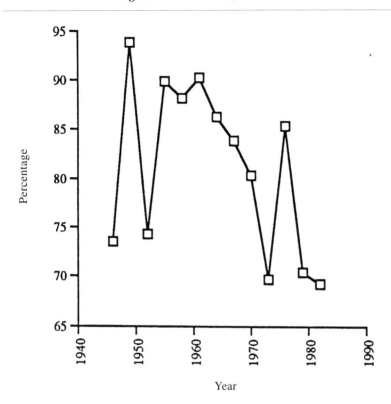

reform initiatives, the regime seemingly never escaped the dangers of dis-integration. This secular component, though present prior to the tumultuous events of the 1980s, underlay and defined the contemporary crisis.

The Conjunctural Component

The second change shaping Mexico's political crisis was a conjunctural change: economic crisis. In and of itself, the economic plunge marking the period eroded popular confidence in the political system, the PRI, and the development model. It limited the quantity of economic benefits handed out by the government to bolster stability. And it altered the regime's foundation of legitimacy. At the same time, it crystallized and magnified the secular-based difficulties just discussed.

Mexico enjoyed decades of solid economic growth, which was both a cause and effect of the nation's political stability. Popularly touted as the

"Mexican miracle," growth rates averaged over 6 percent annually from the 1940s through the 1970s. This period of sustained growth not only transformed Mexico from a rural, agrarian, and illiterate society to a more modern, industrialized, and literate nation, but also anchored the political regime, yielding a wide range of political dividends. Among its effects, sustained growth facilitated the distribution of tangible benefits or rewards to favored labor and peasant organizations incorporated within the PRI family, measures often used as "preemptive" devices to head off labor disputes and temper or weaken tendencies toward the formation of independent labor organizations.[15] Growth also provided domestic business groups with exceedingly low tax rates, high profit margins, and a steady flow of investment capital, thereby fulfilling the government's unspoken desire to keep business "out of politics." Economic growth also provided the state itself with the financial wherewithal to offer special subsidies to the growing urban and middle classes in an effort to forestall or coopt any "uncontrolled" mobilizations from below. It created an abundance of political spoils that could be employed (de jure and de facto) to both unite and discipline the elite alliance. Sustained economic growth, in sum, greased the political machine and nurtured the elite alliance.

In addition to these more tangible benefits, economic progress also served as the linchpin of the regime's political legitimacy. By the 1950s, economic growth had marginalized the nationalist and prosocialist goals of the revolutionary ideology embodied in the Constitution of 1917 and spun during the Cárdenas years. Indeed, sustained growth fashioned an image of progress that provided the regime with a reservoir of legitimacy, helping it overcome its deficiencies. As one observer notes, "We value the government's efficiency by the number of material works realized, without concerning ourselves with the methods or the costs of the apparent progress."[16]

But that was then. Following a spurt of tremendous economic growth fueled by high oil prices and cheap foreign loans from 1978 to 1981, the Mexican economy plummeted. As oil prices dipped, global recession ensued, and interest rates skyrocketed, the Mexican government went bankrupt, and the Mexican economy fell. In dizzying chain reaction, fiscal deficits, capital flight, and inflation galloped as domestic investments, imports, the peso, and real wages plummeted.[17] Sustained economic growth, in short, gave way to economic contraction. GDP fell 0.6 percent in 1982, dropping another 4.2 percent the following year. A sluggish recovery in 1984 and 1985 was short-lived as the economy fell another 3.7 percent in 1986 on the heels of an even more dramatic drop in the price of oil and the devastating Mexico City earthquakes of 1985. Though low levels of economic growth returned in 1987 (well below the levels of the Mexican miracle), the crack in the Mexican *bolsa* in the second half of the year, renewed capital flight, further devaluations, and galloping inflation continued to rock the economy.[18] As shown in Table 1.1., from 1983 to 1988, average annual economic growth stood at a mere .1 percent as inflation ate the value of wages. By 1989, per capita income was 9 percent below the 1980 level.[19]

Mexico's deep economic slide was typical of the problems faced by other Latin American countries during the period. Clearly, this "lost decade" had grave political repercussions, striking hard at the pillars of the political system and challenging the regime's adaptive capacity. First, the economic crisis undermined the people's faith in the future and, consequently, their confidence in their political system to craft it. A majority (54 percent) of those questioned in the 1986 *New York Times* national poll, for instance, felt that Mexico would *never* emerge from the depths of its economic abyss. Such growing discontent undermined the regime's ability to sustain the image of progress that had "helped to paper over the contradictions in the past" and triggered a massive wave of protests against the government and its policies as well as an electoral backlash against the PRI.[20]

Second, at perhaps a time of greatest need, the crisis curbed the flow of tangible resources that had been used in the past to finance consensus and maintain stability. The economic plunge reduced the spoils available to ensure the coherence and discipline of the elite alliance while simultaneously heightening the public's sensitivity to institutionalized abuses of power. It undermined the use of subsidies to allay popular sectors and coopt business and even intellectuals. And it threatened the tangible rewards that nourished allegiance and obedience among the party's official sectors, such as labor. The economic juncture thus seemed to strain the alliances, upset the balances, and forge an increasingly zero-sum equation

Table 1.1   **Selected Economic Indicators (Percentage Change)**

	1981	1982	1983	1984	1985	1986	1987	1988	1989
GDP	8.8	−0.6	−4.2	3.6	2.6	−3.8	1.7	1.3	3.3
Inflation (annual)	28.7	96.8	80.8	59.2	63.7	105.7	159.2	51.7	19.7
Minimum wages	1.0	−0.1	−21.9	−9.0	−1.2	−10.5	−0.2	1.8	6.3
Programmable spending	23.4	−8.9	−15.7	5.7	−5.5	−6.7	−4.7	−5.4	−6.7
Social spending	24.1	−1.3	−30.1	4.3	6.3	−8.1	−4.9	−1.1	3.6

Source: Lustig, *Mexico: The Remaking of an Economy,* pp. 40–41, 80–81.

among the many social groups that had hammered out historic pacts with the government. This tendency not only introduced instabilities, but also forced the government to make difficult choices and then grapple with their consequences. As Viviane Brachet-Marquez argues, "Because fewer goods and services can be distributed through personal favors, the battles waged to obtain such favors may become fiercer and the resulting distribution of benefits even more unequal."[21]

The economic crisis also altered the basic foundations of the regime's legitimacy: economic growth and progress. This had a twofold effect. For one, with its primary foundation of legitimacy weakened, abuses that were perhaps overlooked during good economic times became more and more intolerable, adding to the regime's growing deficit of legitimacy and support. The costs of institutionalized corruption in particular began to outweigh the political benefits, taxing further the low levels of trust the populace had for its politicians. At the same time, the erosion of its legitimizing base forced the government to seek some other criteria to justify its rule. Among the criteria adopted during the crisis were rhetorical promises of social peace and stability and, above all, pledges to democratize and allow free and open elections. Indeed, "rhetoric extolling political democracy has become the linchpin of its new legitimization efforts."[22]

Although emphasizing the electoral route to effect political change was clearly preferable to more violent or revolutionary avenues for both the government and its opponents—in other words, stressing political change by the regime's leaders to bolster legitimacy was the path of least resistance for the government—this development nonetheless further threatened regime stability and challenged the adaptive powers of the PRI-led government. Put differently, although the leaders sought through this tactic to weaken or undermine its critics by usurping the democracy issue, thereby facilitating the regime's ability to surmount the challenges at hand, it still upped the political ante. This added further pressures on the government for sweeping political changes. With opposition support bolstered by the economic crisis and the growing emphasis on elections, the opposition thus threatened to unseat the hegemonic PRI, while fraud threatened to undermine the credibility of the contest and what remained of the regime's legitimacy.[23]

The shift to a democratic criterion to legitimize the regime during a period of growing electoral opposition altered the nature of the political game and the "best strategies" for playing it. Since the PRI was not designed to contest elections but rather to "address an intragroup power struggle," the situation above all challenged the party to reconstitute and redefine itself.[24] This was particularly difficult given the secular-based erosion in the PRI's bases of support noted earlier. Still the task was clear: as President Salinas argued in March of 1988, "we have to change, or someone is going to change us."[25]

In evaluating the contemporary Mexican crisis, Judith Adler Hellman contends that quantitative changes in Mexico had, by the 1980s, produced a qualitative change in the country.[26] To be sure, the economic crisis magnified the secular dimension of the crisis as the economic plunge triggered discontent, multiplied the gamut of societal organizations operating at the margins of government's control, and intensified their demands.[27] The wave of crisis-induced discontent politicized society and overtaxed the already beleaguered structures of demand management located within the state and the PRI, spilling over into the streets, the barrios, and, increasingly, the electoral ring. Labor protests, both from within by dissident factions and from without among independent movements, peaked in the 1980s; social movements emerged, centering on neighborhood associations and workers and focusing on the high cost of living; and autonomous business groups became more politicized and assertive, leading to capital flight. Most threatening, opposition parties became better organized, more active, and more vocal, and they began to win more votes.

The Programmatic Component

On top of the gradual secular erosion of the regime's foundations of support and the more abrupt economic collapse, Mexico's political crisis contained a third strand: programmatic changes designed to address the economic crisis and the exhaustion of the development model on which the regime had long rested. This programmatic component, a major component of the transitional crisis, refers above all to the political side effects of the stabilization program and structural economic reforms adopted by Presidents de la Madrid and Salinas to restore growth. The reforms, however, were part of a restructuring of the alliance, as we will see, prompting the emergence of a new political class, one trained in financial-economic areas and wedded to the nation's larger financial centers of power.[28]

The programmatic changes marking the period encompass both stabilization measures and a restructuring of the state and economy. Begun during the early days of the de la Madrid term, economic stabilization involved massive cuts in public spending, the elimination of subsidies, increases in official prices, and the termination of government jobs to make way for the servicing of the nation's massive foreign debt. Federal expenditures declined by 62.9 percent from 1982 to 1987 as domestic resource use was held below the level of production by an average of 4.8 percent of GDP per year from 1983 to 1988.[29] Figures from the UN's Comisión Económica para América Latina (CEPAL) show a 30 percent decline in real per capita expenditure on social programs for 1986–1988 compared to 1971–1981 (see Table 1.1).[30] At the same time, the government slashed subsidies, reduced price controls, and increased the prices on government goods by the hundredfold. The number of official prices in the economy, for instance, fell from 1,349 to 528 during the period, and even those remaining were tagged closer to the market-clearing levels such that by early 1988, only forty-one product lines remained subject to official prices, representing a mere .5 percent of value of imports and .6 percent of internal products.[31] By 1994, the number of fixed prices was reduced to include only basic household commodities. At the same time, the government also cut jobs. In February 1985, the government froze 80,000 positions in the bureaucracy and cut 51,000 employees during the year. In 1988, another 30,000 positions were cut.[32]

It was initially believed that such austerity measures, combined with minor structural changes to increase efficiency, would be enough to restore growth. The idea was that faithful servicing of the foreign debt would eventually lead to a renewal of foreign investment and that the price of oil would rebound. The failure of these reforms to restore growth thus prompted deeper and more destabilizing structural reforms. This programmatic component involved the fundamental rejection and overhaul of "the system of protection and state-led industrialization on which Mexico has relied since the 1930's."[33] Begun in 1985, it involved a massive reform of the state that included the privatization of state enterprises, an opening of the economy to foreign investment and trade, industrial restructuring, and a range of policies designed to create a propitious climate for capital investments.

The scope of structural economic changes in Mexico during the period was wide, the pace quick, and the impact deep. Of the 1,214 enterprises owned by the state in 1982, for instance, the de la Madrid administration sold, eliminated, or merged 89 percent, reducing the state's involvement to six (down from twenty-eight) industrial categories (petroleum, petrochemicals, electricity, mining, steel, and nuclear energy), the banks, and the media (state newspaper and television stations).[34] President Salinas continued to lighten the state's load, auctioning off all but a few of its banks, its steel plants, its mines and sugar installations, and its television network. By early 1992, the government's portfolio had been reduced to little more than petroleum and electricity, 8.8 percent of the banks, and a few minor commercial enterprises such as Compañía Nacional de Subsistencias Populares (CONASUPO). Moreover, legislative and administrative changes pried open the mining sector to permit private and foreign investment, reclassified products in the electricity and petroleum fields to whittle away at the government's domain in this strategic camp, and even reformed the *ejidos,* Mexico's land reform sector, to permit the sale of *ejido* land and allow the participation of private capital.

The government also dismantled the import substitution regime. De la Madrid lowered the top tariff rate from 100 percent to 20 percent, eliminated official reference prices, and reduced from 92.2 percent to 23.2 percent of the value of domestic production the number of products requiring import permits.[35] In 1986, he even enrolled Mexico in the General Agreement on Tariffs and Trade (GATT), a move that had been publicly debated and rejected just a few years earlier. Salinas followed suit and trumped his predecessor by trimming additional barriers to trade and investment and negotiating and signing the North American Free Trade Agreement (NAFTA) with Canada and the United States in 1993. Throughout, the government courted foreign investors through everything from flexible interpretations of existing laws and legislative reforms, to the maintenance of low real wages.[36] Foreign investments, once officially shunned and limited, skyrocketed from 4.4 percent of GDP in 1980 to 12.2 percent by 1990: a third of all national capital formation.[37] By 1994, Mexico would be the home of over $120 billion in U.S. investments alone and enjoy one of the most attractive and best-performing stock markets in the developing world.

The economic reforms, like the economic crisis itself, harbored severe political repercussions. More than simply a cyclical decline in the level of economic activity, which would have allowed the regime to retain its basic alliances, the new economic policies represented a new phase of capitalist expansion, bringing about permanent structural changes that undermined the bases of support and challenged the regime to reconstitute new bases. The structural changes thus meant a concomitant change in the state's historic relationship with business, the press, labor, the political elite, the people, and even its own past. Perhaps even more important, the changes also threatened to undermine the regime's tried and proven strategies of reformism. As Jaime Tamayo notes, the neoliberal changes "strongly affected the ability of organizations that had been social 'shock absorbers' to negotiate and get a solution to their members' demands."[38]

First, the new neoliberal economic model espoused by de la Madrid and Salinas was incongruent with the traditional mechanisms, alliances, and ideology of the PRI-based political regime. The idea of a liberal, open, and competitive economy clashed with the institutionalized corruption and bureaucratic inefficiencies permitted under a protectionist model of import substitution, practices that most agree helped secure the elite alliance. The model also conflicted with the existing pattern of assimilation and cooptation that, as Wiarda contends, "requires a constantly expanding economic pie so that new 'pieces' can be handed out to the rising groups without the old ones being deprived."[39]

The programmatic changes, moreover, challenged the regime's ability to control the labor movement as it had in the past, despite the fact that labor represented "the very foundation of its [PRI's] permanence in power."[40] For one, the programmatic changes struck hard and often at the interests of labor. Privatization weakened unions by undermining labor

contracts and weakening the unions' bargaining power. One report est-
mated that privatization alone had eliminated nearly 400,000 jobs.[41] Economic restructuring also brought massive layoffs in steel (private and public), in the sugar industry, among doctors (60,000 in 1986 alone), among
nurses and elementary school teachers, and in a range of areas, pushing as
many as 40 percent of the nation's economically active population into the
informal sector.[42] From 1981 to 1987, employment in manufacturing industries fell 17.1 percent and unemployment reached 17.6 percent.[43] Coupled with austerity, labor also faced a fall in real wages. The minimum
wage fell 41.9 percent from 1982 to mid-1987 and 52 percent from 1980
to 1989, while the numbers earning it grew.[44] Meanwhile, salaries in the
manufacturing sector declined 22 percent between 1980 and 1989.[45] Relative to income from capital ownership, wages fell from 64 percent in 1980
to 40 percent by 1988. Moreover, the government had few resources to
protect its alliance with labor. Losing labor as a result of these changes
could fundamentally alter the political game, perhaps triggering the defeat
of the PRI at the polls or the emergence of a more blatantly exclusionary,
authoritarian model.

In addition to altering the state-labor link, the economic policies also
promised to alter the government's relationship with business. Previously,
a situation of political capitalism informed the state's alliance with business.[46] The state enjoyed extensive economic and regulatory controls over
business and was one of the more important economic players in the
game—a situation it could use to reward or punish businesses for their political behavior. Business, consequently, exerted a degree of self-discipline
when treading on political ground. But economic liberalization meant a reduction in these control mechanisms, a concomitant weakening of the
state's bargaining position vis-à-vis business, and hence a change in the
underlying conditions governing the relationship. It would open the way
for a more independent and perhaps a more assertive and participatory private sector.[47] Indeed, much of the pressure in the 1980s would emerge
from business groups and their middle-class allies. Though many of the
economic reforms are compatible with the interests of this group—as we
will see later—this structural economic change looms large as an obstacle
and danger facing the PRI government.

Finally, the new economic model embodied principles contrary to the
nationalistic, prosocialistic tenets of the Mexican Revolution. Gone was
the anointed role of the state to protect peasants and workers against the
onslaught of foreign and domestic business. As Sheahan correctly contends, "The antinational strand in open-economy logic runs squarely
against long-standing Mexican insistence on strengthening the sense of
Mexico as a nation, as a part of the world but a highly distinctive and independent part."[48]

The official attitude toward the United States even changed. Under the old ideological rhetoric the United States was considered partially responsible for Mexico's underdevelopment; under the new logic it became a part of the solution.[49] "Poor Mexico—so close to the United States" seemed either no longer applicable or the opposite. Ideological reversals such as this deepened the divisions within the PRI, eventually leading to the Cárdenas split and forcing the PRI to compete with the Cárdenist-led left during and following the 1988 presidential election for the "legacy of the revolution."[50] Moreover, such changes threatened to weaken the PRI's historic ability to mobilize its ideological bases or employ its "revolutionary capital" to increase popular support. The regime's "revolutionary credentials" were important not only in mobilizing society, but also in undermining and dividing the appeal of opposition parties on the left.[51]

But, although threatening the regime's existing alliances and ideological foundations, the success of the economic reforms depended on these alliances and a degree of legitimacy. Generally, broad-based political support is needed to successfully implement economic reforms and prevent opponents from forcing a delay or reversal in the nation's economic course. Corporate controls over and support from labor are particularly crucial for the implementation of economic reforms, given their strategic position. The regime's historic ability to weather economic crisis has been linked to "the preservation of authoritarian mechanisms for controlling demand" and "the durability of state-labor ties."[52] Hence, factors undermining the state-labor system threaten not only to undermine political stability but also to thwart the economic reforms needed to restore growth.

As with the regime's new emphasis on democratic change, it is important to ask then why such a policy was adopted given the political challenges involved. Though this question will receive greater treatment in a subsequent chapter, it suffices here to note that the domestic and international economic juncture seemingly left the regime few options but those adopted. In other words, the nature of the crisis was such that basic structural changes were needed to restore capitalist growth. In contrast to the reformist measures employed by Presidents Echeverría and López Portillo when confronting economic crisis in the 1970s, neither de la Madrid nor Salinas enjoyed the option of abundant and hence cheap foreign loans, high world oil prices, or even the use of anti-Northern sentiments to rally the nation. Not only did the international economic and political climate differ tremendously from the 1970s to the 1980s—thereby altering the range and weight of the alternatives available to the regime—but the presidents of the 1980s inherited the unpaid bills of their predecessors. The structural economic changes were thus considered necessary to restore growth, despite the inherent political risks. In a sense, the problems associated with doing nothing were considered greater than the disruption caused by the neoliberal reforms.

Conclusion

The secular-based erosion of the foundations of consensus, the outpouring of discontent, and the adoption of democratizing rhetoric by the regime all dovetailed and clashed in the political/electoral arena, creating a deep political crisis. Though prior to the 1980s, elections seemed "peripheral to the real business of Mexican political life" with loyalty counting more than votes, the crisis changed all that.[53] National and even international attention on elections grew, casting each contest as a test of the regime's and particularly the president's willingness to promote (or allow) change. At the same time, opposition parties became more effective at pressuring the government for clean and transparent contests and then threatening to wrest power through the ballot box when such conditions were met. In some cases, the opposition made important electoral strides; when thwarted they would seize government offices, burn government buildings, block international bridges, and stage high-profile protest marches, hunger strikes, and the like to protest electoral fraud and force the government to negotiate to ease tensions. But regardless of outcome, the process became riddled with conflict and seemed to create more problems that it resolved. Between 1985 and 1987, for instance, 1,444 mass mobilizations against electoral fraud and in defense of the vote took place.[54] The 1988 election further intensified and increased such protests.

In addition to the growth and reach of opposition parties and the intense politicization, social NGOs also proliferated and became more politicized. Among them, the Convergencia de Organismos Civiles por la Democracia in the late 1980s brought together 120 NGOs, and Alianza Cívica in 1994 represented over 300 citizen groups.[55] Combined with multiparty organizations such as Asamblea Democrática por el Sufragio Efectivo (ADESE), Consejo para la Democracía (COPADE), Acuerdo Nacional para la Democracia (ACUDE), these civil organizations informed citizens of their rights, scrutinized the government's operations, observed the elections, and pressured the government for progressive changes.[56] Intellectuals and officials of the church also became more involved, raising their voices to condemn electoral fraud, abstentionism, and the abuse of human rights. International human rights organizations would add their voice, publicly condemning the electoral-related repression and the government's use of the military to resolve electoral problems.[57]

In sum, the crisis put forth a delicate dilemma for the political system. On the one hand, the reforms needed to respond to the politicization of elections and to restore economic growth threatened to weaken the regime's foundations of political control and continuity. On the other hand, the inherent dangers of not pursuing such reforms were equally striking.[58] Although the contradictions and dilemmas inherent within the crisis portray an unworkable, irreconcilable, and perhaps zero-sum equation, feeding expectations of fundamental political change, the reformist process does not operate in such an all-or-nothing manner. As Brachet-Marquez points out, "the erosion of a power system does not usually provide sufficient reason for its demise."[59] The dilemmas of the crisis, in other words, shape the reformist equation; they do not determine its outcome. Outcome is, as noted earlier, a product of the interaction of strategic choices among critical actors.

Before focusing on this reformist process and exploring the regime's efforts to surmount the challenges, it is important to complement the analysis by first examining the political actors within the drama—their interests, options, risks, and opportunities—to reassess the crisis from a political and strategic perspective rather than a purely analytical one. Strategic choice theory provides a means of accomplishing this task.

Notes

1. The staples of the Mexican polity have enjoyed substantial analyses over the years. On corporatism in Mexico see Anderson and Cockcroft, "Control and Cooptation in Mexican Politics"; Purcell and Purcell, "The Nature of the Mexican State"; and Spalding, "State Power and Its Limits." On clientelism as it relates to the intricacies of the elite alliance see Smith, *Labyrinths of Power*; and Whitehead, "Why Mexico Is Ungovernable—Almost." For a broad overview on presidential power see Koslow and Mumme, "The Evolution of the Mexican Political System." For detailed analyses on the making of public policy see Purcell, *The Mexican Profit-Sharing Decision*; Teichman, *Policymaking in Mexico*; and Schneider, "Partly for Sale." For a general overview of state-business relations see Maxfield and Anzaldua, eds., *Government and Private Sector in Contemporary Mexico*; and Story, *Industry, the State and Public Policy in Mexico*. For an evaluation of the role of the PRI and elections see Bailey, *Governing Mexico*; Molinar Horcasitas, *El tiempo de la legitimidad*; Garrido, *El partido de la revolución institucionalizada*; and Story, *The Mexican Ruling Party*. Finally, on the role of corruption in the polity see Riding, *Distant Neighbors*; and Morris, *Corruption and Politics in Contemporary Mexico*.

2. During what Molinar Horcasitas, *El tiempo de la legitimidad*, refers to as the preclassical period, 1917–1940, competition against and divisions within the ruling party were common. Changes in the 1940s helped create the modern or classical system, rooted in noncompetitive elections and PRI hegemony.

3. On the debate over whether the principle of no reelection enhances or detracts from authoritarianism see Carpizo, "The No Re-election Principle in Mexico," p. 10; and Brandenburg, *The Making of Modern Mexico*, pp. 3–7.

4. The term "revolutionary family" is attributed to Brandenburg, *The Making of Modern Mexico*.

5. Pereyra, "Estado y movimiento obrero."

6. Many have expressed this view. See, for instance, Bailey, *Governing Mexico*, pp. 64–65; Wiarda, "The Unraveling of a Corporatist Regime?" p. 5; and Baer, "Electoral Trends," p. 40.

7. On the rise of such groups see Klesner, "Changing Patterns of Electoral Participation and Official Party Support in Mexico," p. 97; Loaeza, *Clases medias y política en México*; and Loaeza and Tarres, "Middle-Class Associations and Electoral Opposition."

8. Grindle, *State and Countryside*, pp. 61–67.

9. Loaeza, "Los partidos y el cambio político," p. 36; and Cornelius et al., "Overview: The Dynamics of Political Change in Mexico," p. 14.

10. Pereyra, "Estado y movimiento obrero," p. 67.

11. See Aguilar Camín, *Después del milagro*.

12. Foweraker, "Popular Movements and Political Change in Mexico," p. 15, associates the rise of popular movements to the decline of corporatism, including the neoliberal policies bent on political exclusion. Consequently, popular movements reflect the desire to protect the social pact of the corporatist era.

13. A range of empirical works point to a clear correlation linking the vote for opposition parties to urbanization, education, and income. See, for example, Alvarado, ed., *Electoral Patterns and Perspectives in Mexico*; Baer, "Electoral Trends"; Basañez, *El pulso de los sexenios*; Guillén López, "The Social Bases of the PRI"; and Klesner, "Party System Expansion and Electoral Mobilization." Molinar Horcasitas, *El tiempo de la legitimidad*, p. 166, reviews most of these empirical works.

14. Molinar Horcasitas, *El tiempo de la legitimidad*, extrapolates from past electoral patterns to demonstrate that by the late 1980s the PRI would encounter serious electoral difficulties. This tendency emerged without even taking the subsequent events of the time into account.

15. See Coleman and Davis, "Preemptive Reform and the Mexican Working Class."

16. Loret de Mola, *Las entrañas del poder: Secretos de campaña*, p. 54.

17. Barkin, *Distorted Development*, p. 58, estimates capital flight at $53.4 billion or 60 percent of the increase in external debt during the 1971–1985 period.

18. The *bolsa* crack in October reduced the value of the stock market by as much as 50 percent, triggering capital flight, a 40 percent devaluation of the peso, inflation, and threats of massive strikes on the part of labor. See Basañez, *El pulso de los sexenios*.

19. Sheahan, *Conflict and Change in Mexico's Economic Strategy*, p. 10.

20. Bailey, *Governing Mexico*, contends that confidence and optimism in the future were key ingredients in the regime's legitimacy. The quote is taken from page 6.

21. Brachet-Marquez, "Explaining Sociopolitical Change in Latin America," p. 95.

22. Perey, "The Revolutionary Potential of Mexico in the 1980s," p. 382.

23. Guillén López, "Social Bases of the PRI," p. 250.

24. The quote is taken from Meyer, "Democratization of the PRI," p. 333. The second point is made by Bailey, *Governing Mexico*, p. 90.

25. Cited in Cornelius et al., "Overview," p. 27.

26. The existence of secular changes as a component within the current crisis helps account for the widespread disagreement over when Mexico's crisis actually began. Aguilar, *Después del milagro*, and Basañez, *El pulso de los sexenios*, for instance, hoist 1968 as the crucial year. Newell and Rubio, *Mexico's Dilemma*, underscore the 1970s as the start, when Echeverría and López Portillo altered the political-economic balance. Opposition leader Porfirio Muñoz Ledo (cited in Ortiz Pinchetti, *La democracia que viene*, pp. 311–318) also casts the 1970s as the decisive

moment, but for a different reason: as the critical juncture where the PRI diverted from its historical, revolutionary path. Others, however, underscore crucial events during the 1980s as the detonator of the political crisis, with the economic crisis of 1982 receiving the most votes. Still, Foweraker, "Popular Movements," highlights the role of the 1985 earthquakes in Mexico City as the key moment when society awoke from its slumber. Still others stress the emergence of the Corriente Demo-crática in 1987 and the 1988 presidential elections as the critical events.

Though of limited importance, this debate and disagreement highlight both the role of secular change in shaping the crisis and the multiplicity of factors underlying the Mexican crisis. As noted, this lends support to Hellman's, "Continuity and Change in Mexico," assertion that a series of quantitative changes at some point became a qualitative change.

27. See, for instance, Marvan and Cuevas, "El movimiento de damnificados en Tlaltelolco."

28. Camp, "Opposition in Mexico," for instance, notes the significant decline in the proportion of the federal cabinet with ties to labor. In the 1950s and 1960s, one in four cabinet secretaries were union leaders; by the 1970s this figure fell to 9 percent and by the 1980s declined to a mere 2 percent.

29. Cited in Centeno, *Democracy Within Reason*, p. 192; and Sheahan, *Conflict and Change in Mexico's Economic Strategy*, p. 134.

30. Cited in Ward, "Social Welfare Policy and Political Opening in Mexico," p. 52.

31. See Presidencia de la República, *Las razones y las obras*.

32. Cited in Espinoza Valle, "Reforma del estado y modernización política en México," p. 7.

33. Sheahan, *Conflict and Change*, p. 1.

34. See Bazdresch and Elizondo, "Privatization: The Mexican Case"; Chávez, "Liquidados el 89 percent de paraestatales que había en 82"; and Schneider, "Partly for Sale."

35. Cronin, "Domestic Versus International Influences on State Behavior," p. 1.

36. Indeed, the major factor in the 1980s boom in the maquiladora industry was the fall in real wages.

37. Data taken from Carrasco Licea and Hernández y Puente, "El creciente dinamismo de la inversión extranjera." See also the monthly economic reports provided by the Banco Nacional de México (BANAMEX).

38. Tamayo, "Neoliberalism Encounters Neocardenismo," p. 125.

39. Wiarda, "Mexico: The Unraveling of a Corporatist Regime?" p. 3.

40. *Latin American Weekly Review* 88–46 (November 24, 1988), p. 4.

41. Cited in *Mexico NewsPak* 1 (20), 1993, pp. 5–6. See also Correa and Corro, "40 percent de la fuerza de trabajo, en tianguis y otros subempleos."

42. Alvarez, "Economic Crisis and the Labor Movement in Mexico," pp. 42–43.

43. See Alvarez, "Economic Crisis," and Zamora, "La política laboral del estado Mexicano."

44. Middlebrook, "The Sounds of Silence," p. 195; and Acosta, "Se acerca 1991 con sus elecciones y no mejora la economía popular." According to Alvarez, "Economic Crisis," p. 39, the percentage of families earning less than twice the minimum wage, for example, increased from 47 percent in 1981 to 51 percent a decade later.

45. Acosta "Se acerca 1991."

46. The notion of political capitalism is used and developed by Schneider, "Partly for Sale."

47. Bailey, *Governing Mexico*, p. 59.

48. Sheahan, *Conflict and Change,* p. 61.

49. Pastor, "Post-Revolutionary Mexico," p. 16, associates this shift in attitude toward the United States with divisions in the PRI.

50. Aziz Nassif, "Regional Dimensions of Democratization," pp. 93–94.

51. According to John Womack (cited in Benjamin, "The Mexican Left Since 1968," p. 6), the "precondition for the revival of the left had to be the destruction of the myth of the Mexican Revolution."

52. The first quote is taken from Meyer, "Democratization of the PRI," p. 329; the latter from Middlebrook, "The Sounds of Silence," p. 121.

53. Baer, "Electoral Trends," p. 35. Bailey, *Governing Mexico*, p. 85.

54. Aziz Nassif, "Regional Dimensions," p. 94.

55. *Mexico NewsPak* 2 (7), 1994, pp. 4–5.

56. Aguayo Quezada, "The Inevitability of Democracy in Mexico," p. 122.

57. See, for example, Americas Watch, *Human Rights in Mexico*, and its follow-up report, *Unceasing Abuses.*

58. Other factors being equal, the use of electoral fraud to ensure PRI victories has a built-in multiplier effect. Its use undermines the PRI's appeal as a party "promoting change" and democratization, thereby weakening the party in subsequent elections and thus increasing the level of fraud needed to win. Taken to its ultimate limit, this cycle would eventually undermine the opposition's participation in the electoral game (e.g., by boycotting elections) and/or the reformers' efforts to maintain the system without resorting to more blatant forms of exclusionary authoritarianism.

59. Brachet-Marquez, "Explaining Sociopolitical Change in Latin America," p. 100.

2

Political Reformism
and Strategic Choice in Mexico

Mexico's political crisis defined and divided the major factions. Each faced countervailing winds and critical choices, struggled to navigate seemingly paradoxical currents, and sought to steer the reformist process to its own benefit. Reformers within the government tried to garner credibility by introducing piecemeal changes and then control their effects, hoping to alleviate and overcome the three causal components of the crisis: secular, conjunctural, and programmatic. Other political actors, meanwhile, employed strategic combinations of cooperative and conflictive modes to try to tilt the political equation in their favor, often forcing the government to react to the changing confluence of pressures for and restraints on fundamental political change.

This chapter employs a strategic choice model to help identify the primary actors in the Mexican political drama and their interests and options, and to explore the risks and opportunities they faced during the reformist process. The exercise highlights an assortment of political dilemmas from a strategic perspective—as seen by the actors themselves—and, as such, offers an intermediate step in the leap from the purely analytical treatment of the reformist equation in the preceding chapter to an analysis of the practical political developments marking the process. The discussion is designed therefore to set the stage for a more detailed analysis of the reformist process in subsequent chapters. Beginning with an examination of the four prominent political groups in Mexico, the analysis focuses on divisions and tensions among them and strategic options. The chapter concludes by focusing on the dangers and risks of fundamental political change.

Strategic Choices

Figure 2.1 depicts the economic and political preferences for four of Mexico's most salient political factions.[1] In both realms, the symbol a denotes a preference for the precrisis status quo, and A for liberal, progressive reforms. Politically, a(pol) represents a reliance on and bolstering of the one-party system, including clientelism, corporatism, and even the use of electoral fraud to maintain the PRI in power. A(pol), by contrast, corresponds to a reformist program stressing liberalizing and democratizing politics, particularly opening up Mexico's much maligned electoral process and allowing the opposition parties broader space within the polity and the government, but without the PRI's losing overall power. In the economic realm, a (eco) represents a continuation of the nation's traditional economic policies based on the tenets of political capitalism and import substitution industrialization, an economic policy rooted in the social goals of the Mexican Revolution, albeit with slight modifications to adapt to new global realities. A(eco), by contrast, symbolizes a neoliberal economic program featuring a reduction in the role of the state, greater reliance on market forces, the opening of the economy to national and international capital, the integration of the Mexican economy into the international economy, and an emphasis on economic growth over the social goals of distribution or social justice. Finally, the symbol B represents variants of systemic political change. It embodies a range of possibilities, including the electoral defeat of the PRI at the national level, the disintegration of the ruling party (which would eventually bring about its loss of power), or the rise of a revolutionary situation and/or an authoritarian crackdown, presumably following the total delegitimization of elections and a closure of the peaceful-change option.

The four factions evince different preference rankings along the political and economic dimensions as indicated.[2] Though in a similar type of analysis Hirschman differentiates between strong and weak preferences, no attempt is made here to weight the economic versus political preferences for the various factions. Instead, I assume that the two are mutually and strongly interdependent and that the political solution sought by each actor is shaped by his or her economic preference. Thus, reformers who wish to liberalize the regime politically will "wish to do so" only to the extent that it does not jeopardize the neoliberal economic reform program; the left and right opposition similarly want to effect a political outcome congruent with their economic preferences.

Briefly looking at the four factions, Group 1 can be referred to as *within system conservatives*. It represents many of the politicos and what many call the "political dinosaurs" within the PRI and the government.[3] This group opposed past reforms within the party that sought to weaken their influence vis-à-vis the more bureaucratic/technocratic reformers and broader electoral reforms that opened space for opposition parties. It includes most of the leaders of the PRI's labor and peasant sectors; portions of the PRI's more nationalistic, left-wing members of the satellite parties that traditionally (prior to the 1988 presidential contest) aligned with the

Figure 2.1   Political Actors and Preferences

Group 1		Group 2		Group 3		Group 4	
(System Conservatives)		(System Progressives)		(Nonsystem Right Progressives)		(Nonsystem Left Progressives)	
pol	eco	pol	eco	pol	eco	pol	eco
a	a	A	A	B	A	B	a
A	A	a	a	A	a	A	A
B		B		a		a	

official party; and many of the party's rank-and-file supporters.[4] Group 1 occupies a strategically important position atop many of Mexico's major social organizations and enjoys direct links with lower socioeconomic groups in the country. It is particularly strong in the countryside and among the working class incorporated into the PRI. Representing key corporate organs within the party, members of this faction enjoy (and struggle for) important quotas of power and thus can be found occupying many federal, state, and local governmental posts. Generally, this group exhibits a preference for *a,* being politically loyal to the system that has nurtured them. Economically, the group embraces the social goals of the Mexican Revolution and rejects neoliberal reforms.

Group 2 is composed of *within system progressives,* or what many often tout as the reformers. This amalgam centers on the so-called technocrats who wrestled control of the PRI following the selection of de la Madrid and have effectively dominated the upper ranks of the Mexican government since. This obviously includes Presidents de la Madrid and Salinas and their respective political teams. With limited links to the larger corporate organs within the PRI, this group draws critical support from key segments of the nation's middle class and particularly the business and financial communities, in addition to some of the more liberal-progressive elements within the party. Most of these have been incorporated into the party through its territorial organizations, not through corporate organizations. By virtue of this faction's dominance over internal party affairs, members of the faction have much control over the mechanisms of candidate selection within the PRI and can thus employ this patronage device and the resources of the government to attract and mobilize support for the party and themselves.[5] Politically, the reformers support a brand of "modernization" of the PRI that includes a weakening of its traditional sectors, a purging of its more corrupt elements, and a restructuring of its bases to incorporate new social groups. The reformers even support more "transparent" elections, *A*(pol), and additional concessions to the opposition as means to assuage popular pressures and counter the crisis—provided, of course, that such measures do not threaten their hold on power. On the economic side, the reformers believe in and support the neoliberal reform program, A(eco). They view economic structural changes as necessary to restore Mexico's stagnant economy and a means to recover lost political legitimacy.[6]

Group 3 encapsules *nonsystem right progressives.* This refers basically to the historic, right-wing opposition located within the Partido de Acción Nacional (PAN). This group draws support from business, middle-class sectors, and a growing segment of the working class not incorporated into the PRI. It is strongest in parts of the north (Baja California, Chihuahua, Sonora, Durango, Sinaloa), the west (Guanajuato, Jalisco), the Federal District, and the Yucatán. Rejecting the political status quo, $a,$ the right opposition struggles in the political/electoral arena to unseat the hegemonic PRI (B). It knows that to do so, however, more open elections are needed. It therefore views A(pol), more transparent elections, as a prerequisite for such electoral advances. Economically, its participants opt for the neoliberal economic reform program, A(eco), and reject the state-centered economic model of the past, a.[7]

Group 4 encompasses the *nonsystem left progressives* found among the popular movements, independent labor, and the independent leftist parties and factions that in 1988 united behind and supported the candidacy of Cárdenas.[8] After 1989, the group came to center increasingly on the Partido de la Revolución Democrática (PRD), which was formed by Cárdenas and the members of the Corriente Democrática, though it still encompassed other leftist parties and unaffiliated organizations. This group draws support from the nation's intellectuals, students, and marginalized sectors of urban and rural society. Generally, it represents the second strongest political force in such states as Michoacán, México, Morelos, the Federal District, Tabasco, Veracruz, Chiapas, and Oaxaca.[9] Like the right-wing opposition in the PAN, the left opposition rejects the political status quo, $a,$ officially struggles for peaceful political change through the electoral process, and hence recognizes that political reforms A(pol), are necessary to set the stage for the peaceful dislodging of the PRI from power (B).[10] Yet in contrast to Group 3, this group clearly supports the economic and social goals of the Mexican Revolution. They therefore reject the neoliberal economic program and prefer some form of a (eco) over A. Indeed, PRD leader and Senator Porfirio Múñoz Ledo once characterized the government's neoliberal programs as a "'giveaway' policy."[11]

The Divisions and the Tensions

The two-dimensional distribution of interests among the four groups helps identify important political and theoretical issues in Mexico, dynamic forces, political tensions, strategic alliances, and likely coalitional behavior. Discussion here draws attention, first, to fundamental contrasts between the groups' political priorities, which serve as the source of internal and external tensions between them; and, second, to likely coalitional patterns and strategic tactics.

The PRI Alliance

Group 1 and Group 2 compose the essence of the PRI alliance, though it also includes at times the traditional satellite parties that have historically backed the PRI. Tensions of a strategic nature characterize the division between Groups 1 and 2 and thus strain the alliance: a divisive internal debate over the types of reforms needed to fend off *B* and protect the system.

Politically, Group 1 feels that too rapid a pace of political change or opening, *A*, under the leadership of Group 2 threatens to unleash uncontrollable forces and trigger system breakdown, *B* (reform provokes change). This is the least preferable option. Consequently, the old guard (Group 1) decries the wins of the opposition, or what they see as "the PRI's softening" in state and local elections, and blames the *filósofos* of Group 2 for these ominous trends.[12] The Group 2 reformers, by contrast, hold that "modernizing" the PRI, eliminating the corruption of the past, and creating more "transparent elections," *A*(pol), are necessary concessions to restore system legitimacy and hence prevent the occurrence of *B* (reform as substitute for revolution). The reformers' political project is, as Przeworski stipulates, "to relax social tension and to strengthen their position in the power bloc by broadening the social base of the regime: to allow some autonomous organization of the civil society and to incorporate the new groups into the authoritarian institutions."[13]

The two internal wings of the official party similarly split over the appropriate economic policy, not merely in an ideological sense, but in a political strategic sense as well. The technocrats of Group 2 share Salinas's view that "most of the reforms of our Revolution have exhausted their effects and are no longer a guarantee of the new development the country is demanding."[14] They are convinced therefore not only that the neoliberal economic reforms are economically sound, but that such moves, by restoring economic growth, will actually boost the government's popular support and hence ease the pressures for political change. Particularly given the growing strength of the PAN during the 1980s and early 1990s, the technocrats see the economic reforms as a means to undercut the PAN's growing appeal to middle- and upper-class constituents and even instill within the PAN a perhaps less conflictive and more cooperative posture.

Group 1, however, views the neoliberal economic policies pursued by the government as unpopular, antirevolutionary, antilabor, and hence not only economically disastrous but politically suicidal as well. Many of these reforms, they contend, come at the expense of the popular and work-ing sectors, making it extremely difficult for the PRI to maintain its tradi-tional bases of support or even broaden the party's appeal. This division, in turn, shapes the internal dynamic within the party as those in Group 2 struggle to gain the upper hand within the alliance.

But despite fundamental disagreement over the nature, effect, and pace of political and economic reforms, Groups 1 and 2 agree on the un-acceptability of *B*. Ceding power, even in elections, is antithetical to one of the basic assumptions of reformism. As Bailey contends, "Those bene-fiting from one-party dominance of presidentialism can hardly be expected to cede power gracefully in democratic elections."[15] Even the reformists prefer to "conserve the government even if that means violating the law, rather than sinking with it."[16] This is a concern echoed perhaps most force-fully by labor patriarch Fidel Velázquez of Group 1: "We the revolution-aries shot our way here. Whoever wants to remove us will not be able to do it with votes, he will have to do it with shots also."[17]

On the one hand, the greater the likelihood that the liberal reforms may unleash a process culminating in fundamental political change in Mexico by undermining the alliance—the greater the threat of *B*—the greater Group 2's reliance on the conservatives in Group 1 to retain con-trol at any cost. The "caciques and the 'dinosaurs' who mobilize the vote and manipulate it in the traditional way" are therefore needed to maintain the PRI's level of electoral strength, and these elements cannot be dis-pensed with until a new majority coalition can be built.[18] Again, labor pa-triarch Fidel Velázquez describes Group 1 as "the soul of the party . . . [and the] *filósofos* recognize that the sectors provide the party's organiza-tional structure—and that without them they would be little more than iso-lated groups of bureaucrats and technocrats."[19]

This continuing reliance on the mechanisms of the past to maintain power was demonstrated in 1988. The party and its old guard were deci-sive in mobilizing the vote for Salinas. As Cornelius et al. note, "Without the caciques and the rest of the 'dinosaurs' who mobilize the vote and ma-nipulate it in the traditional way . . . it would have been very difficult for Salinas to win."[20]

On the other hand, the greater the likelihood that too slow a pace of reform threatens the regime's hold on power, the greater the likelihood that the reformers will hasten their attacks on the conservative elements within Group 1 and liberalize the system in order to maintain control. But this will occur only to the extent that the reformers can muster sufficient allies to maintain power. This constant tension between Groups 1 and 2 thus shapes one of the primary restraints on political change and suggests a truncated pattern of reformism, marked by half measures and reform reversals.

The Alliance Versus the Opposition

The second salient division among the four factions revolves around the PRI alliance (Groups 1 and 2) versus the opposition (Groups 3 and 4). This division is two-dimensional, encompassing both a system/antisystem and left-right axes.

According to Adam Przeworksi, the gravest threat to an authoritarian regime "is not the breakdown of legitimacy but the organization of counterhegemony."[21] Such counterhegemony hinges not only on the strength of the opposition, but also on the union of that opposition—the intensity of the system/antisystem polarization. In our model, this polarization stems from the differences in the intensity of Group 2's support for A(pol) and that of Groups 3 and 4. On the one hand, Group 2 wants to ensure that A(pol) does not unleash forces leading to B. As one observer notes, "Salinas and his advisers . . . want to reform the PRI, and at least some elements of the broader political system, but without tearing it apart."[22]

Groups 3 and 4, however, want something different: for political liberalization, A, to set the stage for systemic change, B. Consequently, both external factions pressure Group 2 to pursue political reforms at a pace more rapid than the Group 2 reformers consider appropriate to their own interests. The opposition, as a result, consistently denounces the government's tendency to resort to electoral fraud to retain power, organizes itself to monitor elections and expose fraud, mobilizes to protest electoral "irregularities," and strategically uses threats to boycott the electoral process as a means of exerting political pressure. Put differently, the opposition strives to paint Group 2 as basically indistinguishable from Group 1.[23] As the head of the PAN, Luis H. Alvarez noted as late as July 1992 that Mexican democracy "advances slow, very slow."[24]

Right and Left Opposition

As noted, the potential for counterhegemony hinges not so much on the size of the opposition as on its weight. Yet a cross-cutting left-right division based on economic interests between the two opposition factions tempers this tendency toward polarization. Group 3, though opting for political change, sides with the reformers' economic program, while Group 4 shares Group 1's economic goals.

This division points to two important tendencies among the various groups. First, the cross-cutting pattern underscores a volatile and tenuous alliance among the opposition forces themselves. As with the other participants, there is a built-in tendency for the opposition to reject any political developments that enhance the capacity of its ideological opponents to shape the economic agenda. Though the opposition desires common political change, the economic variable tempers its ability to cooperate and fosters the degree of polarization needed to affect political change.[25] Second, while clearly the gravest danger for Group 2 stems from the strength of a unified opposition, the reformers of Group 2 feel less threatened by the rise of Group 3 than Group 4 as a result of this cross-cutting division. In a sense, the right opposition represents only a political challenge, while the left fashions a revolutionary challenge.[26] As we will see, this produces a range of strategic implications for the reformers and its opponents.

Strategies and Coalitional Patterns

Turning now to optimal strategies, risks, and opportunities for each of the four groups, the combination of preferences depicted here suggests certain likely patterns.

Group 1

The "conservatives" of Group 1 occupy a decisive position in terms of future political developments and yet will seemingly suffer irreparable damage to their status quo position regardless of outcome. Politically the conservative forces are already on the defensive and increasingly alienated from the technocrats of Group 2 in party and governmental affairs. Many of those in Group 1 have been stripped of their privileges and have lost their influence due to both the political and economic reforms heralded by Group 2; some have even been jailed.

Abandoning its within-system coalition with Group 2 to side with Group 4 (its most likely ally given the two groups' common economic preference) Group 1 must accept the least preferable political outcome, B, in return for the most preferable economic outcome, $a(eco)$. Such prospects are heightened only as the strength of Group 4 increases, since this effectively bolsters Group 1's expected utility of such a move.[27] A reduction in the prospects of the left opposition of Group 4, by contrast, or a generalized reduction in the external pressures for change, further weakens the options available to the conservatives of Group 1 but nonetheless eases the need for the reformers to attack their privileges.

Just the mere threat of B, on the other hand—which includes Group 1's threatening to leave the PRI or the heightened strength of Groups 3 or 4—tends to enhance Group 2's dependence on Group 1's skills to maintain power via "traditional" means and thus strengthens Group 1's bargaining position within the alliance. This allows the group to perhaps slow the pace of the reforms and its gradual loss of privilege within the system.

Group 2

Attacked by Group 1 for pursuing change too fast and by Groups 3 and 4 for moving too slowly, Group 2 faces the central paradox of the reformer.

The political success in reforming the system to save it rests first and fore-most on the reformer maintaining some credibility as a reformer in order to arrest the rise of its opponents and instill a cooperative rather than a con-frontational line. But Group 2 must accomplish this manuever while protect-ing its alliance with Group 1. Consequently, a bow to conservative interests to guard against system change tends to delegitimize the PRI and perhaps ac-tually increases the future need to rely on such measures. By contrast, and equally perplexing, electoral defeat of the PRI actually confirms the party's commitment to democratic opening and thus enhances its legitimacy.

This paradox informs the often noted tendency in Mexico for the PRI, in a sense, to win by losing and lose by winning. The use of fraud to main-tain the party's electoral edge represents a clear legitimacy cost to the party and the government: it accomplishes the immediate objective but un-dermines efforts to create a new image for the party and thus actually may strengthen the opposition.[28] As elections have become even more politi-cized during the crisis, the need for and cost of fraud have increased. By contrast, electoral defeats suggest that the government is actually willing to change. In the early electoral contests under de la Madrid, for example, a string of electoral victories by the PAN seemed to provide solid testi-mony as to the democratic intentions of the government and its desire for reform. Many, indeed, "spun" the PAN victories as such for political gain. Under Salinas, the highly acclaimed victories of the PAN gubernatorial candidates in Baja California in 1989 and Chihuahua in 1992 also brought domestic and international praise as unequivocal signs of Mexico's march toward democracy, proof of Salinas's reformist intentions. These, in turn, fed the public's growing confidence in the electoral process as the route to change, enhanced the president's popularity as a reformer, and even helped garner support for the PRI.

Yet such concessions are dangerous, resulting in a zero-sum game. This complicates Group 2's efforts to protect its legitimacy as a reformer. Ceding power through elections may gain legitimacy and even enhance the party's appeal, but it has limits. How can the PRI-led government permit just enough opposition victories to alleviate pressures for change without losing control of the situation and permitting the opposition to unseat it?

To maximize reformist success then, the reformist leaders of the PRI acknowledge the need to reorient the PRI and strengthen its popular ap-peal. Reorienting the party to contend in politicized elections requires the party, among other measures, to broaden its bases of political support, re-activate the party's grassroots, incorporate new groups, and select candi-dates with broader appeal. But such measures run the risk of also dividing the party by weakening the importance of loyalty in the distribution of pa-tronage benefits. Taken to the extreme, such changes could weaken the party to the point of losing elections, and such a prospect, of course, frightens and hence restrains those within the alliance.

This tension highlights then one of the major dilemmas facing the PRI. To maximize reformist success, the reformist leaders of the PRI and the government would like to reform the PRI before opening up the elections—to dispense with the party's most traditional and outmoded elements only after they are no longer needed to guarantee victory. This is because the PRI's continued dominance under more open conditions assumes substantial changes in the party. But this optimal temporal pattern is problematic, raising a number of questions. First, as Barta asks, "Is it realistic to believe that the technocrats would have enough confidence in the existence of a PRI-supporting majority in the electorate to gamble their claim to power in clean elections?"[29]

Second, is it even possible to reform the party to allow it to participate in fair elections without the pressures to do so stemming from electoral defeats? In other words, electoral defeats constitute a major impetus to promote changes within the party. Without these pressures, members of the party may have little reason to relinquish their privileges. Finally, are the two—party reforms and electoral reforms—contradictory? Opposition pressures for democratization, for instance, include calls for an institutional separation of the PRI and the state; yet from the PRI's perspective, the resources of the state provide a ready and strategically superior means to help bolster the appeal and potential of the PRI, thereby enabling it to win free elections in such delicate times.

Facing a tenuous task, Group 2's antipathy for B, along with Group 1 and its common economic preference with Group 3, suggests two possible non–mutually exclusive approaches for the "reformers." First, Group 2 must attempt to draw (or maintain) support from Group 1 and solidify its hold over the "traditional culture." This strategy hinges on some function of (1) convincing the members of Group 1 that a (pol) threatens B more than A—that they have more to lose by clinging to their privileges than what they are losing now as a result of the reforms—and/or (2) altering the weight of Group 1's options—how much they can conceivably gain by leaving the coalition.

Various means exist to accomplish this feat. One way is to weaken the left (Group 4, Group 1's most likely ally) in part by depicting them publicly as extremely dangerous. The reformers (Group 2) thus can use the "specter of *neocardenismo* to frighten the traditional politicos" in an effort to convince them that "they have more to lose than to gain through obstructionism."[30] Another strategy is to provide sufficient benefits to placate the demands of Group 1, thereby maintaining its members' loyalty to the PRI-led system. This would include a conscious reincorporation of the politicos into the political fold, providing them with new opportunities or roles within the framework of the new regime.

A second and complementary strategy for Group 2 is to play on its common economic preference with Group 3 and their shared tendency to favor A (pol) over a. This implies capitalizing on the economic reforms to attract support among the PAN's constituents. A part of this strategy is to enlist the support of Group 3 in order to weaken the pressures coming from Group 4 and thereby temper the tendency for the opposition to unite. This can be accomplished by engaging in a liberalization process that favors the political interests of Group 3 without getting out of hand. Adopting a softer line toward the PAN in conjunction with a harder-line policy toward the left PRD, for instance, helps ensure a more "gradualist" or nonconfrontational posture toward the government by the PAN and temper the likelihood of their allying with the left opposition.

The adoption of a softer line toward Group 3 as well as a policy of shoring up its alliance with Group 1 dovetail with Group 2's strategic need to weaken Group 4, given the latter's revolutionary challenge to the regime. This strategy simultaneously keeps the opposition divided while diminishing the risk that Group 1 will abandon the coalition. Reformers can employ a combination of positive and negative reforms to accomplish this task. Among the positive measures, the reformers can use government policy to deal with the economic issues of concern to Group 4, thereby undercutting their popular appeal. At the same time, the reformers can employ such negative measures as electoral fraud, repression, and nonrecognition to weaken its PRD opponents.

Group 3

The nonsystem right progressives (i.e., PAN) also face divided coalitional lines. They share with Group 2 an economic concern and with Group 4 a political concern. But despite its shared preference for B and thus its tendency to side with Group 4 to promote "free and fair elections," Group 3 (like Group 4) is uncertain as to the economic outcome of B. Thus, threats that Group 4 will prevail under B (the greater the level of Group 4's strength)—and hence institute a (eco)—enhance the likelihood that Group 3 will ally with Group 2 rather than Group 4. Similarly, the greater the prospects that Group 2 will surmount the political crisis without fundamental political change, the greater the probability of Group 3 siding with Group 4.

Group 3, sharing the economic view of the Group 2 reformers, while politically echoing the interests of Group 4, faces a critical paradox. Because the greater the pressures for change on the government (changes that escape the control of Group 2), the greater the alliance between Group 1 and Group 2, the PAN wants to avoid any tendency that strengthens the power of its major nemesis, Group 1—an outcome contrary to PAN's interests. This too suggests a more tempered posture by Group 3, given its economic interests. Yet without external pressures on the government, there is little that strengthens Group 2's efforts to weaken Group 1.

Group 4

Optimal strategy for the nonsystem left progressives (Group 4) is equally twofold: to convince those in Group 1 that accepting B is the price for gaining a (eco) and that this is better than the losses they are suffering under the dual reforms instituted by Group 2. Attracting disaffected labor from the PRI (mainly the rank and file, which then puts pressure on the leadership) and/or effectively appropriating the popular revolutionary legacy emerge as crucial ingredients in the continued growth of the Mexican left. A secondary strategy for Group 4 is similar to Group 3's: to enjoin the support of Group 3 in questioning the reformist credential of Group 2, thereby crystallizing the system/antisystem polarization. This device, however, is limited, since the stronger Group 4 becomes, the greater the likelihood that Group 3 will side with Group 2 to stave off what they see as misguided economic reforms. Group 4, in the meantime, must overcome the divide-and-conquer strategies of the PRI alliance.

For all groups, two-pronged options craft the potential for internal problems and divisions. In the PRD, for instance, a potential division exists between those opting for an alliance with the right based on political concerns and those leaning toward an alliance with the left based on economic matters. The latter may even include siding with the left within the PRI alliance itself in an effort to divide that coalition.

Conclusion

By way of conclusion, it is perhaps useful to set out the forces determining the prospects of fundamental political change (B) under this model and, by implication, the prospects of successful reformism. First, the probability of fundamental change hinges largely on the force and support accruing to the opposition located in Groups 3 and 4. It was, indeed, their increasing political fortunes during the 1980s that triggered the debate over Mexico's political future. The PAN garnered much support in the early 1980s as a result of the economic crisis and the corruption of the prior years, enabling it to win important and critical elections during the period; the PRD, despite growing social opposition in the early period from labor and social movements, emerged particularly strong as a result of the internal divisions within the PRI in 1987 and the presidential contest of 1988. Such strength could be felt not only at the polls, but also in the degree to which these parties could mobilize to defend the vote and their "supposed" victories. But the strength of the opposition is not enough to trigger fundamental political change. The likelihood of such change hinges also on the intensity of the system/antisystem polarization. The fact that the opposition in Mexico is divided thus augurs well for the ability of the PRI to surmount the challenges, since it facilitates a divide-and-conquer strategy and effectively reduces the degree of support actually needed to remain in power.

In addition to the strength and degree of unification of the opposition, the likelihood of fundamental change is also shaped by Group 1's disposition to remain or abandon its alliance with Group 2 and hence accept fundamental political change for the sake of promoting its economic interests. Indeed, as noted, with the politicos in decline vis-à-vis the technocrats, many adopted this strategy before, during, and following the 1988 elections to bolster the strength of Group 4, enhancing the prospects of B. This tendency harbors a bandwagon effect, however, since the threat of B determines the expected utility of this strategy for those in Group 1.

A similar concern relates to the efforts of the reformers to control both the internal process of reform within the PRI and the electoral arena without jeopardizing the economic reforms or its hold on power. Though rhetorically supporting an opening up of internal party affairs, the reformers of Group 2 do not want the reforms to undermine their influence or their vision for Mexico. Hints that internal party reforms or even broader political opening will undermine the economic program are more likely to lead to a retrenchment of the political opening as opposed to the economic opening. This is due in large part to the ideological orientation of the reformers and their commitment to the need for economic reform.

A final factor influencing the probability of B brings us back to our central theoretical question: the relationship between reform and fundamental political change. As noted earlier, despite the internal and external pressures to promote political change, opening the party and/or the electoral process too fast, before the PRI can adapt to the changes, is unacceptable to the members of the PRI coalition. Hence, any indication that political reforms enhance the probability of fundamental change or jeopardize the economic reforms will prompt retrenchment. But even if the use of traditional tactics to maintain power can prevent the short-term rise of B, their long-term impact remains problematic. The possibility exists that intransigence in the face of a unified opposition could further polarize the political situation, strengthen the polar extremes, and weaken the center (as occurred, for instance, in Chile in the 1960s and 1970s, prompting political breakdown). For political reforms to effectively prevent this, the reformers must (1) maintain their coalition with Group 1 to the point at which Group 2 can either participate and win under free elections without their support or decrease the pressures for political change and survive; and (2) weaken the union of its opponents by decreasing the strength of the system/antisystem polarization.

The use of a strategic choice model thus recasts the dimensions of the political crisis and underscores the prime theoretical dilemma. In this light, the remaining chapters of Part 1 chronicle the pattern of reformism marking the de la Madrid (1982–1988) and Salinas (1988–1994) *sexenios*. They identify the major reformist initiatives of the two leaders, assess their political impact, and trace the ebbs and flows of the pressures for and restraints on fundamental political change: the way these paradoxes played out and how the regime survived—despite it all.

Notes

1. This section is adapted from Hirschman, *Journeys Toward Progress,* who employs a similar "preference-centered" scheme to explore economic reformism in Latin America. Przeworski, *Democracy and the Market,* provides a more recent use of strategic choice theory to explore the dynamics of reformism.

2. The four groups identified here parallel the four groups noted by Hirschman, *Journeys Toward Progress,* who employs the terms "hard-liners" and "reformers" for the factions inside the authoritarian bloc, and "moderates" and "radicals" for the opposition.

3. On the *político/técnico* division among the Mexican elite see Camp, "The Cabinet and the *Técnico* in Mexico and the United States"; Hernández Rodríguez, "La reforma interna y los conflictos en el PRI"; and Smith, *Labyrinths of Power.* Centeno, *Democracy Within Reason,* has just recently become available.

4. On the opposition of the conservative wing toward political reform in the 1970s see Middlebrook, *Political Liberalization in an Authoritarian Regime*; and Bailey, *Governing Mexico.*

5. Aziz Nassif, "Regional Dimensions of Democratization," provides a clear account of the PRI's social and geographic bases of support.

6. See, for instance, Salinas de Gortari, "Reformando al Estado."

7. For a general treatment of the PAN see Loaeza, "The Emergence and Legitimization of the Modern Right"; and Gil, ed., *Hope and Frustration.*

8. For an overview of the Mexican left see Carr, *Mexican Communism, 1968–1983*; Carr, "The PSUM: The Unification Process on the Mexican Left"; Carr, "The Left and Its Potential Role in Political Change"; and Carr and Anzaldua Montoya, eds., *The Mexican Left, the Popular Movements, and the Politics of Austerity.*

9. On the social bases of support for these groups during the 1980s see Basañez, *El pulso de los sexenios*, who presents polling data for the 1983 and 1987 period. Chapter 7 also provides additional data on the regional strength of the major political parties.

10. Interviews with members of the Comité Ejecutivo Nacional (CEN) of the PRD in the early 1990s revealed their personal commitment to peaceful change through elections. Still, some members of the party, often referred to pejoratively as "ultras," advance a more violent, armed path toward change. This division was radically demonstrated following electoral protests in the state of Guerrero in 1993, when local *perredistas* actually kidnapped national party officials.

11. Quoted in Gil, *Hope and Frustration*, p. 196. Rother, "Mexican Opposition Finding Unity Elusive," characterized the prospect of the formation of a Cárdenas party in the following terms: "The new party will be one whose objective is to carry out the nationalist program of the Mexican Revolution. . . . It will not be

a Socialist party, but a party that takes as its basis the principles of political and economic democracy, including the just distribution of income and greater public participation in the making of economic decisions."

12. *Latin American Weekly Review* 88–40 (October 13, 1988), p. 9.

13. Przeworski, *Democracy and the Market*, p. 57.

14. Quoted in *Latin American Weekly Review* 89–45 (November 16, 1989), p. 5.

15. Bailey, *Governing Mexico*, p. 35.

16. Reyes Heroles, *El poder: La democracia difícil*, p. 48.

17. Cited in Aguilar Camín, *Después del milagro*, p. 72.

18. Cornelius et al. "Overview: The Dynamics of Political Change," p. 25.

19. *Latin American Weekly Review* (August 9, 1990), pp. 8–9.

20. Cornelius et al., "Overview," p. 25.

21. Przeworksi, *Democracy and the Market*, p. 54.

22. Cornelius et al., "Overview," p. 33.

23. Part of the strategy is to expose the authoritarian character of the government, as PRD leader Múñoz Ledo stresses in Beltrán del Río, "Si al PRI lo quieren modernizar no van a quedar ni sus siglas."

24. Quoted in *La Jornada*, July 17, 1992, p. 5.

25. This also points to a difference in interpretation between the left opposition and the conservative and reformist elements within the PRI. Despite many being former members of the PRI, members of the PRD associate the failure of the PRI to achieve the goals of the revolution under the precrisis economic system to the authoritarian, corporatist, and corrupt political system, *a* (pol), and the emergence of the technocratic/financial group. This view contrasts the opinion of Group 1, which sees the basic political and the economic model as compatible, and the views of Group 2, which rejects the traditional economic program because of its economic deficiencies, not its political failings. See *PRD: 1989 Informe de la situación nacional.*

26. But even here, the two groups exhibit different tendencies in support of the economic reforms. Despite agreement with the business community and the PAN that import substitution-industrialization had exhausted its possibilities and that some form of economic liberalization was needed, the reformers' pursuit of economic reforms is tempered by the need to maintain their internal alliance with the more conservative forces in Group 1. This creates an autonomic source of tension with their potential allies in Group 4, since perceived cautiousness in the pursuit of economic reforms will raise questions as to the reformers' true commitment to economic liberalization. In other words, there is a built-in mechanism that ensures that the business interests rallied into Group 3 will deem the government's economic program too slow, just as it does the political changes.

27. Still, as Przeworski (cited in Collier and Norden, "Strategic Choice Models of Political Change," p. 231) notes, as the prospects of change grow, the opposition actors face the risk of jumping on the bandwagon too late.

28. Guillén López, "The Social Bases of the PRI," p. 250.

29. Barta, "Changes in Political Culture," pp. 65–66.

30. Cornelius et al., "Overview," pp. 25, 32.

3

Political Reformism
Under de la Madrid

When Miguel de la Madrid Hurtado first donned the presidential sash in December 1982, Mexico was suffering an acute economic setback and the PRI languished amidst declining levels of legitimacy and support. The president faced a daunting task. Economically, he sought to restore the nation's financial health while meeting Mexico's obligation to its domestic and foreign creditors. Without fresh capital from abroad, this required the government to reduce drastically its spending, enforce strict austerity measures, and restructure the nation's finances. Beyond stabilization, however, the president also needed to restore growth. This goal, he would conclude by 1985, demanded a broad strategy of economic restructuring, including the privatization of state enterprises, liberalization, and economic opening.

On the political front, de la Madrid faced an even more delicate assignment. First, he had to manage the economy politically: muster support for the economic changes while containing the multiple forces and demands unleashed by the economic crisis, the austerity program, and the restructuring-induced transitional crisis. Second, he faced the task of bolstering the PRI's and the government's waning popular and electoral support, both worsened considerably by the economic crisis. And finally, he sought to control the vociferous demands for democratization arising from the populace and the opposition parties to prevent the further politicization of the electoral process and the polarization of society.

As will be shown, despite some successes, particularly on the economic front, de la Madrid realized few of his political objectives. Support for the PRI dipped—according to one poll from 55.3 percent in 1983 to 29.6 percent in 1987—while the strength of the opposition climbed.[1] Elections, once dormant aspects of the system, became intensely politicized as the incidence of fraud grew more conspicuous and opposition protests more forceful. Polarization also peaked as opposition parties began to unite to pressure the regime for change. These tendencies seemingly culminated in the 1988 federal election, taking the crisis to new extremes. But despite these seeming failures and ominous trends, de la Madrid nonetheless succeeded at forestalling change and transferring power to his hand-picked successor, a clear sign of system continuity and reformist success.

Exploring the reformist dynamic under de la Madrid follows a sectoral rather than chronological path. Discussion centers first on de la Madrid's relations with the private sector and labor, followed by an exploration of the political/electoral arena, with attention to his relationship with the public, the PRI, and opposition parties. Though this arrangement helps us evaluate the development of reform and reaction in specific areas, it should be recognized that trends in one area impacted significantly on the risks and opportunities for reform in other areas. The chapter concludes by focusing on the 1988 presidential election and its impact.

De la Madrid and the Private Sector

Once characterized as smooth and nonconflictual, relations between the Mexican state and the private sector deteriorated when President Echeverría altered the stabilizing development model in the early 1970s. The already tenuous relationship reached a new and critical low some years later when outgoing President López Portillo nationalized the banking system.[2] This desperate, last-minute measure greatly enraged and mobilized the business community. In the months following the decree, for example, the CCE, Consejo Patronal de México (COPARMEX), and some sections of Confederación de Cámaras Nacionales de Comercio (CONCANACO) all launched intense public campaigns to sensitize public opinion to what they perceived as the "progressive socialization" of the country. In so doing, they eschewed their traditional low-key political approach and tradition of political acquiesence, calling on their colleagues to henceforth adopt a more active role in shaping the regime's economic policy and the nation's future.[3]

Many business leaders heeded the call, becoming more active politically though rarely in a monolithic way. The more moderate business leaders representing "nationalistic" small and mid-sized entrepreneurs coalesced in the Conferación de Cámaras de Industria (CONCAMIN) and Cámara Nacional de la Industria de Transformación (CANACINTRA). Favorable toward the government's protective policy, this group sought increased political power through the more established channels, including the PRI. However, a more radical faction revolving around the CCE, COPARMEX, and CONCANACO and centered in Northern Mexico, Puebla, Jalisco, and the Federal District sought a much more radical change both in economic policy and politically, including "a redefinition of the system of representation in the political structure." This group not only promoted "a campaign to defend free enterprise in the areas of

education, social communication and culture," but also encouraged the formation of new pressure organizations, and even pursued "direct involvement . . . in partisan electoral politics."[4]

In response, de la Madrid pursued a number of avenues. He downplayed the "statist" policies of his predecessors, actively consulted and
courted those within business, and embraced an economic program more
to their liking.[5] He publicly recognized Mexico's obligation to service its
external and internal debt, provided financial subsidies to reinvigorate the
private sector, and eventually began to sell state firms and open the Mexican market.[6] These moves sought not only to stimulate capital investment
and to reinvigorate and restructure the Mexican economy, but also to re-
gain the support, confidence, and acquiescence of the domestic and international private sectors and their middle-class allies—more specifically, to
ease tensions with the private sector, attract middle-class support for the
PRI, and ease relations with the international financial community and the
United States.[7]

Though the economic crisis/reform stung many, de la Madrid pursued
an economic policy benefical to the private sector, though at a speed and
scope the radical business group considered insufficient. For instance, the
early reversal of the government's "populist" spending—central government expenditures fell from 27.1 percent in 1982 to 17.1 percent of GDP
in 1988—helped not only to ease business concerns about the nation's
"progressive socialization," but also to pave the way for the servicing of
Mexico's debt.[8] The sale of government-owned industry similarly benefited key elements within the private sector by opening up new profit opportunities and stimulating the Mexican financial and speculative markets.
Even in agriculture, de la Madrid alleviated many of the fears held by the
private sector by publicly declaring that land redistribution had come to
an end.[9]

More specifically, de la Madrid put programs into effect that sought to
counter the ill will brought on by the bank nationalization while reinvigo-
rating the economy. In direct response to the nationalization, he created a
program that provided favorable terms of compensation through Bonos de
Indemnización Bancaria. He returned nonbanking stock to the former own-
ers, auctioned off 34 percent of the stock in the banks to the private sector,
and allowed the banks to maintain most of their management. In addition,
he altered the form of government finance to benefit the private financial
community, relying increasingly on the use of Certificados de la Tesoreia
(CETES) while freezing credits from the Bank of Mexico to the nationalized banks.[10] Such measures not only met the acceptance of the financial
community, but also provided financial relief to the private sector on the
order of 500,000 millon pesos during the 1983–1985 period. If one includes the elimination (or publicization) of private sector debt, that figure

soars even higher. This enabled the former bankers to establish a private parallel financial sector centering on the Casas de Bolsas.[11] All in all, the private financial sector born in part from de la Madrid's policy paid handsome dividends, although creating a somewhat unstable (speculative-based) financial setting. By 1987, Mexico's interest payments on CETES had reached the level of the country's payment on the external debt, and the *bolsa* became one of the world's best performers.[12]

While the government's handling of the banking-financial crisis provided former bankers the means to reinsert themselves into the economic life of the country with renewed vigor (thereby helping to ease their political opposition to the government and the PRI), the government also came to the aid of the nation's larger nonbanking groups. Through the establishment of the Fideicomiso para la Cobertura de Riesgo Cambiario (FICORCA), for example, the government aided and even subsidized the private sector's payment of its foreign debt by offering controlled or subsidized exchange rates. This helped save many of them from bankruptcy and facilitated their restructuring. Later, through Programa de Fomento Integral de Exportaciones (PROFIEX) the government provided tax refunds on imported inputs used for exports. Public funds were also used to finance a range of export-based initiatives through the establishment of an export bank.[13]

Behind these high-profile measures, the government also negotiated, intervened in business affairs, and allowed business a greater say in the making of public policy, all to ease the opposition of business. The government, for example, negotiated agreements with the business community prior to elections in Baja California and Sonora in 1986, making key concessions to them in return for their support. The government even intervened in the internal elections of CANACINTRA to see to it that less confrontational leaders were selected.[14] Moreover, the government allowed business significant input into the policy process. De la Madrid regularly consulted key members of the business community. Business, for instance, played a major role in the drafting of the Programa Nacional de Fomento Industrial y Comercio Exterior (PRONAFICE), one of de la Madrid's blueprints for his economic policy.[15]

Despite the favorable policies and the inclusion of business, the reforms produced only limited political returns.[16] Business generally supported the direction of de la Madrid's economic program and eased somewhat its hard-line posture toward the regime, opting for a more behind-the-scenes style of influence. Likewise, the fear of socialism among the bourgeoisie, so pervasive in provoking political and economic crisis at the end of the Echeverría and López Portillo terms, eased under de la Madrid's leadership. Yet business leaders' support for the PRI, despite growing influence within and upon the party and the government, continued to wane. The more radical and independent entrepreneurs, indeed, seemed to bolster their support for the PAN, particularly in the north. For instance, according to the public opinion polls conducted by Basañez during the period, support for the PRI among *empresarios* fell from 50.9 percent in 1983 to 31.7 percent in 1987, while favorable opinions of the government declined from 39.2 percent to 31.2 percent during the same period.[17] This trend culminated in 1987 with the nomination of Manuel Clouthier as the PAN's presidential candidate, a man who both "headed and personified" this newly politicized and radical entrepreneurial group.[18]

Why, despite an exemplary economic program, did business fail to lend more political support to de la Madrid? A variety of factors combined to undermine the net political impact of the liberal economic reforms of de la Madrid on state/business relations. For one, the economic returns themselves were clearly limited. Despite the reformist efforts, the nation's economy continued to suffer throughout the period. The relapse of economic recession, maxidevaluations of the peso, renewed capital flight, and staggering inflation following the mild 1984–1985 recovery chopped away at the private sector's support of de la Madrid's policies, while forcing the president to embrace more forcefully the neoliberal program. Though the fall in oil revenues and the costs associated with the Mexico City earthquakes played major roles in the relapse, many blamed the timid policies of de la Madrid for the decline, particularly de la Madrid's relaxation of financial controls in 1985.[19]

Other economic factors contributed to de la Madrid's poor political showing in the business community. Rogelio Ramírez, for instance, associates the loss of private sector support to the high costs of borrowing money, a factor tied to the large financial deficits and inflation.[20] Others point to business's problems with de la Madrid's fiscal policy and the maintenance of price controls.[21] The economic reforms also fed a transformation or redistribution of economic and political power within the business community that may have undermined much of business's support for the government.[22] According to Maxfield, for example, total nonbank financial institutions grew from 1 percent of GDP in 1980 to 7.4 percent in 1988 as credit to industrial or agricultural activities fell and became more concentrated.[23] A portion of the private sector was thus hurt by the liberal reforms and offered little support to the government's program. Already stunned from the depressed domestic market, the small and medium-size businesses supplying the domestic market found themselves eclipsed by the newly emerging financial/technocratic alliance.

Beyond the failures of economic policy to restore stability and growth, a critical ingredient in declining business support was arguably political. Much of the intended political effect of de la Madrid's economic program was undermined by the hard-line political/electoral stance taken toward the PAN during the term. This stance hit business and its allies directly, indicating to many the lack of a political willingness on the part of the president to entertain real political reform and to share power. Allying with the more conservative elements within the PRI to stave off the electoral onslaught from the PAN, the president even rhetorically attacked business. In his speech before the Confederacíon Revolutionaria de Obreros y Campesinos (CROC) in March 1986, the president denounced the "minority interests" represented by the more radical business faction, associating their views on economic reform with "ideological models foreign to our way of being."[24] Such statements, coupled with what many interpreted as half-hearted reformist measures, drained the support his economic program might have mustered.

Though offering few immediate political returns, the economic reforms begun under de la Madrid did help set the stage for his successor to reap political benefits, as we will see in Chapter 4. De la Madrid's strict austerity measures, for instance, helped restore the nation's financial health and earned Mexico favorable treatment in debt renegotiations in 1986 and later in 1989 under the Brady Plan. His structural reforms beginning in 1985 and heterodox anti-inflationary pact in 1987 similarly set the stage for the taming of inflation and the restoration of growth. Although during this process de la Madrid did not enjoy the ecconomic returns needed to accommodate those being hurt by the measures, such economic successes would enable his successor to build on this foundation to forge a new, more solid business-state alliance and a new financial/technocratic hegemonic group.

De la Madrid and Labor

While the government's economic policy generally complemented its political goals in dealing with the private sector (though with limited results), the opposite situation characterized the state's relationship with labor. In fact, de la Madrid's economic and political objectives both clashed with the state's traditional pact with labor. Economic objectives demanded austerity, the suppression of wages, reductions in social spending, cutbacks in employment, the elimination of labor conflicts, and an altering of working conditions.[25] Politically, as well, the economic measures demanded a weakening or neutralization of labor's traditional power, a bending of the state-labor pact. The need to increase the regime's political support and broaden the PRI's bases of support similarly meant a curbing of the influence of and the spoils accruing to the entrenched party bosses and sectoral leaders in the party. Even coming to terms with the PAN or opening up the electoral system confronted the staunch resistance of labor leaders within the party.

For these reasons, a range of government and party initiatives struck hard at the interests of the labor sector, a primary pillar of the PRI and the political system. According to de la Madrid and his team, the circumstances of the times demanded an alteration of the state-labor pact, and labor was to pay a significant price. As Arsenio Farell, the secretary of labor, noted in an early meeting with the directors of the Congreso de Trabajo (CT), the interests of workers "regardless of how legitimate they were" had to adjust to the circumstances of the country.[26]

The government attempted to bend the pact in a variety of ways. First, it tightened its administrative review of proposed strikes, prohibited strike coalitions, and altered the procedures covering wage negotiations. This made wage changes more a programmatic change in line with broader economic policy rather than a negotiated or political process.[27] Relying heavily on elite negotiations and corporate bargains (pact making) to control unions and wages, the government effectively stripped official unions of their negotiating power.[28]

Second, the government tacitly set an unofficial limit on wage increases, adopting a hard-line posture toward unions unwilling to abide. Repression was then used in response to "exaggerated" salary demands. Strikes at DINA (1983), URAMEX (1983), TELMEX (1984), SICARSTA (1985), Renault (1986), Luz y Fuerza (1987), Ford (1987), and Aeroméxico (1988)—indications that labor too wished to "bend" the labor pact, and the government's response to them—all illustrated this hard-line policy.[29] In 1987, for example, de la Madrid broke the electricians and telephone workers strikes by taking control of the installations and declaring the strikes null and void.[30]

In addition to its cocksure salary policy, the government also strategically employed bankruptcies, privatization, and decentralization schemes to undermine or break existing labor contracts. This not only weakened the power of labor, but also facilitated the process of industrial restructuring. Strikes at Aeroméxico (1980 and 1988), Mexicana (1982 and 1987), TELMEX (1984 and 1987), CLFC (1987), and Ford, for example, all brought declarations that the enterprises were insolvent. Ford closed its Cuautitlán plant in September 1987 to break a labor strike, only to reopen several weeks later brandishing a new labor contract. Aeroméxico similarly declared bankruptcy in April 1988 as a means to break a strike and nullify the labor contract; almost immediately it resumed operations under a new name.[31]

The government also curbed the power of labor unions by eliminating or reducing key union privileges such as their control over jobs, the rotation of workers, and subcontracting. In 1984, for example, oil workers' control of subcontracting was cut from 50 percent of local contracts to just 2 percent.[32] The government also reduced employment in many of the bloated public agencies and state enterprises and shunned the influence of labor leaders in decisionmaking circles. These moves reflected the liberal economic thinking of the new more technocratic leaders in the government as well as serving their political ends. Also, in an attempt to garner popular support for de la Madrid and nurture his reformist image, the government publicly lashed out against labor's autonomy within the PRI and the privileges (abuses) of the labor elite. These views informed the president's anticorruption message and treatment of the PRI during the initial years of the term.

[The economic objectives of financial stabilization and restructuring required these attacks on the interests of labor; and strikes against corrupt labor leaders were often quite popular. Yet labor support and quiescence remained crucial for the party and the regime. While the crisis and the reforms prompted greater union militancy and mobilization, the PRI counted on the organized strength of the official unions for both electoral and ideological reasons. Political necessity thus tempered and limited de la Madrid's frontal assault on labor. To navigate this dilemma and manage the debilitating consequences, the government relied heavily on a differentiated policy toward labor—a divide-and-conquer tactic (or more appropriately, take advantage of divisions to coopt). The use of both negative and positive measures to encourage (by rewarding) more cooperative behavior and/or discourage (by punishing) more radical conduct would prevent the emergence of a united labor sector or its radicalization.

The approach sought to weaken the labor opposition to the economic program by accentuating the divisions while at the same time maintaining the state's strategic alliance with the major labor confederations for political purposes. As Alvarez suggests, the government "encouraged disagreement among major unions, harassed and weakened independent labor unions, and delineated clear limits on actions undertaken by 'official' labor organizations."[33]

This reformist strategy featured a two-tiered, differentiated approach. The first tier broadly sought to favor the official labor sector over the nonofficial or independent labor movement. The government hence employed repression and strict administrative controls to crush and discourage the rise of independent unions and/or dissident groups within the official unions. It removed dissident leaders of the telephone workers organization in 1982, withdrew official recognition of independent labor sections within the Metro Workers Union in 1983 and within the Sindicato Nacional de Trabajadores de Educación (SNTE) in 1984, closed the Normal Superior in 1983 in a clear swipe at dissident teachers, authorized the decentralization of the educational system to divide the power of the teachers union, and defeated key strikes by independent unions in the automobile, steel, metalworking and mining, university, and nuclear energy sectors in 1983.[34] The government even allowed businesses to employ selective dismissals "to discipline the representative, democratic union leadership."[35] According to Newell and Rubio, moreover, the government used its influence over wage increases to "destroy the independent unions."[36]

In conjunction with its anti-independent labor strategy, the government used administrative reforms, its interpretation of the labor code, and periodic concessions to the benefit of the official labor organizations. Early reforms of Articles 25, 26, 27, 28, and 73 of the constitution in December 1982 guaranteed housing and health care benefits to labor and gave institutional form to the notion of social property. This clause referred largely to the many business enterprises under the control of the official labor groups (a key demand of the labor leadership at the time).[37] In mid-1984, as tensions grew between the government and the Confederacíon de Trabajadores Mexicanos (CTM), and as the threat of coordinated labor activity mounted and elections neared, the government again bowed to a key demand of the CTM by creating the Sistema Nacional de Abasto to help workers purchase basic commodities.[38] De la Madrid made similar concessions in 1985 after the CTM and CT offered an alternative proposal for the economy that featured demands for an acceleration of union-owned enterprises and social welfare programs.

Prompted by difficulties in gubernatorial elections in Nuevo León, Chihuahua, Sinaloa, and Sonora, a wave of strikes among electrical, telephone, university, and textile workers and continued protests from Coordinadora Nacional de los Trabajadores de Educación (CNTE) (dissident faction within the SNTE teachers union) and the belief that the worst of the economic crisis had paced, de la Madrid offered additional concessions to official labor.[39] These included wage increases, an elimination of the 5 percent value-added tax (VAT) on medicines and processed foods, a 30 percent income tax reduction for those earning up to four times the minimum wage, and an expansion of government credit facilities for workers.[40] The government also gave Banco Obrero 5,000 million pesos to support union-owned businesses and subsequently increased its financial support for Fondo Nacional de Cooperacion para el Trabajador (FONACOT).[41] Following the 1985 earthquakes, the government again protected its alliance with the CTM by placing the rebuilding operation in the hands of the confederation through Instituto del Fondo Nacional para la Vivenda de los Trabajadores (INFONAVIT).[42] Later, in 1987, as inflation increased and the economy stagnated, the government eased its hard-line position on wages by allowing the Minimum Wage Commission to increase minimum wages whenever conditions warranted. The government also increased resources—300,000 credits for housing—to INFONAVIT, a move mainly benefiting the CTM.[43]

However, these periodic concessions to official labor in response to their radicalization hardly compensated for the losses labor and labor elite were suffering under de la Madrid. Although concessions helped protect the alliance and the labor leaders' allegiance to the PRI and the state, the demands of the labor patriarchs went largely unheeded in the party and the bureaucracy. Still, the antilabor policies eroded the support and legitimacy of the rank and file. Real wages declined, strikes were routinely declared illegal and/or repressed, and employment declined as more and more workers entered the ranks of the underemployed.

To gainsay these disruptive tendencies and not reward the radicalization and critical posture of the labor leaders, the second component of the government's treatment of labor centered on favoring the more cooperative groups within the official labor sector while attacking the more radicalized CTM. As with independent versus official labor, this tactic sought to make cooperation more beneficial than confrontation, while undermining any tendency toward labor cohesion and cooperation. Facing a critical line from the CTM in 1983 over its austerity program, de la Madrid threw official government support to rival organizations such as the CROC; the Confederación Révolucionaria de Obreros Mexicanos (CROM); and the Confederación de Obreros Revolucionarios (COR)—groups that offered more support for the government's economic program. The government used its control over registration and the social sector (e.g., housing) to discipline the CTM, offering minimum registration requirements to such confederations as the CROC. It also used exclusionary laws (preventing more than one union at a given site) and government control over the internal operations of unions to structure union gains in accordance with this strategy.[44] Publicly, the administration praised CROC's support of the administration's policies, arguing that it, rather than the CTM, might inherit the privileged position within the labor sector.

Overall, de la Madrid enjoyed mixed success in his reformist dealings with labor. First, his adroit handling of labor facilitated the successful implementation of a blatantly antilabor economic program. The government succeeded at cutting spending for social programs and subsidies to state industries to make room for implementing debt servicing; decreasing real wages and the proportion of national income devoted to wages; eliminating a range of government jobs; closing, privatizing, or merging government industries; and initiating a process of liberalization. The initial austerity cutback under de la Madrid, as Sheahan demonstrates, surpassed those of other Latin American countries. Government's solid corporate controls over labor played a key role in fashioning this outcome.[45]

Second, the reformist strategy helped check the power and strength of independent unions and discourage cooperation between the official and nonofficial sectors. Following a dramatic rise in strike activity, independent union mobilization, the creation of *coordinadores* by independent labor and the left, plans for national strikes, and the use of coordinated strategies by the official and nonofficial sectors in 1983, the government's hard-line, differentiated policy effectively defeated the independent unions, clearly placing the movement on the defensive by midterm.[46] Having more at stake in its privileged position in the PRI alliance, the CTM consistently broke with its more independent-minded colleagues despite the overtures toward greater cooperation. Reverting to historic form, the CTM "did not mobilize union members to challenge openly policies that harmed workers' interests."[47] In both 1983 and 1987, the CTM failed to follow through on its initial threats of a general strike.[48]

De la Madrid's strategic concessions to official labor unions not only helped fashion this outcome, but also helped isolate the independent unions and hence ease the government's efforts to arrest the politicization of its relations with labor. As Middlebrook points out, "The state-subsidized labor movement offered overall support for the government's economic stabilization program and persisted in a well-established tradition of incremental, intra-elite bargaining with government officials."[49]

Third, the anti-CTM policy within the official sector was initially successful in managing the crisis by keeping the CT divided and by checking the radicalization and opposition of the CTM. At critical junctures, the CROC and CROM publicly "opposed the CTM's proposals to the Labor Congress for coordinated anti-austerity actions," thereby debilitating the Labor Congress itself[50] and pushing the CTM to adopt a more conciliatory posture.[51] Even during its Eleventh National Congress in late 1983, the CTM decided to focus attention on the less volatile issue of social property rather than concentrate on wages and austerity.[52] This reflected the success of de la Madrid's divide-and-conquer strategy.

Clearly, de la Madrid's antilabor policies and "unprecedented" responses to labor conflict were unpopular.[53] Opinion polls during the period 1983–1987 showed that the greatest fall in support for the PRI and the government took place among the lower sectors (marginal, workers, and peasants).[54] Still, the reformist strategy had largely worked—at least by midterm—by helping keep the opposition diffuse, uncoordinated, and weak, while maintaining the loyalty of the official sector. All this amidst a deep economic setback. This allowed the PRI machinery, despite public opinion, to protect and rely upon its traditional electoral bases of support, among the lower sectors, and help the regime survive the worst of times.

Toward the end of the term, conditions changed, however, chipping away at these gains and setting a potentially dangerous stage for the 1988 presidential election. A number of factors merged. First, the September 1985 earthquakes and the widespread perception of the government's inefficient response reawakened the social or popular movements that had been silent since their 1983–1984 heyday.[55] An alternative to traditional labor union activity, the popular movements enjoyed renewed growth from

1985 to 1987, refocusing popular attention on the issues of austerity and the government's harmful policies toward workers.[56] The formation of neighborhood committees in the Federal District and the proliferation of political demands for the reform of the Mexico City government brought on by the earthquake all offered labor and the left new vehicles through which to articulate their opposition to the government and pressure for change.[57]

Second, this development coincided with renewed economic decline and inflation. The 1986 recession triggered a new wave of strike activity and the radicalization of the CTM through 1987. The number of strikes increased from 284 in 1986 to 1,590 the following year.[58] As had occurred in 1983, renewed labor mobilization brought greater cohesion and cooperation among the left, forcing the government to temper its attacks on the offical labor bureaucracy. The use of corporate negotiations to strike a major wage and price agreement to contain inflation prior to the election year tended to divorce the labor leaders from the rank and file, contributing to what one observer referred to as a "crisis of representation" within the "official" unions.[59] The events also further eroded de la Madrid's reformist credentials in the eyes of the public.[60]

A third factor contributing to the accelerated erosion of the state-labor pact and an undermining of the early successes of de la Madrid's labor reforms centered on the selection of Carlos Salinas de Gortari as the PRI's presidential candidate and the concomitant rise of *cardenismo* as an opposition movement. Though never questioning its alliance with the PRI, many within the labor movement backed precandidate hopeful Alfredo del Mazo during the party's preselection maneuvering. The selection of Salinas, secretary of programming and budgeting and the author of many of the antilabor policies under de la Madrid, demonstrated not only labor's loss of influence and the power of the technocrats within the party and the government, but signaled a continuation of the antilabor policies of the de la Madrid era.

State-labor developments during the final year of the *sexenio* thus laid the groundwork for the rise of Cárdenas in 1988. Coupled with the unpopularity of the economic policies, the mobilization and repression of popular movements, the delegitimization of the labor bureaucracy, and the lukewarm support of the labor bureaucracy for the official candidate, labor became the weak link in the PRI's chain. The diffuseness of labor opposition and the support from "official" labor leaders that de la Madrid had nurtured in the early years evaporated in 1988, giving way to a deepening of the crisis. Not only would Salinas take the resulting electoral blow as workers would abandon the party in droves, but scores of labor leaders would be defeated at the polls.

De la Madrid in the Political Arena

As indicated, de la Madrid faced an arduous political task. In accordance with the assumptions of reformism, he sought to reform the system to salvage it, while carefully avoiding the unleashing of forces that would lead to its demise. His repertoire of purely political reforms was wide, ranging from anticorruption drives to limited political opening and electoral reform.

Taking a historic reformist tactic to new heights, de la Madrid launched a massive anticorruption campaign early in his term. Designed to help him garner credibility as a reformer, divert attention from the weak economy, and disassociate his political team from those of the past, de la Madrid made the "moral renovation" of society the highest priority during his initial years in office. Launching a high-profile rhetorical campaign against corruption, de la Madrid jailed high-ranking officials from the previous administration such as Arturo Durazo of the Mexico City police and Jesús Díaz Serrano of PEMEX (though he found it necessary to block opposition initiatives to investigate the unexplained fortune of former president López Portillo). He passed legislation to create a minimal level of civil service within the public sector, broaden the legal definition of "public servant," and tighten accounting and oversight mechanisms in the government. Most important, he established a cabinet-level agency, CONTROLARIA, to oversee the anticorruption fight and police the public's administration. The campaign also prompted a host of government bureaucracies and state and local governments to strike out against institutional corruption.[61]

A second series of political reforms under de la Madrid centered on the internal operations and structure of the PRI. With the goal of broadening the party's appeal and stimulating grassroots participation, de la Madrid oversaw a program designed to weaken the party's more entrenched and corrupt elements. In many ways, the rhetoric and programs paralleled earlier reforms under Echeverría and López Portillo. Through a program of "direct consultation," for example, the party organized self-styled public hearings throughout the country, inviting the public to openly discuss key policy issues. The intention was to begin a process of establishing, deepening, and bolstering the party's district structure rather than relying on its corporate appendages. Reforms adopted during the party's twelfth and thirteenth assemblies in 1983 and 1987 also pushed the party in this direction, even calling for and actually experimenting with local primaries in Hidalgo, Tamaulipas, San Luis Potosí, and Nayarit to select candidates. These moves challenged the power and privilege of local party bosses, caciques, and corporate leaders.[62]

In the initial year of the *sexenio*, de la Madrid's reformist strategy to bolster legitimacy also encapsuled a tacit policy of electoral opening. This encompassed, above all, a policy of recognizing opposition party victories in local elections regardless of the outcome.[63] Indeed, in striking contrast to the normal electoral pattern, virtually no fraud was reported during a string of 1983 state and local elections. This strategy embodied a wide range of objectives, including the restoration of regime legitimacy and a bolstering of de la Madrid's democratic and reformist credentials. In addition, it was targeted at restructuring the PRI. As John Bailey contends, "Increased electoral competition was viewed as a means of promoting changes within the PRI that would permit the party to compete in a more democratic system."[64]

A fourth political reformist measure under de la Madrid centered on political reform within the Federal District. Promised during his campaign, the president sought early on to establish direct elections for city officals who previously had been appointed by the president. As with the other political initiatives, the move was envisioned not only to preempt popular protests and relegitimize the party and the government, but to wrestle power from the old guard ruling Mexico City.[65]

During the early days of the *sexenio,* these measures seemed to earn the president increased credibility and popular support. Open elections were touted as indications of the regime's willingess to democratize. The party reforms were viewed as important steps in opening up the party and weakening the old party bosses. And the solid blows against corruption were seen as a concerted effort to eliminate this entrenched aspect of the system. One poll, for instance, showed a majority of respondents supportive of the president's anticorruption measures.[66] But while functional in bolstering popularity, they also unleashed dangerous political forces that forced de la Madrid to ease or abandon the initiatives. Such truncations would have multiple effects, undermining the president's progressive image, weakening the office of the presidency, and forcing the government to rely increasingly on negative reform measures such as fraud and repression to muddle through the *sexenio.*

In the open elections of 1983, the PAN won a surprising thirty-one *municipios,* including the important capital cities of Chihuahua, San Luis Potosí, Hermosillo, and Durango. Such an onslught raised the dangerous and unprecedented prospect of the opposition winning a gubernatorial election. Though such tendencies were confined to PAN strongholds in the north, they nonetheless forced de la Madrid to truncate the policy of electoral opening. Bowing to local pressures to abide the status quo, de la Madrid backtracked on his commitment to political change. Subsequent elections featured not only widespread and conspicuous fraud, but also a greater reliance on the party's traditional bases of support and the local bosses.[67] According to Loaeza, the PAN victories forced "a defensive

reaction by political authorities and local PRI forces . . . [and] traditional
norms were reinstated."68

The other reform initiatives followed a similar pattern. The anticorruption campaign, for example, which enjoyed marked success in the early
years, also fell on hard times. For one, the attacks inadvertently contributed to an undermining "of the legitimacy of the political system" and
a weakening of the presidency by dramatizing the depths of corruption.69
Among the public at least, the closing of the political opening made the
anticorruption drive seem less than authentic. It appeared illogical that the
moral renovation did not include clean elections. Among the elite as well,
de la Madrid's increasing reliance on the *politicos* within the party (many
of those benefiting from corruption) made such anticorruption campaigns
counterproductive.70 As a result, not only did the moral renovation campaign grow increasingly discredited, but corruption survived to taint the de
la Madrid regime as much as it did his predecessors. Indeed, the *sexenio*
became known as the "sexenio of impunity."71

The efforts at reforming the internal operations of the party also prof-
fered minimal results and fizzled out during the latter years as political necessity warranted. Though always conditioned on the needs of discipline
and unity and rarely pushed beyond the point of confrontation, the party
reforms threatened to unleash serious internal divisions within the party,
making their implementation more costly than anticipated.72 In Nayarit in
1984, for example, an experimental attempt to have local candidates selected by the CEN rather than by governors and local members of congress
was abandoned after drawing attack from local PRI chieftains.73 An effort
to select PRI candidates based on an internal vote of delegates in accordance with the twelfth assembly in Tamaulipas in 1986 produced severe
conflict that prompted many local PRI members to actually abandon the
party and declare independent candidacies. Three eventually ran under the
Partido Auténtico de la Revolución Mexicana (PARM) ticket.74 In June
1987, the renewed attempt of the PRI to introduce a primary system triggered open conflict, including the burning of 115 precincts in Acapaneta
by disgruntled PRI members. It was clear that the attempted changes
politicized the internal operations of the party and weakened rather than
strengthened it. And this at a time when the growing threat from the PAN
in the electoral arena increased the level of internal unity needed to surmount the challenge. This dilemma depleted the government's willingness
to carry out the party reforms, and in the end little changed. As Gentleman
concludes, "Despite the ambitious character of the project, the political
reform yielded few substantive results. Neither in terms of democratic
consultation, nor in terms of internal democratization within the ruling
party. . . . "75

The democratic reform initiative for Mexico City suffered a similar fate. It died and then was revived in extremely watered-down form. Facing stiff opposition from within the local government and among lobbyists, planners, and career bureaucrats, and convinced that the need for reform was limited, the government abandoned the idea. The issues would re-emerge in the last half of 1985, however, when urban social protests peaked, pushing the government to adopt an extremely weaker version. Rather than establish a representative body, the government created a consultative body that could only make recommendations to the mayor, still a presidential appointee.

De la Madrid's reversal of these political reforms had far-reaching implications. Though functional in maintaining power, the use of negative reforms to counter the growing PAN threat politicized the electoral process and increased system/antisystem polarization. Such developments, in turn, prompted the further erosion of the regime's legitimacy and de la Madrid's credibility as a reformer.

First, electoral fraud triggered widespread protests and conflict. Between 1982 and 1987, postelectoral confrontations erupted in a host of states and localities, including Juchitán, Oaxaca, Monclova, Piedras Negras, Coahuila, Puebla, Monterrey, Agua Prieta, Sonora, Durango, San Luis Potosí, San Juan de los Lagos, Guanajuato, Lagos de Moreno, Jalisco, Chihuahua, Ciudad Juarez, Alcozauca, Cuautepec, and Guerrero.[76] The national legislature became a public forum dedicated to debating electoral fraud. According to Gómez Tagle, the number of contested districts increased from 2 percent in 1979 to 7 percent by 1985.[77]

Fraud also elicited responses from intellectuals, the press, and the church, further crowding the electoral arena and politicizing previously tame forces. Following fraudulent elections in Chihuahua and Oaxaca, for example, a group of twenty nationally prominent intellectuals produced a communiqué condemning the process and calling for the government to annul the results.[78] Combined, the role of and attention to elections increased, crystallizing the democratization issue and making ever more apparent the government's intransigence. Elections attracted greater attention both internally and abroad and each became a major test of the reformist intentions of the president and the reformist capacity of the system. Continued fraud thus seemed to demonstrate the need for antisystem behavior to effect change.

Second, and in response, electoral fraud pushed the opposition to develop more radical approaches and new tactics to pressure for political change.[79] On the right, the PAN shifted internally toward a harder-line, more confrontational posture as indicated by the selection of Luis H. Alavarez as the party's leader in 1986.[80] The PAN mobilized civil disobedience campaigns to protest fraud, undermining the regime's reformist credibility and focusing public attention on the issue of democratization. It also reached out to forge new alliances to augment and channel pressures on the regime for change. The party closed ranks with the United States, the church, and the business community.[81] Even more unprecedented, it sought to internationalize the electoral issue by taking the case of electoral fraud in Chihuahua and Durango in 1985 and 1986 before the Organization of American States Commission on Human Rights.

The left also began to radicalize its tactics and coordinate its activities more in the electoral arena. In Tamaulipas, Oaxaca, Sinaloa, and Guerrero in 1986, three parties on the left—the Partido Socialista Unificado de México (PSUM), the Partido Mexicano de los Trabajadores (PMT), and the Partido Revolucionarios de los Trabajadores (PRT)—ran joint candidates for the first time, setting a pattern that would preface the emergence of Cárdenas's Frente Democrático Nacional (FDN) in 1988. The left also sought to broaden its base of support by forging alliances with intellectuals, popular movements, and independent labor, such as the formation of the Navistas in San Luis, the Coalición de Obreros, Campesinos, y Estudiantes del Istmo (COCEI) in Oaxaca, and the Unidad Popular Gurrerense and Asociación Cívica Nacional Revolucionaria in Guerro, and the Partido Trabajadores Zapatistas in the state of Mexico.[82]

[The growing politicization of elections also heightened the level of polarization by triggering the establishment of broad-based organizations uniting the right with the left into civil organizations. Fraudulent elections in Chihuahua and Oaxaca in 1986, in particular, helped forge the activities of *foro por el sufragio efectivo* and the proliferation of scores of other organizations bent on monitoring the elections, raising the public's awareness, and denouncing fraud.[83] These organizations would echo the demands of parties by putting elections and the need for electoral reforms on the front burner.]

The government's reaction to these developments seemed only to further politicize and polarize. In some cases, the government used repression to crush PAN-led protests over fraud, as occurred in the state of Coahuila in 1984. Such a response, however, seemingly fueled more protests by casting the government as repressive and intransigent. In other cases, the government responded with negotiations. [In Monclava, for instance, the government negotiated with the PAN leaders after the PAN forcibly took control of local government buildings, eventually permitting the naming of a bipartisan mayor.[84] Such an outcome restored a modicum of stability and ended the protest, marches, and hunger strikes; but it also harbored dangerous tendencies, rewarding and maybe even encouraging antifraud and postelectoral mobilizations on the part of the opposition, while undermining the role of elections as a source of legitimacy. Moreover, it created serious tensions within the PRI itself as many local leaders saw their interests sacrificed for the sake of stability.[85] As with the rise of monitoring organizations, these tendencies too would inaugurate a pattern that would carry over into the Salinas years.]

As these tendencies brought a deepening of the political crisis, de la Madrid attempted a new reform initiative in 1986. As with most political reforms in Mexico, the electoral reform package was "designed to generate an appearance of 'opening' without jeopardizing PRI political control."[86] Among other features, the reform increased the seats in the Chamber of Deputies for members of opposition parties (augmenting from 100 to 200 the proportional representation seats), enhanced public subsidies to the opposition parties, provided them with increased media exposure, and granted them a greater role in administering and supervising the elections. At the same time, it limited the PRI to 350 seats in the Chamber of Deputies and created an electoral tribunal to review and rule on allegations of wrongdoing. Theroetically, at least, it held out the prospect (depending on implementation) of cleaner elections.

Though the reform bowed to the new political role of elections in the system and the need to bolster the legitimacy of the process, it provided few dividends. Approved only by the PRI and its satellite parties—the Partido Socialista de los Trabajadores (PST), the Partido Popular Socialista (PPS), and the PARM—the real opposition—the PRT, PMT, PSUM, PAN, and Partido Democrático Mexicana (PDM)—all opposed the measure.[87] Thus, despite the wish to bolster legitimacy, few outside the PRI alliance felt that it had actually moved the country any closer to fair elections or democracy. The reform thus failed to stem the slide toward politicization and system/antisystem polarization infecting the electoral arena.

Despite the politicization of the electoral arena and the growing polarization, the PRI continued to hold power and win elections under de la Madrid. Reliance on the traditional PRI machinery still mustered sufficient electoral support for the PRI to protect its electoral hegemony in most areas of the country. With the PAN centered in small pockets of the country, mainly in the north, and the left weak and divided, the PRI captured the support of the rural areas and the lower classes in the traditional manner (see Chapter 7). Fraud was used when needed to shore up the weaknesses. In the 1985 midterm election, the PRI vote declined, but only marginally, from 69.2 percent in 1982 to 64.8 percent, simply continuing the secular decline of the past, though the degree of competitiveness did increase significantly.[88] The PRI ceded only ten of the 300 majority seats in the Chamber of Deputies to the PAN and thus maintained its solid hold.[89] Part of this outcome reflected de la Madrid's use of populist spending through supplementary budgetary allocations to boost the PRI's appeal, the short-lived economic recovery of 1984–1985, and, of course, fraud.[90]

Some of this support for the PRI was, paradoxically, the result of the politicization of the elections. First, the increased social conflict over elections characterizing the period prompted the regime to change its traditional campaign argument by suggesting that only the PRI could guarantee social stability. This new foundation of legitimacy became a major campaign strategy of the party and the government.[91] Whether this argument reflects the logic that opposition wins would undermine stability or that support for the opposition would prompt members of the PRI to undermine that stability, the reality indeed showed a strong correlation between social instability and the strength of the opposition. Opinion polls in 1986–1988 revealed the fruits of this strategy, showing over half of the respondents agreeing that opposition victory would touch off social unrest. As Cornelius et al. noted, the polls demonstrated "a citizenry still tethered to its traditional political moorings."[92]

Second, electoral fraud functioned indirectly to the PRI's advantage by reinforcing apathy and keeping turnouts low. In 1987, for example, elections in Nayarit brought a 70 percent rate of abstentionism, while in the state of Mexico the opposition estimated actual abstentionism at from 50 percent to 80 percent.[93] Such high abstentionism made elections easier to manage and manipulate for the PRI and the government.[94] Both these aspects aided the PRI's ability to surmount the crisis.

But underneath de la Madrid's apparent success at managing the crisis, the forces of crisis conspired. Broadly, two tendencies converged to deepen the political crisis as the *sexenio* neared its conclusion. The first centered on the politicization and polarization of the elections, which brought heightened public attention to elections, strengthened the opposition, and in effect cast the 1988 presidential contest as a plebiscite on the government's professed desire for democratic change. Most significantly, the politicization of elections, particularly the Chihuahua election of 1986, mobilized the PAN in preparation for the 1988 national contest. Combined with the failure of the economic program to broaden the PRI's middle-class and business support, the PAN thus became a national threat positioned on the PRI's right flank.

The second force leading up to the 1988 election was set in motion by de la Madrid's attacks on labor and the politicos. In late 1986, a faction of the politico class under the initiative of Cárdenas and Múñoz Ledo founded the Corriente Democrática, challenging the technocrats' hold on the government and hence the PRI. Born perhaps from the efforts of de la Madrid to "open" the party, the Corriente attacked not only the neoliberal economic policy of de la Madrid, but also the most sacred practice of the party: the traditional method of selecting the presidential candidate. Throwing tradition to the wind, the dissidents openly campaigned for Cárdenas as the PRI's candidate. Staunchly opposed by both the progressive technocratic wing and the more conservative wing of the party, the dissidents were subsequently expelled from the party after Cárdenas accepted the nomination of the PARM.[95]

The diminished power of the nationalistic wing of the revolutionary alliance, coupled with the regime's general political weakness, heightened the attractiveness of attacking the system from outside rather than brokering for position from the inside. This new approach for internal opponents, in turn, required them to focus on the issue of democratization as a tactical device to promote change. The Corriente thus served as a beacon attracting the diffuse opposition nurtured by de la Madrid's economic and political reforms. As Carr posits, "Almost overnight, an independent mass movement of impressive size and national character had arisen in Mexico."[96] In other words, the ranks of the "progressive nonsystem left" in Mexico exploded.

In Mexico, "the great political changes . . . have had one common characteristic: they have been preceded by divisions within the . . . power elite."[97] The significance of the split at the heart of the PRI in 1987 was therefore substantial. For the first time in decades, the center-left presented a united force behind an individual with substantial revolutionary and national credibility. This forced the PRI to confront the presidential election alone, without its traditional allies and against someone with even greater historical appeal.[98] And for the first time, the PRI faced a two-front battle with strong opposition poised on both its left and right.[99]

The 1988 Elections

The denouement in the political drama under de la Madrid was the July 6 national election. Touted as a watershed event, the contest "officially" left the PRI presidential candidate, Carlos Salinas de Gortari, with a bare majority of the popular vote (50.4 percent) and the hegemonic PRI with a slight advantage in the Chamber of Deputies (256 versus 244 for the opposition). Clearly resulting in the party's worst showing in history, both the process and the outcome had a manifold impact on the reformist equation.

First, on a psychological level, the surprising performance of Cárdenas, coupled with the government's sloppy handling of the election, delegitimized the incoming president, demythologized the one-party system, weakened the office of the presidency, and actually made credible the notion of a PRI electoral defeat. Or as Robert Pastor pointed out, it made "opposition legitimate and democracy possible."[100] Not only did the "official" vote for Cárdenas (31.4 percent) surpass the level obtained by any opposition candidate in history, but the perception of fraud in the eyes of the public and among the opposition was widespread and pervasive.[101] According to a Los Angeles Times poll in 1989, 74 percent of the respondents did not believe that Salinas had won.[102] To be sure, the curious events surrounding the election, particularly the period of official silence when the computers went down on election night, helped craft this image. The opposition eventually filed over 400 complaints before the Electoral Review Tribunal, contesting the results in 256 of the 300 electoral districts.[103]

In addition, because scores of PRI deputy candidates lost, the election also overturned an important psychological postulate within the official party itself: being a candidate for the PRI no longer ensured victory. This change would alter the operations of the party.

Second, the election further politicized the electoral process. Following the election, Cárdenas claimed to have won and rallied his supporters across the nation. Before initating a "journey for democracy and respect for popular sovereignty" throughout the nation, which called on protests "in every neighborhood, on every ranch" days after the results were released, he attracted a crowd of over 200,000 in the Zocalo. He called for a sit-in in congress, filed criminal charges against Manuel Bartlett, the head of the electoral commission, for not releasing the results from 45 percent of the polling precincts, and called for new elections. This demand was even backed by the PAN candidate, Manuel Clouthier, who like Cárdenas rejected the legitimacy of Salinas and refused to accept the results or "recognize those authorities which emerge from fraudulent elections." For his part, Clouthier called for a "civil disobedience campaign" to pressure the government.[104]

Though his calls went unheeded, due in part to a tacit agreement between the PAN and the PRI, the countless "popular mobilizations" of Cárdenas helped focus public attention and thrust elections permanently into the political forefront. The events prompted the opposition parties and society to organize to supervise and scrutinize the operation of future elections, and it made the government's handling of elections a critical determinant of regime legitimacy and its leader's reformist image. Indeed, 1988 became the decisive event shaping political acts for the foreseeable future.

Third, for the PRI itself, the election demonstrated the party's inability to deliver the vote in the traditional manner.[105] The defeat of scores of labor candidates within the PRI field in particular signified the inefficiency of the sectors to mobilize support for the party. Though the PRI victory hinged on the party's traditional bases of support, the outcome suggested that the party had either to revive itself, face the prospect of defeat in the future, or rely on repression and fraud to maintain its political hold. As Dresser concluded, "The 1988 election revealed that top-down change without the support of organized constituencies could probably not be sustained."[106]

Finally, the election had a fundamental institutional impact. For one, it transformed the Chamber of Deputies from a basically apolitical rubber-stamp institution to a forum of intense public debate. With only a handful majority, the PRI had to bargain in good faith with its opponents in order to alter the constitution. And even though the PRI could use its majority control to pass legislation, it became clear that only through compromise with the opposition could it garner the legitimacy needed to govern effectively. The PRI's slight majority in congress, furthermore, enhanced the bargaining power of the PRI's legislative group and concomitantly heightened the importance of party loyalty, since only few departures could undermine the party's legislative majority.

Perhaps even more important though, the election forged a viable, unified center-left opposition, first in the FDN behind Cárdenas, and post-1989 in the PRD. For the first time, the PRI's opponents now pinched from both sides of the political spectrum, contrary to the past when its only major opponent sat to its right. On the one hand, this institutional change heightened the prospects that the left could mobilize the "popular movements" spawned by the crisis-ridden eighties and thus mitigate "the contradiction between electoral and social struggles" that had long characterized the political scene.[107] This also meant that the PRI, for the first time, had to struggle to maintain its monopoly over the legacy of the revolution. On the other hand, the presence of a powerful center-left coalition helped temper the PAN's opposition to the PRI and the government's hard-line posture toward the PAN—a situation Salinas would attempt to exploit.

Conclusion

Putting the period in context, it is clear that de la Madrid's early reforms reflected the interests of the progressive reformers (Group 2). The government eventually reversed course, however, relying on negative measures and the more conservative elements in the system (Group 1) to protect the alliance. This reflected in large part the failure of de la Madrid to totally overcome the tensions with the private sector and diminish their growing support for the PAN (Group 3). Fearing the further rise of the PAN, as evidenced in a series of local elections as well as the growth of urban social movements following the 1985 earthquakes, de la Madrid came to rely increasingly on the old guard and their tactics to maintain power.

Even so, the liberal reformers (Group 2) were generally successful at putting through their economic agenda, though it was slow and cautious for political reasons. By the end of the term, Mexico was in the process of dismantling the import substitution model and installing a more liberalized, export-oriented one, though many of the controls remained. Still, de la Madrid's inability to turn the economy around prevented him from enjoing the political rewards. It triggered a massive departure from within the PRI alliance, as many of those within the conservative camp (Group 1) actually abandoned the party. This significantly bolstered the strength and unification of the left opposition (Group 4). This further reinforced de la Madrid's reliance on the remaining old guard within the party to mobilize the vote in 1988 and prevent a further erosion of support for the system.

In sum, despite de la Madrid's intentions to alleviate Mexico's crisis, his major reform initiatives marking the early 1980s proved unsuccessful at truly taming it. Political/electoral opening, anticorruption initiatives, party reforms, and swipes at the system's traditional pillars were all either gradually abandoned in the face of growing pressures, discredited, or watered down. Relying on the traditional pillars and aged practices to protect power, the regime muddled through and survived. Yet despite it all, the political crisis deepened. As a result, by the end of the term, elections had become staunchly politicized, the PRI was divided, and the nation seemed dangerously polarized. Within this setting, the reformist imperative to maintain the PRI's hold on the government through whatever measures necessary in the short term clashed with the reformist goal of restoring regime legitimacy to protect its long-term survival. This zero-sum context left incoming President Carlos Salinas a system ever closer to the brink of breakdown or political breakthrough.[108]

Notes

1. Basañez, *El pulso de los sexenios*, pp. 217–247, reports the results of national polls conducted in 1983 and 1987.

2. For an overview of state-business relations see Maxfield and Anzaldua, eds., *Government and Private Sector in Contemporary Mexico*. Newell and Rubio, *Mexico's Dilemma: The Political Origins of Economic Crisis*, as noted earlier, locate the roots of the crisis in the disruption of the traditional pact with business in the 1970s.

3. Presidencia de la República, *Las razones y las obras,* p. 19.

4. Luna et al., "Businessmen and Politics in Mexico," p. 14.

5. Schneider, "Partly for Sale," p. 108, makes the argument that the success of the PAN in the early 1980s pushed de la Madrid toward a policy of privatization.

6. In 1985, the government eliminated permits for imports on some 4,300 product lines and lowered tariffs. By 1986, 89.6 percent of products had been liberalized. From 1985 to 1987, the number of products with set prices declined from 1,348 to 581 (see Presidencia de la República *Razones y obras*, p. 524).

7. On de la Madrid's handling of the financial crisis and relations with the financial community see Basañez, *El pulso de los sexenios*; Garrido Noguera, "Relaciones de endeudamiento, grupos económicos y reestructuración capitalista en México"; and Maxfield, "The International Political Economy of Bank Nationalization." On the economic crisis/reforms generally, see Bizberg, "El México neocorporativo"; Sheahan, *Conflict and Change in Mexico's Economic Strategy*; Whitehead, "Mexico's Economic Prospects"; and Wyman, ed., *Mexico's Economic Crisis.*

8. *Latin American Weekly Review* 89–21 (June 1, 1989).

9. Foley, "Agenda for Mobilization."

10. Prior to the use of CETES, the government relied on a high *encaje legal* (reserve requirement) of 50 percent to finance itself. In 1984, the figure was lowered to 10 percent. See Garrido Noguera, "Relaciones de enduedamiento."

11. One indication of the rise of the parallel sector was the drop in deposits at the nationalized banks, which fell from 25 percent of GDP in 1980 to 15 percent by 1988. In real terms, deposits fell 13 percent in 1985 alone. See Maxfield, "International Political Economy."

12. Despite a declining or stagnant economy, the Mexican stock market was bullish, reflecting the benefits for some of the financial restructuring program. The index of the Mexican *bolsa* climbed to 2,451 points (fourfold increase) in 1983, 4,038 in 1984, 11,197 (117 percent increase) in 1985, 47,101 points (320 percent increase) in 1986, and 114,586 during the first semester of 1987. At the same time, the number of investors increased from 84,476 in 1983 to 373,822 in August 1987. By 1986, however, the breach between the real value of the stocks and their value on the *bolsa* grew, drawing more investors into the volatile and largely unregulated market. As a result, the market crashed in October 1987. The crack reduced the value of the stock market by as much as 50 percent, triggering capital flight, a 40 percent devaluation of the peso, inflation, and threats of massive strikes on the part of labor. This paved the way for corporate-level negotiations and the signing of the "Pact" to control inflation (see Alvarez Bejar, "Economic Crisis and the Labor Movement in Mexico"; and Basanez, *El pulso de los sexenios*). Basáñez, who links the creation and treatment of the financial sector and its instability to the "bolsa crack," views this as an example of how resolving one crisis eventually forges another.

13. Garrido Noguera, "Relaciones de enduedamiento," p. 33.

14. Luna et al., "Businessmen and Politics," p. 24.

15. Cronin, "Domestic Versus International Influences on State Behavior," pp. 17–19.

16. Bizberg, "El México neocorporativo," p. 49.

17. Basáñez, *El pulso de los sexenios*, pp. 225, 229.

18. Meyer, *La segunda muerte de la Revolución Mexicana*, p. 93.

19. Part of the economic problems and the inability of the reforms to counter opposition from the private sector stemmed as well from de la Madrid's inability to maintain a coordinated strategy. As Sheahan, *Conflict and Change,* points out, up until 1987, the government shifted from an emphasis on promoting exports (via devaluations) to one of controlling inflation (via allowing the peso to become overvalued). To a large extent, the establishment of the anti-inflationary pact in 1987 resolved this paradox, setting the stage for a slow recovery and the reduction of inflation.

20. Ramírez de la O, "The Mexican Crisis," p. 174.

21. Luna et al. "Businessmen and Politics," pp. 25–26.

22. Garrido Noguera and Quintana López, "Financial Relations and Economic Power in Mexico," p. 123.

23. Maxfield, "International Political Economy."

24. Cited in Bravo Mena, "COPARMEX and Mexican Politics," p. 91.

25. See Ortega and Solís de Alba, *México: Estado y sindicatos*, p. 9.

26. Zamora, "La política laboral del estado Mexicano," p. 113.

27. Alvarez Bejar, "Economic Crisis," p. 45.

28. Ortega and Solís de Alba, *Estado y sindicatos*, p. 13.

29. Zamora, "La política laboral," p. 114.

30. Whitehead, "Mexico's Economic Prospects," p. 78.

31. Alvarez Bejar, "Economic Crisis," p. 45.

32. Centeno, *Democracy Within Reason*, p. 92.

33. Alvarez Bejar, "Economic Crisis," p. 46.

34. See Alvarez Bejar, "Economic Crisis," p. 46; and de la Garza, "Independent Trade Unionisn in Mexico," p. 177. On the weakening of the independent movement during the de la Madrid period see also Couffignal, "La gran debilidad del sindicalismo mexicano"; Franco, "Labor Law and the Labor Movement in Mexico"; and Ortega and Solís de Alba, *Estado y sindicatos*.

35. Alvarez Bejar, "Economic Crisis," p. 44.

36. Newell and Rubio, *Mexico's Dilemma*, p. 127.

37. Presidencia de la República, *Razones y obras*, pp. 16–80.

38. Durand Ponte, "Corporativismo obrero y democracia," *Revista Mexicana de Sociología* 52 (3), 1990, p. 100.

39. Durand Ponte, "Corporativismo obrero y democracia," p. 102.

40. Middlebrook, "The Sounds of Silence," pp. 206–207.

41. Zamora, "La política laboral," p. 128.

42. Alvarez Bejar, "Economic Crisis," p. 48.

43. See Durand Ponte, "Corporativismo obrero y democracia," pp. 98–102. See also Alvarez Bejar, "Economic Crisis," p. 48; and Presidencia de la República, *Razones y obras*, p. 777.

44. Middlebrook, "Dilemmas of Change in Mexican Politics." See also Aguilar Camín, *Después del milagro*, p. 70; Durand Ponte, "Corporativismo obrero y democracia," p. 100; Franco, "Labor Law and the Labor Movement in Mexico," p. 114; and Middlebrook, *Unions, Workers and the State in Mexico*, p. 12.

45. Sheahan, *Conflict and Change*, for instance, attributes the functioning of the wage/price PACT to Mexico's strong corporate controls.

46. Ortega and Solís de Alba, *Estado y sindicatos*, p. 21. The independent labor unions and the left created a variety of *coordinadores*—such as the Fondo Nacional de Cooperacion para el Trabajador (FNDSCAC), the Comité Nacional de Defensa de la Economía Popular (CNDEP), and the Asamblea Nacional de Obreros y Campesinos Populares (ANOCP)—to protest austerity and the government's antilabor leanings. By the mid-1980s, such organizations turned to progressive political parties to forge electoral pacts, a development that eroded the historic atomization of the left. According to Alvarez Bejar, "Economic Crisis," p. 29, by mid-1984, these coalitions had shrunk or disappeared because of the CTM's adoption of a more conciliatory line. On these movements see Craig, "Institutional Context and Popular Strategies"; Durand Ponte, "Corporativismo obrero y democracia"; and Tamayo, "Neoliberalism Encounters Neocardenismo." On their linkages with the left, see Carr, "The Left and Its Potential Role in Political Change," and Couffignal, "La gran debilidad."

47. Middlebrook, *Unions, Workers and the State*, p. 11.

48. The CT called a general strike for February 12, 1987, and demanded a 23 percent pay increase. The strike was postponed three times before the CT agreed to push its unions to engage in individual negotiations. Another threat of a general strike was made in December but also ended with nothing, showing a generalized weakness of the labor movement. Despite the disagreements, the CTM held that its relationship with the government was not open to discussion (see Zamora, "La política laboral," p. 134).

49. Middlebrook, *Unions, Workers and the State*, p. 11.

50. Durand Ponte, "Corporativismo obrero y democracia," p. 100.

51. See Middlebrook, "Sounds of Silence."

52. Ortega and Solís de Alba, *Estado y sindicatos*, p. 18.

53. Tamayo, "Neoliberalism Encounters Neocardenismo," p. 122.

54. Basañez, *El pulso de los sexenios*, p. 225.

55. Tamayo, "Neoliberalism Encounters Neocardenismo," p. 122.

56. Alvarez Bejar, "Economic Crisis," p. 47.

57. Foweraker, "Popular Movements and Political Change in Mexico," p. 17.

58. Zamora, "La política laboral," pp. 128–129.

59. Ortega and Solís de Alba, *Estado y sindicatos*, p. 29.

60. Cornelius et al., "Overview," p. 13.

61. For a more detailed description and analysis of the Moral Renovation campaign see Morris, *Corruption and Politics in Contemporary Mexico.*

62. On internal party reforms under de la Madrid see Bailey, *Governing Mexico*; Cornelius, "Political Liberalization in an Authoritarian Regime," Meyer, "Democratization of the PRI" and *La segunda muerte;* and Presidencia de la República, *Razones y obras.*

63. Cornelius, "Political Liberalization," p. 22.

64. Bailey, *Governing Mexico*, pp. 145, 154.

65. An excellent anaysis of this reform effort is provided by Davis, "Failed Democratic Reform in Contemporary Mexico."

66. See Chapter 5 of Morris, *Corruption and Politics.*

67. Cornelius, "Political Liberalization," p. 23.

68. Cited in Molinar Horcasitas, "The Future of the Electoral System," p. 269.

69. Baer, "Electoral Trends," p. 39.

70. Cornelius, "Political Liberalization," p. 23.

71. Cited in *Proceso* 659 (June 19, 1989), p. 18.

72. PRI President Adolfo Lugo (cited in Bailey, *Governing Mexico*, p. 119) referred to this as a strategy of gradualism: "The commitment to the process [consultation] remains firm; consultation will be attempted flexibly, according to the specific conditions in each state; the indispensable conditions are unity and internal discipline; the process will proceed gradually with political realism; and despite the great deal that has been accomplished in deepening democratic life in the heart of the party, that—due to the survival of local fiefdoms [*cacicazgos*]—we encounter obstacles and resistance."

73. Cornelius, "Political Liberalization," p. 24.

74. Presidencia de la República, *Razones y obras*, pp. 439–443, 140–146.

75. Gentleman, ed., *Mexican Politics in Transition*, p. 57. The political reversal accompanied a watering down of the antilabor side of the economic program. In the face of a growing electoral threat from the PAN and with the midterm elections approaching, the government closed ranks with the CTM, made concessions to labor, and increased its social spending.

76. See Baer, "Electoral Trends," pp. 48–49; and Basañez, *El pulso de los sexenios*, pp. 91–92.

77. Gómez Tagle, "Democracy and Power in Mexico," p. 165.

78. Basañez, *El pulso de los sexenios*, pp. 90–91.

79. Much of the politicization produced by the electoral fraud reflected the somewhat amateurish nature of the fraud—a factor, according to Riding, *Distant Neighbors*, reflecting the technocrats' lack of experience.

80. Molinar Horcasitas, *El tiempo de la legitimidad*, pp. 186–187.

81. Basañez, *El pulso de los sexenios*, pp. 90–91.

82. Presidencia de la República, *Razones y obras*, pp. 140–146.

83. Basañez, *El pulso de los sexenios*, p. 90.

84. Cornelius, "Political Liberalization," pp. 24–25.

85. On antisystem polarization leading up to the election see Molinar Horcasitas, *El tiempo de la legitimidad*, pp. 185–210.

86. Baer, "Electoral Trends," p. 50.

87. See Presidencia de la República, *Razones y obras*.

88. Molinar Horcasitas, *El tiempo de la legitimidad*, p. 159.

89. On the 1985 elections see Molinar Horcasitas, "The 1985 Federal Elections in Mexico."

90. Philip, *The Presidency in Mexican Politics*, p. 150.

91. Sánchez Susarrey, *La transición incierta*, pp. 29–30.

92. Cornelius et al., "Overview," p. 16.

93. Presidencia de la República, *Razones y obras*, pp. 507–514.

94. Bailey, *Governing Mexico*, p. 162. Others would make this argument during the initial years of the Salinas term.

95. On the initial features of the Corriente see, for instance, Flores Maldonado, *¿Cuál será el destino del PRI?* For a complete analysis of the Cárdenas break with the PRI see Garrido, *La ruptura*.

96. Carr, "The Left and Its Role," p. 371.

97. Meyer, *La segunda muerte,"* p. 91.

98. This was the first time in history that the candidate for the PRI failed to be postulated by another political party. It is important to note that the 1986 electoral reform actually reduced the PRI's reliance on the satellite parties to control the electoral machinery, thereby weakening their bargaining strength vis-à-vis the PRI. This, of course, set the stage for their abandonment of the PRI in 1988 (see Molinar Horcasitas, *El tiempo de la legitimidad*, pp. 194–195, 200).

99. Meyer, *La segunda muerte,"* p. 40.

100. Pastor, "Post-Revolutionary Mexico," p. 8.

101. For an analysis of electoral fraud in 1988 see Barberán et al., *Radiografía del fraude*.

102. Cited in Montanño and Lund, "Erosion of PRI Support and Credibility."

103. Cited in the *Mexico Journal* 1 (42), August 1, 1988, p. 6.

104. Still, both opposition leaders demonstrated restraint; much of the *cardenista* following would have resorted to armed revolt had their leader supported that path to change. See the series of reports in the *New York Times,* July 11, 1988, p. 1; July 16, 1988, p. 6; July 17, 1988, p. 5; July 22, 1988, p. 3; August 11, 1988, p. 11; and August 15, 1988, p. 5; and the *Mexico Journal* 1(42), August 1, 1988, p. 8.

105. Francisco Ortiz Pinchetti, "La solución para el PRI sería el suicidio pacífico."

106. Dresser, *Neopopulist Solutions to Neoliberal Problems*, p. 3.

107. Eckstein, "Formal Versus Substantive Democracy," p. 214; and Paré, "The Challenges of Rural Democratization in Mexico," p. 91.

108. Perhaps even more dangerous than zero-sum, Molinar Horcasitas, *El tiempo de la legitimidad*, p. 172, characterizes the 1988 election as a type of negative-sum equation because the government lost control (by losing its absolute majority in congress) and legitimacy.

4

Political Reformism
Under Salinas

The 1988 election made Carlos Salinas de Gortari president but intensified and altered Mexico's political crisis. Economically, Salinas needed to curb inflation, encourage investments, and strengthen growth. To do so, he sought to maintain strict fiscal discipline and the anti-inflation pact while deepening the neoliberal restructuring program initiated by his predecessor. Politically, he faced the precarious task of depoliticizing and depolarizing the situation fostered by the 1988 election. Although achieving his economic goals would presumably play a role in easing popular pressures, he still needed to restore regime legitimacy, nurture the reformist image, arrest the internal and electoral deterioration of the PRI, and undermine, divide, and weaken the opposition.

Salinas accomplished many of these objectives. A popular leader, he centralized and used the power of the presidency to slightly and subtly reshape the state-business pact, the state-labor alliance, state-society linkages, and the internal operations of the PRI. As a result, the PRI rebounded in the midterm election of 1991. Still, like his predecessor, Salinas faced renewed economic and political crisis during the final year of his term. Marked by renewed economic recession, an armed uprising in the state of Chiapas, disputes within the ranks of the PRI, and the assassination of the PRI's presidential candidate, 1994 brought renewed risks and dangers of breakdown. Yet, true to historic form, the regime brokered the dilemmas and held on to power. On December 1, 1994, Salinas followed a well-established pattern by handing over power to his hand-picked successor, friend, and PRI colleague.

In focusing on reformism under Salinas, I follow the same pattern I used to examine reformism under de la Madrid. I begin with an examination of the state's evolving relationship with business and labor and then turns to the political realm and an examination of Salinas's moves to gain popular credibility, bolster the PRI, and divide opponents. The discussion ends with an examination of the crisis/reform pattern during the first half of 1994, converging around the presidential election.

Salinas and the Private Sector

Salinas's relationship with the private sector was shaped in large part by his economic reform program. While similar in design to de la Madrid's, Salinas's economic policies were more consistent, more extensive, and yielded better economic and political outcomes. Like his predecessor, Salinas continued to scale back the economic role of the state. He oversaw the sale of 250 state firms, including such major enterprises as Telmex (the telephone monopoly), the banks, and the state's television station, reducing the number of state firms by 1994 to an estimated twenty-seven.[1] He continued to cut government spending, thereby lowering, and by 1992 actually eliminating, the budget deficit.[2] Along with the periodic renewal of the corporate-based anti-inflationary pact and a strict wage policy, this contributed to the taming of inflation. Price increases fell from the 159 percent high registered in 1987 to an estimated 13 percent in 1992 and less than 10 percent by 1993.

Besides restoring fiscal health, Salinas also bolstered investments and hastened the economy's global opening. This he accomplished through such devices as the maintenance of high domestic interest rates and a series of sectoral changes designed to facilitate foreign and private investment, promote exports, and free imports, such as the 1989 reform of the foreign investment law. Clearly the symbolic and institutional centerpiece of this effort was NAFTA.[3] Initiated in 1990 at Salinas's request, the mere negotiation of the agreement triggered a wave of investments that spurred economic activity. During the period 1987–1991, private investments increased more than 10 percent per year.[4] Much of this came from abroad as Mexico became the preferred child of foreign investors, capturing over $49 billion during the Salinas term (through June 1994).[5] Such investments, according to Nora Lustig, provided the spark for renewed economic growth.[6] Thus,following an average growth rate of .1 percent during the entire *sexenio* of de la Madrid, the economy grew at an average rate of 3.45 percent for the first four years under Salinas.

Like de la Madrid's, Salinas's specific policies provided a solid boost to the private financial market. The maintenance of high domestic interest rates, for instance, particularly during the first four years of the term, paid handsome dividends. In 1992, estimated earnings on CETES reached over $35 billion.[7] The privatization of the banks, the creation of a bank-controlled retirement program, and reforms of the INFONAVIT housing funds under Salinas also increased profits and spurred financial activity.[8] Structural reforms covering foreign investment, agriculture, fishing, and mining and the "locking-in" of the liberal changes through NAFTA also opened a range of opportunities heretofore closed to private and foreign investors.[9] To accommodate business interests in the countryside, Salinas even overhauled the *ejido* land system in 1991 to allow for private investments, joint ventures, and the sale of *ejido* land. Though Salinas had long provided special benefits to the agribusiness sector over peasant interests, the reform proved popular among the business sector because it institutionalized the changes already in practice.[10]

In providing further favor to business, Salinas also responded partially to one of its more consistent demands: a watering down of the nation's liberal labor law.[11] The product of three years of intense corporate negotiations, the 1992 Acuerdo Nacional para Elevar la Productividad y la Calidad (ANEP) undercut the bargaining power of unions. It eliminated the practice of industrywide labor negotiations, forcing labor to negotiate at the plant level and depoliticized wage increases by tying future raises to productivity.[12] This move was coupled with a generally hard-line policy toward labor unions and the suppression of wages (to be discussed in the next section).

The substance, implementation, and impact of these policies contributed to an easing of tensions with business. In an annual survey of business opinion by Banco Nacional de México (BANAMEX) during the second half of 1991, for example, over 60 percent of those interviewed found the business environment highly favorable.[13] But such a situation went even further by setting the stage for the forging of a new state-business pact. The new pact was based less on the domestic-oriented industrial firms associated with the import-substitution model and more on the more powerful financial and export-related business benefiting from the economic program.[14] The new pact featured an enhanced role for business in politics.

The new alliance went deeper than economics, coinciding with a growing presence and involvement of big business in the government and the PRI. First, government effectively incorporated business into the policymaking process. As one observer notes, business almost became "a part of the corporate system."[15] Through an open line of communication, the president ordinarily consulted business leaders on major economic matters. The most conspicuous example was the prominent role of private sector representatives alongside government officials in the NAFTA negotiations. In many areas, the private sector representatives actually led the negotiations. The private sector also spearheaded the massive pro-NAFTA propaganda campaign within the country and the United States.

Business also became more active within the PRI. Rodríguez Reyna even goes so far as to suggest that beginning in 1988 the PRI began to add a fourth sector: the entrepreneurial sector.[16] The private sector provided critical financial support for the party. In Nuevo León, for example, officials of such high-profile economic groups as CEMEX, VISA, and Metalasa sat on the finance committee for the PRI's gubernatorial candidate, Sócrates Rizzo.[17] A similar group backed the PRI at the national level.

Business groups participated, for instance, in the creation of a PRI credit card in 1993 and the establishment of a Fondo de Financiamiento General. Such support reached scandalous proportions in early 1993, when it was revealed that twenty-five wealthy businessmen had been asked by the PRI to contribute $25 million apiece to the party's campaign. Though this touched off a mini public relations scandal, many such contributions were reportedly made. In fact, Emilio Azcarraga, the multibillionaire media giant, stated publicly that he had made so much money under Salinas that he was willing to give $75 million to the party. Such financial support came at a critical time: when opposition parties and the public began to complain about the illegal and illegitimate use of public resources to finance the PRI.

Besides money, the business community also provided personnel to the PRI as candidates for gubernatorial seats, congressional posts, and other state and local offices, particularly in more hotly contested states. Favored by centralized decisionmaking in the party and the move toward territorial-based organs, the ranks of business candidates grew. The LV legislature (1988–1991), for instance, counted more that thirty-five members from the PRI delegation associated with the nation's major business organizations.[18] In critical state elections, the PRI tapped local business leaders, such as Eduardo Villaseñor in Michoacán, to counter the threat of both left and right opposition. And business provided votes for the ruling party. Arresting the tendency during the de la Madrid period for business to publicly side with the PAN, Salinas and the PRI attracted members of the business community back to the tricolor. Polls indicated that much of the newfound support for Salinas during the 1991 election came from among the more educated and higher socioeconomic groups—a measure easing the secular aspects of the political crisis.[19] Indeed, the PAN's vote in 1991 stagnated. Support for Salinas and his reforms among big business was so strong that it even led one such group to openly float a trial balloon calling for Salinas's reelection.[20] Though the PAN performed much better in 1994, exit polls revealed a similar pattern wherein the PRI did well with the private sector.

Not all was to their liking to be sure. Small and medium-size businesses, for instance, enjoyed fewer benefits from the economic reforms. Even so, the healthier state of the nation's finances seemed to offer Salinas some room to respond to their concerns. Thus, in 1991, he crafted the Programa Nacional de la Micro, Pequeña y Mediana Industrias.[21] The program provided financial relief and assistance to this segment of the business community—a measure that not only could be used to help them financially, but that also could be withheld to discipline their opposition to the regime if needed. According to Poitras and Robinson, the program in fact went a long way in garnering the support of the outspoken CANAC-INTRA for the free trade agreement.[22]

The private sector generally criticized the government for its use of price controls and its fiscal policy. Through more vigilant interpretation and application of fiscal law, for example, the Salinas government enhanced and broadened its taxing powers. Such moves were disconcerting to business. Coining the term "fiscal terrorism," business openly criticized the unpredictable nature of fiscal administration. In April 1992, the CONCANACO claimed the fiscal law had undergone 505 changes during the preceding twelve-month period.[23] The government generally stuck to its guns on the issue of prices and taxes, enforcing cooperation based on threats of sanctions, audits, and loss of government contracts.[24] But, it also provided exemptions and help on a case-by-case basis, offering generalized tax cuts and subsidies to business beginning in 1993.

Just as the restoration of growth and hence the easing of the conjunctural component of the crisis provided the government the wherewithal to accommodate the losers in the transitional crisis, it also helped the regime withstand renewed crisis. Thus, when recession hit during the second half of 1993, bringing the yearly growth rate down to just .4 percent, the government found itself better positioned to respond. At the end of August, international reserves stood at $22.6 billion and the government held a $4 billion surplus. This enabled the government to put into effect a stimulus package that plowed an estimated $6 billion surplus back into the economy, doubled the number of individuals not paying taxes, provided rebates to an estimated 6.9 million workers, slashed prices by as much as 40 percent on government products, cut the corporate tax rate by 1 percent (while permitting faster depreciation and easier terms), and increased social spending by 27 percent.[25]

In sum, Salinas orchestrated a new convergence of state–private sector interests in Mexico. He ended the antibusiness rhetoric of the past, followed policies favorable to many businesses, and then built a new coalition based on the program's main beneficiaries.[26] Though differences in policy approaches continued to surface from time to time, business groups generally downplayed the confrontationalist style that had marked their relationship with the state during the late 1970s and early 1980s. Pleased with the new economic program and its greater involvement in the creation of that program, the private sector fell back into its historic pattern of pressuring the regime in a less public and more subtle way, generally acquiescing to the authoritarian nature of the system and its slow pace of political change. Such an outcome was precisely what the government needed to arrest the growing convergence between business and the PAN, to restore economic growth, and to overcome the crisis.

Salinas and Labor

Among the many lessons of the 1988 election was the decline in the capacity of the official labor unions to mobilize support for the PRI. Congressional candidates from the party's labor wing, including such deeply entrenched labor bosses as Gamboa Pascoe, were in fact among the big losers in the 1988 election. This realization of the political liability of corporatism fit snugly with the economic views held by the technocratic reformers. The conclusion: for both political and economic reasons, the state-labor pact had to change. For equally important political and economic reasons, of course, the need to alter the historic pact was tempered by the government's continued reliance on and need to protect the basic structure of the corporatist system.

This goal of bending the pact without breaking it encompassed a host of objectives and implied a range of instruments. One of the major ingredients in Salinas's anti-inflation and labor strategies was to curb and discipline worker demands. To do so, the government adopted a hard-line approach toward strikes. It routinely ruled strikes illegal, sided with management and the "official unions" to facilitate the firing of worker dissidents, and deployed police repression to break workers' resolve. Facing a threatened strike in the Cananea Mining Company in 1989, for example, the government declared the state-owned copper firm bankrupt, reorganized the company, and resumed operations under a new labor contract.[27] Likewise, declaring the strike at the beer plant Modelo in 1989 illegal, the government permitted the firing of workers and the hiring of strikebreakers.[28] Conflict at Ford in late 1989 and 1990 also featured the repression of workers, their firing, and the hiring of replacement workers provided by the CTM itself.[29] In July 1990, the government violently removed striking workers at TAMSA (Tubos de Acero de México),[30] and in June 1991, Salinas ordered the requisition of port facilities in Veracruz in response to labor conflict. In like fashion, the Volkswagen strike in 1992 ended with the firing of all 15,000 union employees and the repression of the workers, while a seven-month strike in CIVSA concluded with an agreement between the company and the governor allowing for the firing of striking workers.[31]

While such a policy was targeted at workers generally, the government also took swipes at the privileges of official unions and their leaders as a means to curb labor's influence. It cut back (without eliminating) unions' control over subcontracting, reformed the social security and housing programs to diminish labor's long-standing control over resources, and even curbed labor's control over pensions.[32] In addition, Salinas removed some rather deeply entrenched labor leaders. A military raid early in 1989, for example, led to the arrests of longtime petroleum worker leaders Joaquín

Hernández Galicia ("La Quina") and Salvador Barragán Camacho, and their associates.[33] In similar fashion, Salinas intervened to remove Jongitud Barrios, the deeply entrenched leader of the teachers union, SNTE, in 1989.[34]

As part of this hard-line approach toward labor—what one group of labor lawyers characterized as "dictatorial, blackmailing and authoritarian"—the government promoted a "new syndicalism."[35] As Salinas himself stated, this involved a new worker-government bond based on "new forms of participation, new themes, and new ways to relate to one another."[36] Above all, new syndicalism meant the "depoliticization" of the larger, more powerful labor confederations, a weakening of their influence over public policy and within the ranks of the official party, a debilitation of their negotiating strength, a reduction in the role of government in mediating labor disputes, the installation of a labor leadership less prone to the use of the strike tactic to pressure for worker benefits and more supportive of the neoliberal program of restructuring, and even the end of unions' affiliation to political parties, including the PRI.

Though touted as a clean strike against labor corruption, for instance, the new leader of the oil workers union, Sebastian Guzmán Cabrera was hand-picked in the same style that La Quina had been selected years earlier by President López Mateos.[37] Yet Guzmán lent support to the government's economic policy, including the massive scaling down of the petroleum industry, the dismissals of thousands of workers, restructuring, and even some privatization.[38] Indeed just a few years after the removal of Hernández, Sindicato de Trabajadoes Petroleros de las República Mexicana (STPRM) membership had been cut in half.[39] Though Barrios was removed to restore order, his removal similarly facilitated the restructuring of the educational system and a depoliticization of the large teachers union. Indeed, shortly after Barrios's ouster, more cooperative SNTE leaders agreed to Salinas's educational reform package, the Acuerdo Nacional para la Modernización de la Educación Básica. This reform decentralized salary and contract negotiations and even provided for the elimination of the obligatory affiliation of the organization with the PRI, despite the solid allegiance of the union's leadership.[40]

Promoting new syndicalism also meant favoring more cooperative organizations over the more combative CTM in true divide-and-conquer strategy. While rebuffing demands from the CTM and even publicly questioning a number of its affiliates because of its resistance to change, the government heaped praise and rewards on more cooperative, supportive, and pliable organizations such as the CROC and particularly the Federación de Sindicatos de Bienes y Servicios (FESBES). Preferential treatment even included wage increases.[41] These organizations in turn praised Salinas and his economic program, calling on the rank and file to adopt a new and more "modern" attitude toward labor. As Nestor de Buen notes, the CROC was "more than satisfied by the demonstrations of affection that they received from the president of the Republic."[42] Indeed, during their ninth national congress in March 1992, Alberto Juárez Blancas, the confederation's general secretary, called the secretary of labor "CROC's best friend." Secretary Farell, in turn, praised the growth of the CROC during the previous ten years—a pattern strongly influenced by the role of the government—and averred that CROC "is now part of modern syndicalism, in accordance with the circumstances not only in Mexico, but in the world."[43]

New syndicalism also began to take shape through two negotiated pacts. The first, the Worker-Peasant pact, was hammered out within the PRI in June 1992. This agreement, rather than eliminating the corporate unions, brought the CTM and the Confederación Nacional de Compesinos (CNC) into a new alliance that refocused their activities and delineated a privileged area of activity for them under the new economic regime. Among its features, the accord sanctioned productivity increases based on greater worker training, freed the CTM to engage in union activity in the countryside, and linked the CTM to the projects of Solidarity and the CNC, particularly in agroindustry. The agreement also provided financial subsidies to help support these new social endeavors by labor unions. The other pact, the ANEP, also helped carve out a new relationship between the workers and the state.[44] For its part, labor promised to promote consciousness among workers in support of the liberal economic changes of Salinas, accept increased benefits in return for productivity gains, and conduct negotiations at the plant level, where labor's bargaining strength is the weakest.[45]

Critical to the success of these moves was garnering the support of the official unions and preventing the rise of independent unions. To do so, the government usually tempered its hard-line labor policy with either concessions or with only lukewarm enforcement of its policy. For example, Salinas and the PRI shielded labor leaders from the attacks of the opposition in the congress. They continued to provide the old guard with a quota of nominations within the party, including important gubernatorial seats. And they used imposition and other means to prevent the rise of dissident leaders or unions (thereby favoring the official unions). During the strikes at Ford, Modelo, and VW, for example, the government clearly sided with the official unions against dissident workers. The union, in turn, not only supported the firing of labor dissidents, but even offered to send in replacement workers.

At times, government even acceded to labor's demands, particularly when political times warranted.[46] In May 1992, for instance, Salinas agreed to provide credit from NAFINSA to the Compañía Industrial de

Orizaba (CIDOSA) to avoid the laying off of 3,000 textile workers; this was apparently a concession won by and for the PRI gubernatorial candidate in the state of Veracruz. According to a representative of the CTM, this measure would "assure that the social peace in Orizaba would be conserved"—and would guarantee CTM backing in the upcoming state elections.[47] In 1993, Salinas went even further in easing up on his hard-line policy. He restored a large part of the CTM's role in managing and enjoying the housing funds, removed Genaro Borrego as head of the PRI, and officially slowed the internal party reforms detrimental to the labor sector.

Such a strategy nestled the CTM, the largest and most staunchly conservative of the labor confederations, between the sword and the stone, forcing it to "navigate between criticizing the neo-liberalism of the government's project and the expression of a power that does not want to lose certain privileges."[48] In response, it too adopted a critical yet restrained posture. On the one hand, it openly attacked the government for everything from the military-style capture of the petroleum labor leaders to the salary caps. During just the first half of 1992, Fidel Velázquez criticized the government for violating the right to strike, accusing Labor Secretary Farell of "causing prejudice among the population in general and particularly the working class,"[49] and assailed the government's wage policy, noting that "Mexican workers are constantly becoming poorer, pauperized, [and are] currently unable to afford clothing, pay the rent or much less to eat."[50] He even went so far as to argue that the government had eliminated workers' rights and privileges and hinted that perhaps mass mobilizations were necessary. Labor would then attempt to use these points in strategic fashion to withhold support for the various corporate agreements, including the anti-inflationary pact, which required periodic renewal. The CTM, which controlled 40 percent of the vote within the CT, for example, even refused initially to support the ANEP, demanding first that the government scrap the salary caps (which the government insisted were nonexistent) and that a guarantee be made that workers would benefit following increases in productivity.[51]

On the other hand, the CTM pulled back on its criticism to protect its privileges in the system. It rejected radical stances or strategies and declined to mobilize its constituents, undertake a general strike, or attack the president personally. In fact, it offered statements of strong support for the government while simultaneously attacking it. After assailing the government's labor policy, for example, Juan Moisés Callejas, a CTM representative, clarified that the president "will always be on the side of the workers."[52] In similar fashion, the CTM promised in 1992, despite the statements noted earlier, to work for the PRI and "unconditionally support the party," while reminding party leaders that the CTM constitutes the "majority force within the party," particularly at the state and local levels.[53]

In sum, the state-labor relationship under Salinas was marked by periods of tension followed by relaxation and compromise, generally on new terms somewhat detrimental to labor. Decisive blows against unions provoked a reaction by labor leaders that led to negotiations and, eventually, reconciliation. After the attacks on the petroleum leaders in early 1989 soured the relationship, better relations emerged in April 1990, with the CTM coming out in support of the government's actions against the strikes in SNTE, RUTA-100, Cananea, Ford, and Cervecería Modelo.[54] Conflict heightened again over the government's wage policy and attempted reforms in the PRI during 1991 and 1992, preventing Salinas from successfully negotiating the ANEP. In the end, however, a series of concessions, official support, and a watering down of the government's antilabor stance prompted the CTM to support the measure. Further pressures on the labor sector eased even further in 1993 with the removal of Borrego and the watering down of changes within the party detrimental to official labor. Yet throughout the give and take, it was clear that the government had bent the pact without breaking it.

Through such tactics, the government successfully enforced an implicit salary cap that kept wage increases below the rate of inflation. A study by the CT in 1992, for instance, showed that while the price of basic necessities had increased 210 percent since 1987, salaries had risen by only 105 percent.[55] A similar study in 1993 by the CTM, "Salarios y Empleo," revealed that the real minimum wage had declined 64.5 percent from 1977 to 1992.[56] Despite this, the government maintained official labor's control over the labor movement, stalled the emergence of independent unions, weakened the use of the strike, and maintained labor unions' allegiance to the president and the ruling PRI. Though never dismantling the old corporate system and even strengthening it somewhat toward the end of the term, Salinas altered the state-labor pact, putting in place the beginnings of a new syndicalism.

Salinas in the Political Arena

Turning to the political arena, our attention centers on reforms by the Salinas government in three areas: (1) those targeted broadly to nurture the reformist image and recast the state-society linkage, (2) those designed to arrest the internal and electoral deterioration of the PRI, and (3) those marshaled to weaken and divide the opposition. In many ways the three interacted and cross-cut the reforms with business and labor just discussed.

Nurturing the Reformist Image

Since the 1988 election did little to legitimize Salinas, a primary objective of the president centered on establishing and nurturing his credentials as a

reformer. To this end, Salinas employed a combination of old and new political tactics, ranging from strikes against corruption, electoral reforms
and selective political opening, and a revamping of church-state relations,
to the creation of a massive populist social program.

[Like de la Madrid, Salinas early on attacked institutionalized corruption. He orchestrated the downfall of many political figures for corruption,
extortion, malfeasance, tax evasion, and the stockpiling of arms. These included financial giant Agustín Legoretta; entrenched union leaders Joaquín
Hernández Galicia ("La Quina") and Salvador Barragán Camacho of the
powerful petroleum workers union and Jongitud Barrios of the teachers
union; *narcotraficantes* such as Felix Gallardo; police chiefs Miguel Nazar
Haro and José Antonio Zorrilla Pérez; ex-officials such as Eduardo Pes-
quería, former head of Agriculture and Hydraulic Resources, and Emilio
Ocampo Arenal, former director of Compañía Minera de Cananea; and a
range of state and local leaders, among others. Some of these officials, like
Hernández and Barragán, were apparently removed for having opposed
Salinas during the 1988 election; others, such as Jongitud Barrios, were
purged because they were unable to maintain stability; and still others,
such as the many governors, were removed because they had become a political liability.[57] Whatever the reason, the purges helped Salinas distance
himself from the patterns of the past in the minds of many, demonstrate his
reformist intentions and tough style, and consolidate his control over the
political elite.

A critical factor in nurturing his own credentials as a reformer was to
restore legitimacy to the electoral process left crippled by the events of
1988. To do so, Salinas rhetorically recognized the historic end of the one-
party system and then promised free and open elections. In conjunction
with the rhetoric, he overhauled the country's electoral law: once in 1990,
twice in 1993, and again in 1994. The 1990 reform, known as COFIPE
(Código Federal de Instituciones y Procesos Electorales), revamped the
electoral system. Among its many features, it enhanced non-PRI representation on the newly created body charged with organizing the elections
(the Instituto Federal Electoral, IFE), strengthened the oversight function
of opposition parties, went further in ensuring the neutrality of the workers handling the election, created an electoral tribunal to handle complaints
of fraud, and called for a new voter registration list.[58] The extensive reforms in 1993 went even further by introducing proportional representation in the senate that would increase the opposition presence in that body,
and by bolstering the supervisory role of opposition parties during voter
registration. It also set campaign finance and contribution limits, called for
equal access to the media, and legitimized the role of election observers.
Of utmost political importance, moreover, these measures enjoyed the support of the PAN and other minor opposition parties and in many cases responded to their demands.[59]

Beyond such legal reforms, Salinas also sought to nurture the image of himself as a democratic reformer through a policy of political opening or *concertación*. This included negotiations with and a broadening of the political space allotted primarily to the PAN. Efforts to negotiate with the PAN date from the very beginning of the term when the opposition initially refused to recognize Salinas's occupation of the presidency—Salinas was declared president-elect by congress with 263 *priístas* voting yea, 85 *panistas* voting nay, and the *cardenista* faction not voting, in protest. As a result, Salinas bargained with the PAN leadership to obtain the Compromiso Nacional por la Legitimidad y la Democracia. Reversing its hard-line position, the PAN agreed that the Salinas government could take power in return for future political reforms.[60]

The trend of cooperation between Salinas and the PAN set during the initial days continued throughout the term. Subsequent negotiations found the PRI and the PAN agreeing to a range of economic and political reforms. During both the 1989 and the 1993 electoral reforms, for example, not only did the PAN support the measures in the end, but the government even attended to many of the PAN's demands for change in order to garner their support. Concomitantly, the PAN seemed to begin to enjoy new political terrain. During the 1989 state election in Baja California, Salinas reportedly intervened directly to overturn fraud, enabling the PAN candidate, Ernesto Ruffo, to taste victory and become the first recognized opposition governor.[61] Though the PAN would continue to suffer from electoral fraud in other state elections, the party still made significant strides, including a gubernatorial appointment in Guanajuato in 1991 and its third gubernatorial post in Chihuahua in 1992. This growing convergence of interests reversed the hard-line political posture of de la Madrid, prompting many to see the PAN as a cogoverning party alongside the PRI.

Salinas also used upper-level negotiations and compromises to ease tensions and restore order following destabilizing state elections. Most dramatically, in San Luis Potosí (1991), Guanajuato (1991), Veracruz (1992), Tabasco (1992), Michoacán (1992), and the Yucatán (1993), Salinas resolved massive opposition-led protests by requesting the resignation or "leaves of absences" of key PRI officials, by creating joint municipal administrations, or, as occurred in Guanajuato, by actually appointing an opposition governor. Though the outcome tended to marginalize elections and often upset local PRI officials (a point to be returned to later), Salinas's negotiations contributed to his image as a reformer intent on overturning local fraud. The negotiations also prevented local protests from further polarizing the political climate.[62]

A third political initiative aimed at enhancing Salinas's reformist credibility involved an alteration of state-church relations. Through changes in five articles of the constitution in late 1991, the reform went a long way in reversing the anticlerical flavor of the regime. Among its features, the reform recognized the legal status of the church, legalized convents and monasteries, permitted the presence of foreign priests, granted the clergy the right to vote and criticize the government, and allowed religious organizations to publish newspapers and promote their views through radio and television. Though Salinas touted the move as part of a strategy to bring the law up-to-date with reality, most saw the move as designed to ease political tensions with the church, which had become an outspoken critic of the government's human rights policy, and to attract support away from the PAN.[63]

Aware of the political dangers of totally dismantling the revolutionary ideology, but also of the importance of controlling "democratizing" reforms—and having learned from de la Madrid's failed "moral renovation" program—Salinas did not tout any of these reforms as his centerpiece reformist project. Instead, Solidarity or the Programa Nacional de Solidaridad (PRONASOL) came to assume that role. Set in motion in early 1989 as an antipoverty program, PRONASOL grew to become a multifaceted, multipurpose "populist" program delivering a range of public works (schools, roads, clinics, lighting, water) to poor districts of the country, providing direct credit to peasants, and in many cases actually mobilizing local organizations to confront pressing social problems. Moreover, it served as a vehicle for Salinas to exert a type of paternalistic, populist appeal unmatched by his predecessors.

A departure from the austerity characterizing the de la Madrid administration (1983–1988), Solidarity enjoyed a hefty budget, accounting for over 60 percent of the federal government's investments by 1991. In 1992 alone, the program spent $2.14 billion and in 1993 enjoyed a budget of $2.46 billion.[64] In 1992, the program even absorbed the nonperforming loans of Banrural, the government-owned bank dealing with *ejidos* and small landowners. From a variety of angles, the increases in spending through Solidarity were notable, as shown in Table 4.1.

But more than just increased spending, the program also sought to reconstitute state-society ties.[65] As Jorge Alcocer argues, Solidarity seeks to

Table 4.1   Spending on PRONASOL

	1989	1990	1991	1992
Expenditures (billions of pesos)	22.86	37.36	47.16	60.78
As % of GDP	.45	.71	.88	1.08
As % of programmable public spending	2.63	4.16	5.07	5.95

Source: Lustig, "Solidarity as a Strategy," p. 89.

"rearticulate state-society links [and] recover lost legitimacy, taking into account the new social processes and actors."[66] Solidarity pursued this strategy by working with social and popular organizations, sidestepping both local governments and the PRI in the process. Under the new framework, social organizations created Solidarity committees that were linked directly to federal government programs without forsaking their autonomy. Indeed, the approximately 70,000 Solidarity committees that were reportedly formed were conceived "to replace traditional PRI-affiliated corporatist organizations like the CNC and the CTM as vehicles for political incorporation, organization, and ultimately, control."[67]

PROCAMPO (Progreso para el Camp con Justicia y Bienestar), a stepchild of PRONASOL, was also critical in the reformist arsenal. Crafted as a market-oriented program, PROCAMPO began in late 1993 with 11,790 million new pesos in land subsidies for the benefit of 2.2 million low-income agricultural producers. Like PRONASOL, the program not only provided relief to those in need and offered an avenue for Salinas to nurture his image, but it also tried to "break . . . alliances between bureaucratic actors and particular interests," weakening the old corporatism and establishing a new alliance between state and society.[68]

Underlying all these measures was Salinas's resolve to cultivate public opinion. Though he showed his toughness by crippling entrenched leaders like Hernández, Solidarity best provided the president with an "untainted" vehicle to stage an ongoing political campaign to bolster his popularity and legitimacy. In the name of Solidarity, Salinas routinely traversed the country, personally listening to community demands and then dispensing political goodwill in almost caudillistic fashion.[69] In conjunction, the government devoted considerable resources to publicizing the program and praising its achievements.[70] With similar concern for public opinion, the president struggled to cast his economic program and economic developments as not only solutions to Mexico's more immediate crisis, but as a means to thrust Mexico into the ranks of the developed, industrialized countries, despite widespread poverty and worsening income distribution.[71] Thus, he sold the debt agreement in 1990 as the "end of the debt crisis," despite the fact that Mexico's foreign debt continued at roughly the same level. He touted the occasional opposition victories and the electoral reforms as irrefutable evidence of the country's march toward democracy, despite continued fraud and his own intervention to overturn fraud to demonstrate that he too was battling the intransigent forces of the system. He even "spun" the work of the high-profile Human Rights Commission, created in 1989 in response to the political crisis, as working toward the elimination of human rights abuses, despite their actual increase across the nation.[72] In sum, he sought to cast the regime as progressive, distinct from the ancien régime.)

Refashioning the PRI

In dealing with the PRI, Salinas faced the difficult task of stopping and reversing the party's internal and electoral deterioration. Like his labor policy, this presented contradictory demands. The first required the president to shore up support within the party, to protect the old alliances and ease the divisions that had resulted in the massive departure of dissidents during the close of the de la Madrid period. The latter task, however, demanded a broadening of the party's popular appeal.[73] The party's leader from 1989–1992, Luis Donaldo Colosio, stated in 1990 that the party had to "adapt our structures, our internal forms of conduct, not only within the party but also toward society."[74]

First, Salinas sought early on to ease tensions with the politicos or the system conservatives, a serious problem with the departure of the *cardenista* faction in 1987. To do so, he tapped many of the PRI's more traditional politicians to serve in his cabinet, to occupy gubernatorial posts, and/or to sit on the party's newly formed Consejo Político.[75] To improve relations with those of the party's long-neglected left wing, he gave them a major role in the fourteenth national assembly in 1990 and had the assembly approve a measure recognizing the legitimacy of dissident movements. He also incorporated many of them into the Solidarity program. The first leader of PRONASOL, Manuel Tello, was in fact the finance minister under López Portillo.[76] Indeed, in fine cooptive fashion, many *cardenista* supporters eventually came to work for the PRONASOL program.[77]

At the same time, Salinas and the party's secretary-general struggled to restructure and change the operation of the party to broaden its appeal and weaken the more entrenched party leaders. This included a range of initiatives. During the fourteenth assembly in 1990, for example, the party reduced the sectors' representation to only 20 percent of the 8,600 voting delegates, made affiliation in the party "individual and free," reduced the number of secretariats within the CEN to streamline operations, and set up thirty-two state-level councils and a National Political Council to direct the party.[78] In addition, it issued a specific proposal to democratize candidate selection.[79] Called *consultas a la base,* the process required potential candidates (except the presidency) to obtain the support of directive bodies of organizations or a certain percentage of voters at the district level to secure the party's nomination.[80] Part of weakening the traditional sectors involved the party's nominations for public office. Labor sector nominations fell from seventy-five in 1988 to fifty-four in 1991 and from fifty-eight to forty-eight for the peasant sector. These reductions made way for an increase in the number of candidates from the popular sector, particularly those in the federal and state governments tied to the Salinas team and members of the local business community.[81]

The party's fifteenth assembly in 1992 pushed in virtually the same direction: weakening the old while structurally making room for the new. Rooted in Salinas's call for a *refundación* of the party based on his economic and political program of "social liberalism," the assembly sanctioned a plan to totally restructure the party.[82] In place of the labor, peasant, and popular sectors, the plan envisaged four pillars: the Movimiento Popular Territorial (MPT), Frente Nacional Ciudadano (FNC), Movimiento Sindical (MS), and el Pacto Obrero-Campesino.

The MPT was to become "the political and social arm of the party," concentrating on creating a network among popular organizations, particularly *colonos* (poor urban residents) and the new Solidarity committees.[83] The FNC, in turn, would target individuals and the middle class, though it would also include bureaucrats and teachers. The ambiguity was captured by PRI's secretary general, Borrego, who described the proposed FNC as "more than a structure, it is a strategy, since it does not deal with an organization of organizations, but rather a program of political attention to the middle classes of the country."[84] Both the MPT and the FNC were to emerge from the PRI's popular sector, (UNE, previously the CNOP). The idea of the MS was even more ambiguous. It was envisioned to incorporate the traditional labor sector but also the new syndicalism of the Salinas period: "The idea is to create it without affecting or originating confrontations with the labor congress and the strong leadership of Fidel Velázquez."[85] Finally, the fourth component of the newly restructured PRI was to include the labor-peasant pact noted earlier. It was designed to facilitate the establishment of new enterprises between workers and peasants.[86]

Practice, however, differed from design, and reality fell short of intention. As Federico Reyes Heroles succinctly notes: "The PRI reforms do not coincide with the events."[87] Perhaps most conspicuous, the democratic selection of candidates was almost always overridden in favor of "unity candidates": nominees selected from the top, not the bottom, in pure *dedazo* (finger painting) manner.[88] In fact, for the 1991 midterm election, over 90 percent of the candidates were selected through this centralized manner, while in the twelve state elections in 1992 (ten hosting gubernatorial contests), input from below was kept to an absolute minimum.[89] Even the official policy of recognizing dissident currents in the party was overshadowed by the practice of quieting them and allowing them no input into party affairs.

The sixteenth assembly, in 1993, went far in officially reversing many of the earlier reforms. Bowing to the demands of the party sectors, particularly the interests of official labor, the assembly replaced Secretary-General Borrego with Carlos Ortiz Arana, a move that, according to one report, "annulled the hopes of the 'renos' [reformists] that their party would modernize, as they had been led to believe since 1988."[90] In addition, it altered statutes to give the labor and peasant sectors key positions on the CEN and granted the labor sector a larger role in candidate selection.[91] The move even found Salinas officially stating that the reforms of the party would take years. He echoed the reversal of the party reforms by slowing reforms detrimental to labor leaders, such as the reorganization of INFONAVIT.[92] Later, Ernesto Zedillo, during his campaign for the presidency, reembraced many of the old politicians that had been "out of the circle" under Salinas and de la Madrid.

The truncation of the party reforms stemmed in part from the instability that they ignited. Experiments at opening the candidate selection process triggered divisions, pitting local against national leaders. For example, in Tabasco, the site of one of the first efforts to open up the process under Salinas, local militants protested, prompting state and national leaders to overturn the results. In response, one group staged a hunger strike outside the office of national party leader Colosio; another group occupied the city party headquarters; and the so-called Movimiento Popular Priísta mobilized a "marcha por la dignidad y la democracia priísta." After their arrest by state authorities, the group subsequently closed ranks with the Comité de Derechos Humanos en Tabasco, the Academia Mexicana de Derechos Humanos, and the PRD candidate.[93]

Similar disputes over the selection process prompted local PRI militants to stage public protests, block highways, kidnap party delegates to local conventions, take control of party offices, and stage hunger strikes. In Hidalgo, for instance, "members of the PRI denounced their own party for impositions, favoritism . . . in the procedures to select candidates", and staged disruptive public protests. Conflict also marked the candidate selection processes in Tamaulipas (October 1989), Coahuila (July 1990), Hidalgo (August 1990), México (September 1990), Yucatán (October 1990), Morelos (January 1991), Tlaxcala (September 1991), Veracruz (September 1991), and Guanajuato and Campeche (October 1991). In Yuriria, Guanajuato, for example, nonconforming *priístas,* upset over the candidate selection process, set fire to the local PRI office in October 1991, while in the state of México, one report indicated that "in almost half of the 34 electoral districts there were serious disagreements over procedures and nominations." In the municipality of Ecatepec, this led to public demonstrations by nonconforming *priístas*, while in Huixquiliucán hundreds of *cenecistas* (CNC supporters) reportedly took control of the municipal party headquarters. In Veracruz, the selection of candidates led to protests, with nonconforming militants blocking highways, etc.[94] As one observer concluded: "Where direct consultation took place, nonconformity predominated."[95] In some cases, the problems even prompted activists to either rally the citizenry to vote against the PRI or led to their closing ranks with the PRD.[96] Such developments at times brought PRI defeats, as occurred in local races in the states of Hidalgo and Yucatán.[97] This projected a dangerous scenario for the party and undermined its electoral potential.

Not only did such instability prompt the decision to truncate the reforms, but most critically the experimental process seemed to produce results contrary to those desired by the national leadership. At heart, the reforms sought to undermine the party's corporate sectors and the old style politicos, thereby enhancing the appeal of the party; instead, the democratization process at times seemed to favor the conservatives. The official response to disputes in Guanajuato over candidate selection, for instance, made reference to the "caciques who refused to lose their power."[98] But as Hernández shows, the lack of democratization within the party was due less to the position of the conservatives and more to the methods of the new politicos to consolidate power.[99]

Beyond the push and pull of strengthening certain segments of the party while weakening the older guard, Salinas also struggled to reorient the party to the task of winning elections. This he accomplished through a combination of old and new tactics, negative and positive reforms. On the more negative side, the party relied increasingly on electoral fraud to help bolster its recovery and maintain power. This was particularly true during the early half of the *sexenio* and in areas where the PRD was strong. One of the first elections of the *salinista* era, in Michoacán, for example, was deemed by one analyst "the most fraudulent electoral process in history," undercutting the legitimacy gained from the PAN's "respected" victory in Baja California at the same time.[100] Subsequent promises to make the Guerrero elections a "laboratory of electoral transparency" also contrasted the fraud and violent-ridden results.[101] Widespread perceptions of fraud in state elections in Durango, Oaxaca, Morelos, Coahuila, Michoacán, Tabasco, Sinaloa, México, San Luis Potosí, Guanajuato, Veracruz, and Baja California Sur further chipped away at Salinas's reformist image.[102] In fact, virtually none of the post-1988 elections failed to provoke some debate in the Chamber of Deputies.

Widespread accusations of fraud also shadowed the 1991 federal contest and the PRI's recovery. The opposition parties continued to attack the electoral process, citing the gross advantages in resources enjoyed by the PRI, the pro-PRI slant of the media,[103] the inexplicable delays and irregularities in formulating the electoral rolls, changes in the location of voting precincts, the lack of a secret vote, incomplete voting documents, delays in opening precincts, the shaving of names from the voting lists, the continuing control of the process by the PRI at virtually every stage, delays in reporting results, and other problems. The independent watchdog ACUDE (Acuerdo Nacional para la Democracia) concluded that the vote occurred under conditions that failed to satisfy democratic criteria.[104] The PAN, noting that "unfortunately they [the government and the PRI] have returned to tactics we thought we had overcome," lodged formal protests in 158 of the 300 electoral districts.[105] The PRD, for their part, contested forty-nine districts and walked out of the IFE session of August 21 in protest.[106] As always, these doubts fueled even greater hesitation as to the usefulness of participating in the electoral game. For example, the "defeated" coalition candidate for governor in the state of San Luis Potosí, Salvador Nava, concluded that "democracy cannot be reached by electoral means."[107] This situation prompted Salinas to promise further reforms in the electoral arena, culminating in the 1993 reforms referred to earlier.

Within this pattern, however, a second phase in the party's electoral development emerged—one hinging increasingly on the use of more positive reforms to revive the party's appeal and reshape its internal alliance. Part of this shift centered on more effective organization by the party in contesting elections. This included the widespread use of extensive public opinion research to compile electoral information and guide the campaign.[108] In critical state elections in Chihuahua in 1992, for example, the party formed the Consejo Estatal de Organización para la Movilización Partidista, headed by the gubernatorial candidate. It brought together 38,000 *promotores del voto* (vote promoters) or *jefes de manzana* (block chiefs) to bring ten people to the polls. This new structure was not based on the traditional sectors.[109] Indeed, in interpreting the party's resounding 1991 electoral comeback, the outspoken *priísta* Demetrio Sodi de la Tijera noted the intense campaigns on the part of the PRI, centering on personal contacts "in the city, in dairies, markets, schools, and above all, visits in homes and canvasing street by street."[110]

This more positive change also included the massive injection of resources into the party's electoral campaigns. Many of these resources came suspiciously from the government, primarily the Solidarity program.[111] The first full-fledged Solidarity experiment in January 1989, for instance, targeted Cárdenas's home state of Michoacán.[112] In Morelos—another state that Cárdenas won in 1988, public investments increased 93 percent from 1988 to 1989. According to Beltrán del Río, PRONASOL delivered 4,500 property titles in Cuautitlán, engaged in highway construction, inaugurated two health clinics, and initiated various public works in Chalco on the eve of state elections in México.[113] Dramatic "paternalist presidentialism" peaked during the weeks leading up to the 1991 federal election as Salinas covered ten states in fewer days, interspersing PRONASOL handouts with campaign messages. The opposition PAN called Solidarity "paternalist waste, with clear propaganda purposes and oriented by selective criteria of an electoral tint."[114] Solidarity even upstaged the PRI itself, prompting many state and local politicians to jump on the Solidarity bandwagon. "In many places Solidarity has practically substituted for the PRI," with PRONASOL propaganda replacing party propaganda.[115]

In three key 1992 elections, for example, the resources and the conspicuousness of Solidarity in supporting the official party were staggering. Reports estimated that the PRI spent $32 million for the gubernatorial campaign in Michoacán, $20 million in Durango, and $20 million in Chihuahua. A study by the Instituto Mexicano de Opinión Pública (IMOP) revealed that of the 160,000 billion pesos used by the PRI in Chihuahua and Michoacán, 40 percent came from the Secretaría del Estado, 20 percent from the parastate sector, 30 percent from state government, and 10 percent from private enterprise.[116] Many of these resources, they contended, were funneled through Solidarity, while an increasing number were devoted to highly advanced publicity campaigns for the government and the party.

Dividing the Opposition

The flip side of the coin with regard to reestablishing PRI's electoral appeal involved weakening the support of the opposition. Here, Salinas employed a differentiated strategy (divide and conquer) of concerting and negotiating with the PAN, while isolating and undermining the support accruing to Cárdenas and the PRD. The first step, negotiating with the PAN, was discussed earlier. Salinas sided with the PAN to pass both economic and political reforms, while intervening to provide the PAN virgin political space. To accomplish the objective of undermining the popularity of Cárdenas and the PRD, Salinas and the PRI relied on a wide range of devices, including legal reforms, selective opening, the Solidarity program, and propaganda designed to portray their opponents as violent and dangerous in the popular and foreign arenas and repression and the sabotaging of the efforts at local governance.

Among the initiatives, Salinas used the electoral reform of 1989 to weaken the potential for oppositional coalitions, raise the threshold needed to gain power, and generally weaken the opposition. It included a controversial "governability clause" that reduced to 35 percent the plurality needed to guarantee majority control in the Chamber of Deputies. It encapsuled provisions making it difficult to mount electoral coalitions similar to the FDN's in 1988. At the same time, it boosted proportional representation for the PRI itself and smaller parties while enhancing the PRI's majority on the highest body overseeing elections. The reform also contained a highly ambiguous clause that, it was feared, could be used to deny legal recognition to parties that question election results or provoke electoral protests.[117] Though the 1993 reforms overturned the governability clause, the difficulties of uniting the opposition were actually strengthened, essentially making it impossible for the opposition to unite behind a single presidential candidate. Indeed, as occurred with the 1989–1990 reform, aspects of the 1993 change actually enhanced the PRI's control over the electoral process.[118]

Second, Salinas politically targeted and courted real and potential PRD supporters. He endeavored early on to prevent the traditional satellite parties of the PRI—the PPS, the Partido de la Frente Cardenista para la Reconstrución Nacional (PFCRN), [previously the PST], and PARM—from institutionalizing their one-time electoral 1988 union with Cárdenas.[119] To do so, he negotiated with their leaders upon taking office and brought members of the coalition into the government.[120] Evaristo Pérez Arreola, for example, the leader of the powerful university union, was named special adviser and later became mayor of Ciudad Acuña, Coahuila, under the PFCRN banner. Martínez Nateras also split with the FDN to become an adviser to state governments in Michoacán and Guerrero, later becoming mayor of Tuxpan and plurinominal candidate for the PRI in 1991. Perhaps the best example was the ambassadorial appointment of Ignacio Castillo Mena, member of the PRD's CEN and congressional delegation, in 1991.[121]

At the same time, Salinas wooed old politicos within the party to prevent the trickle of *priístas* to the PRD from turning into a flood. He relied on such programs as Solidarity to undercut the appeal of the *Cardenistas,* attract members of the left and many from the intellectual community into his government, and hinder PRD efforts at forging popular ties with burgeoning social movements and intellectuals.[122] The policy of selective opening mentioned earlier aimed at weakening the tendency toward polarization. Aligning with the PAN to bring about electoral and economic reforms and permitting the PAN to enjoy electoral gains helped bolster PAN's more cooperative and less confrontationalist mode and separate it from the more radical PRD. By altering the expected utility for the PAN of confrontation, it weakened the impact of the PRD's more confrontationalist approach.

Salinas and the PRI also sought to divide and weaken their opponents by portraying the *cardenista* party as violent and communistic, with links to unsavory drug traffickers, or as simply incompetent. Among the diatribes against PRI's PRD opponents was one by labor leader Fidel Velázquez: "There are many armed people in Mexico who have plans to destabilize the country . . . authorities at the highest levels know there are opposition members—specifically the PRD—who are involved with drug traffickers."[123] Ads and columns placed in the Mexican and U.S. press sported similar claims, warning of communists among Cárdenas's ranks.[124] Denouncing Cárdenas's "confrontational" approach, while nurturing and then playing on the fears of ungovernability, helped muster support for the "gradualist" and "controlled" process of reform heralded by Salinas. One PRI candidate on the campaign trail best captured the prevailing theme (and the hidden threat) in the following manner: "Your vote decides: three years of violence or three years of peace."[125]

Such campaigns not only sought to delegitimize the PRD by instilling fear, particularly in the eyes of the middle class and the United States, but they also helped justify and warrant Salinas's conspicuous deployment of security forces and the related increases in repression (or provocation). A fourth measure designed to ease the pressures from the left was thus repression targeted primarily at the PRD's constituents. Indeed, Americas Watch pointed with concern to the "increasing reliance on the military to resolve political problems and police matters such as drug trafficking," an upsurge in human rights abuses, and the use of the criminal justice system "as an instrument to intimidate the far left."[126] Examples of heightened repression include the April 1990 crackdown involving the arrest of 166 people associated with the left, the high number of deaths and disappearances as a result of raids on occupied city installations following local elections, and a series of political killings and intimidations.[127] In fact, in *La defensa de los derechos humanos: Un sexenio de violencia política*, the PRD claims that 250 of its militants were killed during the Salinas *sexenio*.[128]

A final initiative designed to undermine its center-left opponents and perhaps exorcise the ghost of Cárdenas-past (the father) rested on sabotaging the PRD's efforts at local governance. Though allowing the opposition to govern could have served strategically by "having the left in the municipal palaces, governing, and not mobilizing in the streets," it also offered a unique opportunity to cast the PRD as incompetent and unable to govern, undermining its viability as an opposition.[129] PRD-governed municipalities thus frequently found the PRI-run state and federal governments uncooperative, withholding needed resources and at times even triggering social disturbances.[130] The PRD mayor of Morelia in Cárdenas's home state of Michoacán, for instance, discovered the city treasury empty upon taking office and its coffers unreplenished by state funds for months.[131]

Gauging the Political Fallout

(The reformist results of these measures were generally impressive. The anticorruption campaign, the electoral reforms, and Solidarity, coupled with improvements on the economic front, all fueled an outpouring of support and faith in Salinas's abilities, truly painting him as a dedicated reformer. Indeed, Salinas projected a sense of confidence and optimism that, bolstered by a carefully managed media, seemed to spill over into society, shaping popular impressions about change and Mexico's future.] In October 1990, he enjoyed a 65.7 percent approval rating; in mid-1991, it stabilized above the 60 percent level; in January 1992, it climbed to 80 percent; and in May 1993, it still surpassed the 60 percent mark.[132] At midterm in

November 1991, 64.9 percent surveyed felt Salinas had fulfilled his campaign promises.[133] Such views were accompanied by expressions of optimism toward the future.[134] Even the continuing repression and fraud were made to seem exceptions rather than the rule. As Dresser so aptly described it: "Salinas has beat Cárdenas at his own game: he has now presented himself as the agent of change."[135]

Even the electoral reforms, the tolerable PAN victories, and Salinas's interventions in resolving electoral disputes seemed to help rather than hinder Salinas's ability to garner credibility for himself and elections. These factors seemed to lend support to the view that Mexico was undergoing a process of democratization, albeit slow. Those expressing a lack of confidence in the electoral process fell from 53 percent to 32 percent from 1988 to 1991, a shift that would rebound and echo within the PRI's electoral recovery that year.[136]

The push and pull of the reforms within the party, despite the problems, also enjoyed mixed though, one could easily argue, "sufficient" results. The PRI proved successful at arresting the disintegration of the party that had marked the late years of the de la Madrid term. The flood of departures from the party thus slowed and even slightly reversed itself during the term despite some leakage. The measures did ignite instability within the party, which generally forced the leadership to retreat or soften the reforms, but in the end, the old guard conservatives not only continued within the party, along with the corporate organs, but they were even able to reassert themselves as the term approached its conclusion. Salinas incorporated new elements into the party, making it more popular and, more important, more efficient at the electoral game. It incorporated supporters from the ranks of business, refashioned the role of labor and peasant organizations while maintaining their incorporation, and helped channel support via Solidarity. This vamped PRI dispensed benefits in a centralized and authoritative manner to those supporting the Salinas agenda and demonstrated a capacity to mobilize the vote for the party through a territorial rather than corporate-based structure. In a sense, by altering the conditions of party participation, the reforms forced the old to adapt to the new rules.

Once this renewed PRI began to emerge, Salinas and the reformers enhanced their reliance on the party and curbed the use of such negative reforms as electoral fraud. Though early on they generally viewed the party as a liability, they eventually came to see it as an asset as these reformist patterns began to take shape.[137] Thus, the group that initially wanted to totally alter the party later opted to promote it anew.[138]

Finally, Salinas and the PRI enjoyed success in their campaign to undermine and divide the opposition. The PAN vote, for example, despite its cooperative posture toward Salinas, stagnated in the 1991 midterm election, as noted. More significantly, in September 1992, the PAN suffered a critical division at its uppermost ranks. The dissident *foristas,* complaining that their proposals were not being respected and that the candidate selection process was unfair, abandoned the party to forge the Partido Foro Democrático. The primary difference, however, centered on their opposition to the PAN's new conciliatory approach toward the government.[139]

Salinas enjoyed even more success at undermining the PRD. He prevented former allies in the 1988 election from joining the PRD organizationally, electorally, and congressionally—though a history of divisions within the left and a record of PRI support among such satellite parties as the PPS, PARM, and the PST (now the PFCRN—or *ferrocarril*), of course, aided the process. It also effectively isolated the more threatening PRD. During the 1989 (and 1993) reforms, for example, Salinas and the PRI enjoyed the backing of all opposition parties in the Chamber of Deputies save the PRD. This allowed Salinas and the PRI not only to gain broad-based legitimacy for the electoral process, but also to isolate the PRD and thereby make it appear overly intransigent. Salinas's policy of opening, which allowed the PAN some breathing room and even brought the PAN into state government, also tended to isolate the PRD and weaken the appeal of its hard-line opposition. At the same time, it helped inscribe a negative public perception of the PRD and Cárdenas.[140] One poll found 32 percent of the respondents harboring a negative opinion of the party (the highest negative rating in comparison to the PRI and PAN), with even fewer expressing a positive view (26 percent).[141] Such sentiment obviously contrasted those expressed at the polls in 1988. The vote of the PRD consequently fell tremendously during the midterm election. Much of the government's legitimacy and Salinas's reformist credibility came to be associated with the PRI's ability to guarantee stability, an indication of the fear tied to the PRD. Political mistakes on the part of the PRD, particularly its internal divisions, contributed to this pattern.

More important than weakening his opponents individually, Salinas tempered the tendency for the opposition to join forces and push for change. Selective negotiations with the PAN, Solidarity, and other programs prevented Cárdenas from solidifying the leftist alliance and the PAN and the PRD from forging a unified front. Indeed, Cárdenas's efforts to bring PAN-PRD together to design *una transición pactada,* or to promote a broad-based *acuerdo nacional democrático,* for instance, died due to the lack of support from the PAN. Momentum for the PRD's Acuerdo Nacional Democrático (AND), for example, was mortally wounded by Salinas's electoral reform package of 1989, passed with the support of the PAN.[142]

Combined, the reforms helped restore the party's electoral dominance. The PRI captured approximately 87 percent of the electoral contests in

1989, despite the conspicuous wins of the PAN in Baja California and the PRD in Guerrero and Michoacán. This translated into a 54–65 percent increase in the vote, with the PRI winning 1,007 of 1,100 mayoral races and 223 of 253 local legislative seats and surpassing its previous tally in all but three states (Tamaulipas, Guerrero, and Yucatán).[143] The party's 1990 record was no less impressive. (The PRI even swept the crucial state of México in November, a state in which the party itself had expected to perform poorly.[144] This trend culminated with the virtual return of the *carro completo* during the federal elections of 1991 as the PRI garnered over 60 percent of the national tally, capturing 290 majority seats and twenty proportional representation seats in the 500-member Chamber of Deputies and winning all six of the gubernatorial posts, all but one senate seat, and even prevailing overwhelmingly in its weakest territory, the Federal District. The PRI's control of the Chamber of Deputies hence increased from 266 in 1988 to 310 in 1991, providing the legislative edge that Salinas needed to further engineer the postcrisis system. This pattern continued throughout the period. In 1993, for instance, the PRI enjoyed huge victories in most state and local contests with protests and instability racking only a handful of contests. Most of the favorable vote for the PRI reflected the image of Salinas. When asked the reasons for voting for the PRI in 1991, for example, the public usually responded that it was because of the actions of Salinas.[145]

But despite the clear signs of change and recovery, conflict continued to rack the party. Much of this stemmed from the absence of democratic reforms, as reflected in the disturbances, protests, and departures of such prominent *priístas* as Rodolfo González Guevara, Demetrio Sodi de la Tijera, and, more painfully by 1994, Manuel Camacho Solís. In Ciudad Juárez, local *priístas* blamed defeat on imposition.[146] In his report to the national leadership, Mario Tarango (PRI state leader in Chihuahua) blamed defeat on the selection of the gubernatorial candidate.[147] Dissident voices within the party continued to emphasize the need for the party to democratize its procedures and assert its independence from the government. Yet despite the internal bickering, the PRI was able to push the PRI's 1994 presidential candidate, Ernesto Zedillo, to victory.

By the same token, the reform of Article 27 transformed peasant politics and altered the support they provided for the PRI. For one, the corporate sector became more divided, with the Congreso Agrario Permanente representing eleven organizations with many of these, such as el Barzón in Jalisco, becoming intensely politicized and tied to opposition parties. In addition, open support for the PRI declined. Though in 1988 the leader of the CNC, the largest peasant organization, had promised 10 million votes for the PRI candidate, by 1994, the new leader publicly rejected the corporatist vote. The peasant organizations, however, still enjoyed a large quota of the party's nominations.[148]

In addition, elections continued to be highly politicized. Electoral disturbances continued to rock the foundations of the system. Protests in Nayarit and Yucatán in 1993, for example, prompted upper-level negotiations, further diminishing the credibility of elections and rewarding antisystem behavior. Few considered the playing field level, recognizing the government's and media's favorable treatment of the PRI. Uncovering, denouncing, and protesting the slightest hint of fraud, opposition parties along with social organizations clamored to force the regime to make real changes in the operation and handling of elections. They even tried to persuade their militants and others in society that greater confrontation may be needed to effect real change.

1994: Renewed Crisis

Despite the seemingly spectacular reformist successes that Salinas enjoyed through 1993, his government faced renewed political crisis in 1994. The causal components were many, the impact fierce, and the reformist response swift and sufficient. The first causal factor was economic recession, beginning in the latter half of 1993. Always troubling, the economic slowdown meshed with signs that the benefits of Salinas's economic growth had been poorly distributed all along.[149]

A second and even more critical ingredient was the New Year's Day guerrilla uprising in the southern state of Chiapas. Led by the Ejercito Zapatista de Liberación Nacional (EZLN) and its charismatic leader, Subcomandante Marcos, the rebels shocked the nation when they took control of a handful of towns. By so doing, they raised the threat of revolution while dramatically concentrating Mexico's and the world's attention on the nation's political and economic problems, including the lack of democracy and basic human rights.[150]

A third contributing factor involved the eruption of internal bickering within the PRI and among Salinas's closed circle of associates following the selection of the PRI's presidential candidate in late 1993.[151] Extending well into 1994 and deepened by other events, these divisions not only threatened to seriously divide the party, but also raised the possibility of another renegade challenger from within the ranks. Finally, perhaps the most devastating blow to the system, was the March assassination of the PRI's presidential candidate, Luis Donaldo Colosio Murrieta. This was the first such upper-level political assassination since the killing of Obregón more than sixty years earlier.

These factors together had a tremendous impact on the political situation facing Salinas.[152] For one, they effectively undermined the credibility that he had so carefully nurtured during the previous years. The uprising, for instance, undermined the credibility of the Solidarity program, which ostensibly had alleviated poverty, prompting Colosio to campaign without even mentioning it by name (despite the fact that he had headed the program).[153] Combined with the economic recession, the dramatization of poverty in Chiapas also undermined the public's perception of the economic reforms. And by drawing public attention to the political demands of the rebels, the uprising also undermined the credibility of elections and Salinas's political reforms. As Tim Golden of the *New York Times* perceptively noted, "What Mr. Cárdenas had been unable to do in five years as the main leader of the opposition—galvanize calls for change in the way elections are run—the masked rebel leader . . . Marcos seemed to manage in a matter of weeks."[154] The percentage of the population expecting fraud consequently climbed to 46.5 percent as political and popular pressures for political change peaked.[155] Coupled with the assassination of Colosio and a rash of kidnappings and drug-related violence, the uprising finally undermined the notion of stability that had become one of the more critical achievements of the PRI-run government and a linchpin of its legitimacy.

The erosion of credibility brought a concomitant boost in the credibility of other groups in the country, weakening the government's ability to control events and perceptions. International news agencies covering Chiapas, for example, paid close attention to independent human rights groups in the nation, helping them shape public opinion regarding the events in the region. This was particularly true of the National Network of Civil Human Rights Organizations. Events also enhanced the credibility of other independent organizations, such as the Alianza Cívica, which brought together over 300 organizations to supervise and monitor the 1994 presidential campaign and elections. Among the more unusual civil organizations that emerged to shape public opinion and the political equation were the EZLN and the San Angel group.

After negotiating a political solution with the government's peace commissioner, Manuel Camacho, and then rejecting it, the EZLN continued as a political force with popular sympathies. It made credible the threat of revolutionary upheaval if the government and/or the PRI employed fraud to stay in power, and it served as a political device to mobilize the left and attract attention to a series of political and economic demands. The EZLN-led Convención Nacional Democrática (CND) in July deepened the popular demands for democratic reforms before and after the August election.[156]

Another organizational ingredient in what Ricardo Alemán characterized as a "civil uprising" during the year involved the Group of San Angel.[157] Named for the location of their first meeting, the group brought together prominent intellectuals and political, university, and labor leaders to discuss the nation's political situation and pressure the regime for real changes. The group included such nationally known figures as Jorge Casteñada, Carlos Fuentes, Enrique Krause, Federico Reyes Heroles, Raúl Paudilla, Miguel Basañez, and, at least during some initial meetings, Manuel Camacho. Expressing concern over the danger of "ungovernability," the group raised the public's and the government's belief that the absence of political change would risk a massive social explosion, that real change was imperative, and that perhaps a transitional government may be needed. Like the more radical EZLN, the centrist group of San Angel went a long way in shaping the public agenda and forcing the government and the candidates to respond. In addition, the groups implicitly provided a framework for either a revolutionary organization to undermine the social order and defeat the government or a transitionary government if such a rupture were to take place.

In addition to undermining regime credibility and enhancing that of others, the crisis also weakened the regime itself by triggering serious internal divisions within the government and the official party and by forcing it to back a less popular substitute candidate at mid-campaign. Already divided over the selection of Colosio, members of the government divided initially over how best to respond to the rebels. While some, such as Fidel Velázquez, believed the rebels should be exterminated, and others were of the opinion that PRONASOL money could be used to resolve the issue, Camacho publicly stated that only "a commitment to democracy" would overcome the crisis.[158] Camacho's statements not only overshadowed the campaign promises of Colosio, but they were also backed up by an implicit and often explicit threat that if the government did not share his vision, Camacho would launch an independent bid for the presidency. In a press conference in March, for example, instead of ruling out such a move, Camacho stated: "If there is no advance in democracy and there is more polarization, I would take the necessary political decision to advance democracy in Mexico."[159] Though eventually Camacho decided to resign temporarily from politics rather than mount a challenge, his resignation was accompanied by a blistering attack against the new presidential candidate, Zedillo, and the PRI.[160] The attack provided support to the opposition's claims that the government, despite the reformist veneer of Salinas, had no intention of changing politically.

The Colosio assassination furthered the internal tensions within the PRI and the debilitation of the party. On the one hand, given the split between Camacho and Colosio over the nomination, the assassination furthered the distance between Camacho's supporters and the party. Camacho was even accused and verbally attacked by Colosio's mourners as the intellectual author of their leader's death. Moreover, the death of Colosio pitted the various internal factions against one another in the struggle to select a replacement. The old guard, particularly the labor leaders, postured

publicly and privately for the selection of Fernando Ortiz Arana, while
Salinas opted for his former budgeting and education secretary, Ernesto
Zedillo. Echoing the concerns of some liberals within the party, the old
guard even attacked the traditional power of the president to appoint the
candidate.[161] Though Salinas's decision prevailed, the assassination nonetheless weakened the government and the party even more by leaving the
PRI with a little-known candidate well into the campaign season. Unlike
Colosio, Zedillo had neither a strong following, a seasoned political team,
nor name recognition.[162]

The Reforms

Salinas, Colosio, Zedillo, the government, and the PRI responded to the
crisis through a variety of initiatives. Vis-à-vis Chiapas, the government
quickly abandoned its reactive policy of repression and issued a unilateral
cease-fire. Salinas then fired Secretario de Gobernación Patrocinio
González (former governor of the state of Chiapas and the one considered
responsible for many of the grievances voiced by the rebels) and replaced
him with former human rights ombudsman Jorge Carpizo. Relying on the
skillful Camacho, the government then opened negotiations with the gov-
rebels, arriving at a tentative agreement in early March in which the government agreed to hold a special session of congress to discuss electoral
reforms, a new agrarian reform law, a law against the discrimination of Indians, the establishment of new local governments to serve Indian needs,
the protection of the Indians' autonomy, improved health and education
services, more roads, and a new criminal law for the state that outlaws the
expelling of Indians.[163]

Vis-à-vis other parties and society, Salinas agreed to another overhaul
of the nation's electoral law. Sketched out in January, negotiated with opposition parties into February, and hammered out during a special session
of congress in late March, the fourth electoral/political reform under Salinas broadened the power of the independent citizen representatives on
IFE's board of directors and strengthened the laws against electoral fraud,
including the appointment of a special prosecutor, equal access to the
media, a reduction in campaign spending limits by nearly 80 percent,
agreement to commission-independent audits of the voter lists and exit
polls, official recognition of and permission for national election observers, and even the carving out of a role for foreign observers. The reforms, according to Miguel Angel Granados Chapa, effectively displaced
the PRI from the IFE, while weakening the potential for fraud.[164]

Compelled by the events and facing the risk of losing the reformist initiative, Colosio, Zedillo, and Salinas all rhetorically promised and embraced change as an ally. During his campaign, for instance, Colosio issued

a proposal for substantial political changes, including a weakening of the power of the presidency.[165] Zedillo likewise emphasized the notion that continued stability requires fundamental political changes. In one speech, he even promised if elected to end the historic practice of the *dedazo:* "I am totally resolved to not intervene, in any way, in the process to select the PRI's candidates for positions of popular representation."

At the same time, Zedillo promised to strengthen the state of law, enhance the division of powers, limit the power of the presidency, use dialogue to arrive at a political consensus, renovate federalism and the autonomy of the *municipio,* broaden the participation of society and NGOs, provide greater freedom of press and expression, increase the autonomy of organizations that provide official information, promote pluralism within the party system, maintain the separation between the PRI and government, promote reform within the PRI and create conditions for the democratic selection of candidates, and present a complete report on campaign spending following the election.[166] Salinas, of course, echoed these promises. In a breakfast speech in June before the nineteenth national assembly of the radio and television workers' union, Salinas similarly voiced his support for change, proclaiming his intention to hand over power "to whoever triumphs in the honored election next August 21, regardless of the political party to which he belongs."[167] While perhaps disingenuous, the statement nonetheless captured the headlines and brought official responses from all the presidential candidates.

(A third ingredient in brokering the crisis involved the negotiations of two elite pacts. This included the January civility pact (Pacto Político de Civilidad) and the July agreement for civility, concord, and justice. The former, signed by all but the PPS, codified the promise for free and fair elections; the latter, negotiated by Jorge Carpizo and signed by all save the PRD, centered on avoiding postelectoral violence and a social explosion. More specifically, the July agreement called on all parties to: (1) participate in elections according to the law; (2) deny the use of violence and promise to use dialogue to work out any differences; (3) encourage better access, openness, objectivity, and equity in the media; (4) promote respect, tolerance, and citizen participation in the process; (5) ensure impartiality of public officials; (6) strengthen democratic culture; and (7) ensure that the next government is made up of the best people.[168] Politically, both accords were designed on the one hand to convince the public of the government's willingness to allow and actually promote change, and on the other hand to restrain the opposition from using destabilizing methods to ensure it.

While such moves sought to ease political tensions and demonstrate the government's willingness to change (critical in restoring reformist legitimacy), the PRI still faced the arduous task of mounting an effective campaign and winning the elections. A critical ingredient in promoting this objective was Zedillo's efforts to solidify the party and capitalize on its intense mobilizational resources. Zedillo thus reached out to embrace many of the old politicos within the party, including former governors and caciques that had been left out of Salinas's circle and Colosio's campaign. This included the naming of Ignacio Pichardo and Luís Tellez of the team of México state boss Hank González as PRI president and campaign manager, respectively, and the inclusion of Xicotencatl, the deposed governor of Baja California, to a party post.[169] Using the generous contributions from the big financial enterprises that had come to constitute the new state-business alliance, the PRI then spent lavishly to promote its candidate and its pace of political change. This included not only slick commercials, free videotapes of its candidate, and the lavish courting of the press, but also such traditional tactics as the selling of goods during the campaign,[170] counterfeit crowds, and blackmail and coercion.[171]

During this time, Salinas, of course, continued to travel the country dispensing political favors. He combined the stimulus package of late 1993 with other measures to try to ease social pressures. With PRONASOL's activities concentrating on means to use its resources and organizational structure to enhance the PRI's electoral appeal, PROCAMPO's subsidies in the countryside, and numerous broadcast messages praising the government's accomplishments and IFE's pledge to provide clean elections, Salinas promised additional resources to a range of groups. In June alone, for example, Salinas promised to increase federal contributions to the states to the tune of $1.2 billion pesos, handed out 23,465 land certificates to *ejiditarios* in the state of Puebla, and promised farmers additional funds through PROCAMPO.[172]

The Outcome and the Future

Though the crisis considerably weakened the Salinas government, the PRI won the presidential election with roughly 50 percent of the national vote and maintained its strong majority in the congress. Though the PAN practically doubled its 1988 vote totals and strongly surpassed its 1991 performance, the PRI solidly reasserted its dominance over Cárdenas, reducing the PRD's vote to less than 20 percent. Perhaps more important than winning the vote, the government also seemed to win the battle for legitimacy. Not only did the electoral reforms, particularly the presence of observers, seem to lessen the preelectoral expectation of fraud, but initial reports supported the view that the election was at least "cleaner than in the past" (and hence a step in the proper direction).[173] Most of the opposition lent credence to this interpretation by accepting defeat. Even those, like Cárdenas, who considered the results fraudulent were unsuccessful at mobilizing any significant protest movement. Though the EZLN in the state of Chiapas promised to fight the fraud and create a climate of instability in the south, momentum had clearly shifted and the rebel group did not even attempt a coordinated national response.[174]

Initial explanations for the PRI's strong showing amidst political crisis pointed to a range of variables. They included the open and public support offered by many business leaders, including the head of CCE, Luis German Carcoba, and the leader of the Asociación de Banqueros Mexicanos (ABM), Roberto Hernández;[175] the general support and optimism associated with the Salinas economic program; the lack of any feasible organized alternative; the patron-client networks of the PRI and the government; and, perhaps most critical, the overriding fear of instability. Though the events of the year crystallized the need for change, they also helped instill a fear of change. If so, the reformist initiatives of Salinas, the government, and the PRI could be credited for successfully tilting the equation in such a way as to convince the public that only the PRI could provide an acceptable balance between these two forces.

In sum, Salinas not only survived renewed crisis, but he also guaranteed the PRI's control into the next century. And though Zedillo will perhaps begin his term with a degree of legitimacy Salinas lacked, many pressures and restraints will continue to exist to forge a dynamic reformist setting in the interim. Like many others, José Crespo, one of the citizen representatives on the IFE, contends that Zedillo will have to promote yet another electoral reform early on to consolidate the recent changes, though he concludes by suggesting that "one cannot discard [the possibility] that, as occurred under Salinas, irrationality will again take hold of the governing elite and close once again their eyes to the new reality."[176]

Perhaps most critical for the regime were reports concerning further divisions within the ranks of the PRI. The assassination in September 1994 of PRI's secretary-general, Francisco Ruiz Massieu, the party's ideological leader and bridge between the politicos and the *técnicos,* coupled with the subsequent accusations against and the arrest of prominent members of the party, threatened to weaken the party.[177] Some have even predicted the dissolution and complete breakdown of the PRI during the coming years.[178] Of course, to paraphrase Mark Twain, such predictions of the death of the Mexican political system have often been premature.

Conclusion

As we have seen, Salinas surmounted the crisis using negative and positive reform measures and balancing change with continuity. He effectively forged a new state-business alliance based on the liberal economic reforms and supported by the businesses benefiting from those policies without losing the support of other businesses within the alliance. By the same token, he weakened the power of traditional labor without destroying the corporatist arrangement, allowing him to reinvigorate and rely on that support when needed. Moreover, he fashioned Solidarity as a means to reestablish the links between the state and society while using it to alter the internal logic of the party and the government. At the same time, he nurtured the reformist image and enjoyed significant popular support, thereby allowing him greater latitude in orchestrating the pace, nature, and direction of political and economic change. In so doing, he was able to depoliticize and depolarize society and weaken and divide opposition parties sufficiently to maintain power and muddle through.

Putting the period in context, it is clear that Salinas, first, broadened the appeal and support of the progressive/technocratic reformers (Group 2), while solidifying and strengthening their control over the government and the party.[179] Efforts to create a new coalition with big business, to forge a "new syndicalism," and to use Solidarity to recast state-society ties all contributed to the rise of this faction. Second, Salinas protected the PRI/government alliance between the progressive reformers (Group 2) and the more conservative elements (Group 1). The divide-and-conquer strategy with labor, periodic concessions, Solidarity and party patronage, and the declining prominence of the left-progressive opposition (Group 4) all prevented further ruptures in the alliance and the allegiance of the corporate-based elements in the party and government (Group 1). Third, Salinas used government policy to undercut the appeal of both his opponents. Economic reforms, political opening, the adoption of candidates from business, and even a change in church-state relations stole much of the PAN's thunder, while Solidarity muffled part of the PRD's roar. This not only made it difficult for either group to bolster its appeal, but actually prompted internal divisions and factional debate. Finally, Salinas checked the tendency for the left and right opposition (Groups 3 and 4) to cooperate to push for change. This he achieved primarily by emphasizing the common economic preferences the reformers (Group 2) shared with the right opposition (Group 3) and their preference for political change. He nurtured that alliance sufficiently to not only prevent the left (Group 4), which had little to lose through confrontation, from forging a strong political alliance with the right opposition (Group 3), but also to effectively isolate the left opposition (Group 4) and thereby weaken its appeal.

Notes

1. In all, Salinas sold or dissolved 80 percent of the 1,155 firms—a move that brought in more than $21 billion (see *La Jornada*, November 2, 1991, p. 23; and Alcocer V., "Tres Años").

2. From 1987 to 1990, for example, government spending as a share of GDP fell from 31 percent to 21 percent (cited in Centeno, *Democracy Within Reason*, p. 192).

3. President Salinas clearly sees NAFTA as a key to restoring economic growth and development. See, for example, the interview with Salinas in Maza, "El Tratado de Libre Comercio es el único medio para satisfacer a los 82 millones de mexicanos."

4. Data are taken from a variety of monthly reports by BANAMEX.

5. Of this amount, roughly 53 percent was invested in the Mexican stock market and other highly liquid assets (see González Pérez, "De 49 mil 776 mdd, la Captación Sexenal de Capital Extranjero").

6. This is one of the primary conclusions presented in Lustig, *Mexico: The Remaking of an Economy.*

7. Ortega Pizarro, "Inestable, especulativa, peligrosa."

8. Though both the retirement program, SAR, and the reforms to INFON-AVIT were openly opposed by the CTM and others, these reforms were touted publicly as beneficial to the worker while placing massive amounts of funds in the private banking sector (see Acosta and Corro, "Más recursos para el gobierno, más beneficios para la banca").

9. The new foreign investment law, Reglamento de la Ley para Promover la Inversión Mexicana y Regular la Inversión Extranjera, passed in May 1989, simplified the procedures and administrative regulations covering foreign investments. Among its provisions it allows for Inversión Automática, investments without seeking permission; Inversión Nuestra, which permits foreign investment in the stock market; and Régimen de Inversión Temporal, which permits involvement through trusts in areas previously restricted.

10. For an overview of the politics involved in the *ejido* reform see Cornelius, "The Politics and Economics of Reforming the Ejido Sector."

11. According to the Asociación Nacional de Abogados Democráticos, the pact was "an attempt to modify the Federal Labor Law by way of collective and individual contracts" (cited in *La Jornada,* June 3, 1992, p. 3). Though the reform was pushed and supported by the private sector, ostensibly to enhance competitiveness, it did not go nearly as far as they wanted. COPARMEX, for example, wanted the government to eliminate the clause requiring workers to join unions and allow companies to hire other workers during a strike (see *La Jornada,* May 7, 1992, p. 22; and Ortega Pizarro, "Todo en manos privados, por ley, exige la Coparmex").

12. For an overview of the components of the agreement see *La Jornada,* June 5, 1992, p. 11.

13. This contrasted a comparable figure of 20 percent registered in the 1986 *New York Times* poll (see Aziz Nassif, "La fragilidad de la democracia").

14. Aziz Nassif, "La fragilidad de la democracia." The concentration of the benefits of the economic program is clear. According to an official report by the Treasury Department, almost a third of the 180 public enterprises sold under Salinas wound up in the hands of just five economic groups (cited in *La Jornada,* July 16, 1992, p. 37). In fact, just two financial groups, BANAMEX-Accival and Bancomer, came to control over 67 percent of stocks on the Mexican market (*La Jornada,* July 7, 1992, p. 38). Not only did privatization concentrate control, but exports (and export opportunities) were equally concentrated in a handful of large enterprises, primarily those enjoying international contacts and able to obtain capital.

15. See Garza and Ortega Pizarro, "Monterrey tiene a la mitad de los bancos y el mayor consumo de tortibonos."

16. Rodríguez Reyna, "Nuevo empresariado," p. 3. The Monterrey economic elite nurtured particularly close ties with the Salinas team as a result of the government's program.

17. See Garza and Ortega Pizarro, "Monterrey tiene a la mitad de los bancos."

18. Rodríguez Reyna, "Nuevo empresariado."

19. See a review of the data presented in Chapter 5.

20. See Jáquez, "Comerciantes de la laguna piden que haya reelección presidencial."

21. These industries represent 98 percent of all establishments, 50 percent of the employment in industry, 43 percent of industrial production, and 10 percent of GDP (see "Cambios en la estructura industrial y el papel de las micro, pequeña y mediana empresas en México" by Nacional Financiera 1992, cited in Carrasco Licea and Hernández y Puente, "Nafín: Micros, pequeñas y medianas").

22. Poitras and Robinson, "The Politics of NAFTA in Mexico."

23. *La Jornada*, April 23, 1992, p. 27. See also Acosta," El causante, obligado a justificar lo que gana"; and Ortega Pizarro, "Propuesta de una ley que iguale al fisco a los causantes."

24. Centeno, *Democracy Within Reason*, p. 196.

25. See articles in *Mexico NewsPak* 1 (17), 1993, pp. 9–10, and 1 (18), 1993, pp. 4–5. Note that following two quarters of negative growth in the latter half of 1993, positive growth returned in 1994, reaching a 2.2 percent yearly rate for the first semester, according to the government. For a summary of the report see Howard, "Sorpresivo crecimiento reporta SHCP."

26. Rubio, "La transición administrada," p. 44.

27. Described in *Latin American Weekly Review* 89–35 (September 7, 1989), p. 8.

28. Discussed in Russell, *Mexico Under Salinas*, pp. 300–301.

29. A letter leaked from Labor Secretary Farell to Commerce Secretary Serra Puche, for example, showed government discussions with Ford on joint union busting—a measure designed to keep dissident unions from gaining control from the CTM. Whether such led to any concerted action is not clear, though the effort was indeed successful. The CTM won the June vote by workers at Ford (see *Latin American Weekly Review* [June 20,1991], p. 8).

30. See Robles, "Trabajadores de TAMSA torturados, presos y con una deuda de miles de millones."

31. See *Mexico NewsPak* 1 (21), 1993, pp. 3–4; and *La Jornada*, March 17, 1992, p. 11.

32. The reform of INFONAVIT was justified in part as curbing corruption. The plan definitely enjoyed the support of the private sector (see *La Jornada*, April 3, 1992, p. 17).

33. La Quina was the head of the Ciudad Madero union local of PEMEX in 1959 when he became secretary-general, thanks to the backing of President López Mateos. He continued to rule from behind the scenes following his three-year term, exerting strong-arm control over the union's leaders. He reportedly sold jobs for as much as $4,000 and purportedly took as much as $100 from 90,000 temporary workers (Russell, *Mexico Under Salinas*, pp. 8–10).

34. Jongitud Barrios, who had used strong-arm tactics to take control of the SNTE in 1972 and reportedly sold teaching jobs and controlled over $1 million a

month in union dues, had served as governor of San Luis Potosí and was one of the state's senators at the time of his arrest (Russell, *Mexico Under Salinas*, p. 11).

35. Cited in *La Jornada*, May 21, 1992, p. 11.

36. Cited in *La Jornada*, April 25, 1992, p. 9.

37. Though facilitating change, Sebastian Guzmán was generally considered to be of the same cut as the ousted Hernández Galicia (see Correa, "El único cambio en el sindicato petrolero"). Elena Poniatowska, in fact, referred to him as La Quina's "moral twin brother," who was equally tainted by charges of corruption (cited in Russell, *Mexico Under Salinas*, p. 11).

38. Correa "El único cambio."

39. *Mexico NewsPak* 1 (11), 1993, p. 6.

40. It is important to note that this reform reflected in some measure the fact that many workers were already siding with the opposition. Due to instability and wages, for example, many teachers had thrown their support behind the opposition (see *La Jornada*, July 21, 1992, pp. 4, 13).

41. One study by the Asociación Metropolitana de Ejecutivos en Relaciones Industriales found that contractual revisions had produced fewer gains in 1992 than in 1991. It put the average increase in February 1991 at 21.86 percent and in the same month of 1992 at 16.76 percent. The study also pointed out that increases for the CTM, which had the most revisions, were slightly less than average (15.96 percent) and that increases for independent unions were even less (15.84 percent) (cited in *La Jornada*, April 3, 1992, p. 17).

42. It is important to note that the CROC represents more service sector employees, who generally enjoy higher wages than the industrial workers of the CTM (see de Buen, "Primero de mayo").

43. Cited in *La Jornada*, March 15, 1992, p. 12.

44. This view was presented in a study by the Centro de Estudios Sindicales of the Instituto de Proposiciones Estratégicas of the private sector (tied to COPARMEX) (see *La Jornada*, February 2, 1992, p. 9).

45. For its part, business agreed to offer training and human development programs for workers and reward productivity gains through increased benefits (though not higher salaries). The government, in turn, promised to elaborate a Plan Nacional de Desarrollo and create a Comisión de Seguimiento y Evaluación for the benefit of workers. All parties (government, business, and labor) agreed to cooperate to promote a new labor culture (see *La Jornada*, May 26, 1992, p. 12).

46. In April 1992, for instance, a legislative request for an investigation and audit of INFONAVIT funds (operated largely by the labor confederations) was blocked by the PRI delegation over the objections of virtually all the opposition (see reports in *La Jornada*, March 17, 1992, p. 25; May 2, 1992, p. 5; and May 2, 1992, pp. 1, 16).

47. *La Jornada*, May 9, 1992, p. 13.

48. Aziz Nassif, "El movimiento obrero," p. 4.

49. See the various statements in *La Jornada*, March 26, 1992, p. 15; March 24, 1992, p. 13; and March 19, 1992, p. 13.

50. Cited in *La Jornada*, May 8, 1992, p. 17.

51. The government relied on the more supportive leaders of the Sindicato Mexicano de Electristas (SME) and CROM to try to mediate between the CTM and business (see *La Jornada*, April 29, 1992, p. 4).

52. Cited in *La Jornada*, March 19, 1992, p. 13.

53. See *La Jornada*, January 19, 1992, p. 5; February 24, 1992, pp. 1, 14; and June 28, 1992, p. 12.

54. See *Latin American Weekly Review*, April 5, 1990, pp. 4–5.

55. Cited in *Mexico NewsPak* 0, 1992, p. 2.

56. Cited in *Mexico NewsPak* 1 (22), 1993, p. 7.

57. According to Acosta, "Gobernadores, funcionarios, empresarios, líderes, caídos ante el poder presidencial," pp. 8–9, the governors were removed because "they were considered responsible for the resounding defeat during the 1988 presidential election, and worse [because] they could not guarantee, in subsequent elections, better results for the party."

58. COFIPE replaced the Código Federal Electoral (CFE) passed under de la Madrid three years earlier. Note that according to Aziz Nassif "¿Nuevo padrón electoral?" p. 4, the PRI agreed to the new Padrón Electoral to gain support in congress for the electoral reform package. For an overview of the 1989 reforms see Beltrán del Río "El COFIPE, 'Triunfo de México.'"

59. The 1993 reforms altered fourteen articles of the constitution. They changed Article 82, allowing Mexicans of foreign parentage to run for the presidency, effective in the year 2000, and set limits on fund raising for the parties to $650,000 per individual and five times that amount for organizations. For a discussion of the 1993 reforms see *Electoral Reform in Mexico* and *Mexico NewsPak* 1 (17), 1993, pp. 4–5.

60. According to Alemán, "Clase Política," the PAN agreed basically to allow Salinas to govern under the assumption that his government would be one of transition, that the government "could legitimize itself before the Mexicans by the proper use of its power and, more especially and immediately, through its behavior during the first elections under its responsibility."

61. *Latin American Weekly Review* 89–34 (August 31, 1989), p. 8.

62. This does not mean that violence and repression did not make up part of the pattern. As will be discussed in Chapter 7, violence racked many postelection protests. In the state of Michoacán following local elections in late 1993, for example, the opposition took control of more than twenty town halls, with battles in the towns of Yurécuaro and Turícato, leaving eight dead and three wounded.

63. For an overview of church-state relations see Grayson, *The Church in Contemporary Mexico.*

64. See Bailey, "Centralism and Political Change in Mexico." One estimate, cited in *Mexico NewsPak* 1 (17), 1993, p. 10, projected total spending over five years at $10 billion, 55 percent of federal expenditures in 1993.

65. The program also created more opportunity for government employment, an important patronage tool. According to Espinoza Valle, "Reforma del estado y modernización política en México," p. 15, by 1991, Salinas had actually increased the number of people working in the government by over 12,000 from the previous year.

66. Alcocer V., "Salinas y su pronasol," p. 38.

67. Dresser, "Bringing the Poor Back In," p. 156. Knight, "Solidarity: Historical Continuities," p. 7, makes reference to the number of committees formed.

68. For a good discussion of the program see de Vries, "Procampo and the Politics of State Intervention." The quote is taken from page 7.

69. Ibarra and Corro, "El PRONASOL, medio de liquidación del federalismo."

70. Publicity was indeed a critical ingredient in the program. In highlighting the importance of publicity in the program, Dresser, "Bringing the Poor Back In," p. 162, for instance, cites polls showing that while in November 1990, 78 percent of the population were unfamiliar with the program, by July of 1991, 72 percent knew of the program.

71. Applying for admittance (and eventually being accepted) to the exclusive Organization for Economic Cooperation and Development (OECD) lent a veneer of credence to that claim.

72. Not only did human rights abuses increase during the period despite the high-profile commission, but in many cases the commission's recommendations were ignored or not carried out. It was reported that the commission received 27,841 complaints during the Salinas period (through July 1994). In July 1994, the Comisión Nacional de Derechos Humanos (CNDH) noted that of the 103 pending cases, fifty were only partially resolved and thirty-three had been ignored by officials in eleven states, despite the fact that Salinas had given them thirty days to respond (see *Siglo 21,* July 22, 1994, p. 21).

73. Peschard, "PRI: Los desafíos de la recuperación."

74. Cited in *La Jornada,* July 16, 1990, p. 3.

75. See Chávez, "Exhorta la corriente crítica a desconocer dirigentes."

76. Noted in *Latin American Weekly Review,* September 20, 1990, pp. 4–5.

77. This statement is made based on a series of interviews with employees of Solidarity I conducted in Mexico during my many visits. It should be recognized that this is more than mere cooptation, since many of those within the left are the most experienced and most motivated to work with the poor in social programs.

78. See, for instance, *La Jornada,* June 10, 1992, p. 4; *Proceso* 723, pp. 24–27; *Latin American Weekly Review,* August 9, 1990, p. 8; and Corro, "Ante las siempre toleradas críticas de Fidel Velázquez."

79. Many have long considered the internal democratization of the PRI as a sine qua non for overall system democratization (see, for instance, Meyer, "Democratization of the PRI."

80. *Latin American Weekly Review,* September 20, 1990, pp. 4–5.

81. See Reyes del Campillo, "Candidatos: Hacia una nueva Cámara."

82. At the same time, Salinas announced that "ya no sería el partido del gobierno" [it will no longer be the party of the government] (see Albarrán de Alba, "El PRI acaba la era Salinas derrotado").

83. *La Jornada,* June 24, 1992, pp. 1, 11; and June 25, 1992, p. 3.

84. Chávez, "En medio de exaltaciones al Presidente." See also *La Jornada,* June 25, 1992, p. 3.

85. Cited in *La Jornada,* June 24, 1992, pp. 1, 11.

86. See *La Jornada,* June 25, 1992, p. 3, and June 27, 1992, p. 3. Note that though these measures curbed the influence of the corporate sectors, the party never considered abandoning the corporate-based structure of the PRI. Indeed, the new organizational layer supplemented rather than replaced the party's corporate structure. Such moves, nonetheless, brought stinging opposition from the labor sector.

87. See Galarza, "El Presidente rehusa arriesgar su proyecto económico por la democratización."

88. Party documents, reformed in the fifteenth assembly, called for more democratic processes in the selection of candidates, but at the same time they authorized the council to adopt "unity candidates" (a euphemism for *dedazo*) whenever it deemed it necessary for the good of the party.

89. Taken from an unpublished document from the executive council of the PRI dated October 22, 1991.

90. Albarrán de Alba, "El PRI acaba la era Salinas."

91. See *Mexico NewsPak* 1 (5), 1993, pp. 11–12; and 1 (8), 1993, pp. 7–8.

92. *Mexico NewsPak* 1 (8), 1993, pp. 7–8.

93. See *La Jornada*, November 2, 1991, p. 14.

94. *La Jornada*, November 27, 1991, p. 11.

95. See Beltrán del Río, "El PRI de Colosio pierde la linea."

96. See Beltran del Rio, "En su estudio, el PRI preveía la perdida de 49 municipios del Estado de México ante el PRD."

97. See Beltrán del Río, "El PRI de Colosio"; and Guzmán and Ramírez, "Deserciones y protestas de priístas."

98. See Beltrán del Río, "El PRI de Colosio." It is possible that the National Assembly simply escaped the leaders' control.

99. Hernández Rodríguez, "La reforma interna y los conflictos en el PRI."

100. Cited in Anders, "The Electoral Game." Despite official results in Michoacán showing PRI wins in twelve of the eighteen electoral districts, the PRD provided substantial documentation to demonstrate it won fifteen electoral districts and that in the other three, irregularities were so widespread that is was impossible to determine the outcome. PAN results largely agreed with those of the PRD (see also *Latin American Weekly Review* 89–30 (August 3, 1989), p. 10).

101. See *Proceso* 678, p. 18.

102. State elections in México, for example, showed the PRI winning 117 of the 121 municipalities and all thirty-two state congressional seats. This landslide contrasts a preelection poll conducted by the *Centro de Estudios de Opinión Pública* showing 42 percent favoring the PRD, 38 percent for the PRI, and 17 percent for the PAN, and preelection studies by the PRI itself predicting huge losses to the PRD (see Beltrán del Río, "En su estudio").

103. Hinojosa, "Televisa priísta," quotes the president of Televisa, the virtual monopoly of Mexican television, Emilio Azcarraga Milmo, as claiming to be "part of the governmental system and as such support the campaigns of the candidates for the PRI."

104. See, for example, Reding, "Las elecciones en Nuevo León."

105. Cited in *La Jornada*, August 22, 1991, p. 3.

106. *La Jornada*, August 23, 1991, pp. 12, 14.

107. Cited in *La Jornada*, August 26, 1991, p. 5. Many observers envisioned high rates of abstentionism as part of a PRI electoral strategy. As one observer noted: "In their denunciations, PAN and the PRD concur that an important part of the official strategy in the state of Mexico is to achieve a low level turnout"—what the PAN calls the "Chihuahua 90" strategy and PRD calls *uruapanazo* (see Beltrán de Río, "División de priístas, que se culpan ya de la derrota en el Estado de México"). Post-1988 elections indeed featured lofty levels of abstentionism: 70 percent in Chihuahua, 75 percent in Michoacán, and 80 percent in Veracruz (this compares to the 50 percent rate in the 1988 election). Despite such views, the 1991 midterm elections exhibited both a high voter turnout (67 percent), and a strong PRI showing, demonstrating perhaps the shift from a reliance on "negative" reforms such as fraud to more "positive" measures based on popularity.

108. For an overview from the PRI's perspective of the new tactics and techniques, see Colosio, "Why the PRI Won the 1991 Elections."

109. According to one party official (cited in *La Jornada*, May 23, 1992, p. 6), it involved "a design in which the traditional sectors of the PRI (the CTM, CNC, and UNE) did not exist."

110. Sodi de la Tijera "¿Por qué ganó el PRI?"

111. Empirical analysis by Molinar Horcasitas and Weldon, "Electoral Determinants and Consequences of National Solidarity," demonstrates the political determinants of Solidarity spending.

112. Beltrán del Río, "Solidaridad, oxígeno para el PRI."

113. Ibarra and Corro, "El PRONASOL," p. 11; and Beltrán del Río, "Solidaridad, oxígeno para el PRI."

114. See Beltrán del Río, "Solidaridad, oxígeno para el PRI." See also Consejo Consultivo del Programa Nacional de Solidaridad, ed., *Solidaridad a debate*; Dresser, *Neopopulist Solutions to Neoliberal Problems*; and Cornelius et al, eds., *Transformaing State-Society Relations in Mexico.*

115. Beltrán del Río, "Solidaridad, oxígeno para el PRI," p. 11.

116. See Chávez, "Michoacán: Cada voto del PRI costó 239,188 pesos."

117. The new formula of representation in the Consejo General, the highest electoral organ under the COFIPE reforms, for example, increases the PRI's majority from the 19–16 edge it enjoyed previously in the CFE to 13–9. It is important to recall, however, that law requires political will; and even the short-lived and, according to many at the time, unfair system under de la Madrid produced the greatest PRI electoral lashing in its history. Hence, much of the political impact of COFIPE corresponds to image and tactic (see Beltrán del Río, "El COFIPE").

118. See *Mexico NewsPak* 1 (15), 1993, pp. 1–2.

119. Note that there were certain benefits—e.g., financial subsidies and congressional seats—of keeping the parties within the FDN separate (Russell *Mexico Under Salinas* p. 97).

120. According to Russell, *Mexico Under Salinas*, pp. 97–98, Salinas met with the leaders of the PARM in December 1988 and the leaders of the PFCRN in March 1989. The mere meetings indicated a departure of these leaders from the Cárdenas line of not recognizing the legitimacy of the Salinas government and refusing any contact or negotiations.

121. Beltrán del Río, "Mil días bastaron a Salinas."

122. In referring to PRONASOL, for example, Heberto Castillo of the PRD noted that it was satisfactory "to see how the PRI, which in the beginning questioned the PRD, has little by little . . . adopted in its campaigns the proposals of the PRD" (*La Jornada*, August 11, 1991, p. 8). See Eckstein, "Formal Versus Substantive Democracy," for a discussion of this reformist strategy as it relates to the politics of Mexico City.

123. Americas Watch, *Human Rights in Mexico*, p. 5. Note that the organization concluded (p. 6) that there was "no evidence to indicate that this concern is well-founded."

124. *New York Times*, October 22, 1988, p. 2, and October 31, 1988, p. 16.

125. Cited in Beltrán del Río, "Las elecciones en Michoacán."

126. See both reports by Americas Watch, *Human Rights in Mexico* and *Unceasing Abuses.*

127. See Americas Watch, *Human Rights in Mexico*, pp. 5, 6, 30.

128. Cited in Correa, "Manchado de sangre, de principio a fin," p. 6.

129. Beltrán del Río, "El alcalde perredista de Morelia."

130. The paramilitary group Antorcha Campesina, which many feel has links to the government, was active in provoking violence in certain regions, particularly in the state of Michoacán. In Morelia in March 1990, for instance, the group stormed city hall and took city officials hostage, demanding the resignation of the PRD mayor, Maldonado. The military then entered the fray, arresting 103 *perredistas* (see Nevaer, "Mexico's Heartland Hit by Growing Political Turmoil").

131. See Beltrán del Río, "El alcalde perredista." On similar difficulties for the PAN see Galarza, "El alcalde panista de SLP"; and the report in the *New York Times*, May 22, 1990, p. 15.

132. See the presentation of data in *Nexos* 170, pp. 83–85; *Este País* 5 (August) 1991, pp. 2–6; and *Este País* 28 (July), 1993, p. 41.

133. *Nexos* 168, 1991, pp. 69–71.

134. In 1991, for example, 48.3 percent of the respondents predicted personal economic improvement for the following year (see *Nexos* 170, pp. 83–85).

135. Cited in *Mexico NewsPak* 1 (3), 1993, p. 3.

136. Basañez, *El pulso de los sexenios*, p. 6. See also Rodríguez Araujo, "En la hipótesis de la ingeniería electoral."

137. According to Coppedge, "Democracy: You Can't Get There from Here," p. 132, Salinas initially tried to mount his presidential campaign without relying on the mobilizational expertise of the party—a decision he subsequently reversed. Interestingly, Colosio, the PRI's 1994 candidate, also tried to shun many of the party's bosses in the early days of his campaign (see Chávez, "Cambio con Zedillo").

138. See the article by Granados Chapas in *La Jornada*, March 4, 1992, pp. 1, 4.

139. See the string of reports in *Proceso* throughout the month of December 1992; *Mexico NewsPak* 0, 1992, p. 13; and *Siglo 21*, August 10, 1994, p. 10.

140. Another means of accomplishing this: In late 1988, the state laws in Veracruz and Tabasco were interpreted so as to prevent the running of unified candidates (*New York Times*, October 22, 1988, p. 2).

141. Basañez, "Encuesta electoral 1991."

142. Beltrán del Río, "En 5 años, unas 10 propuestas de civilidad y democracia." *Proceso* 888.

143. Cited in *Novedades*, December 14, 1989, p. 18. See also Buendía Laredo and Zuckermann Behar, "Escenarios."

144. Beltrán del Río, "En su estudio."

145. See the series of polls reported in *Nexos* and those presented in Chapter 5.

146. Cited in *La Jornada*, July 17, 1992, p. 10.

147. Cited in *La Jornada*, July 18, 1992, p. 5.

148. For a solid overview of the peasant sector under the late Salinas period, see *La Jornada*, August 16, 1994, p. 18.

149. Most agree that the recession reflected such factors as the excessively high interest rates, the layoffs associated with industrial restructuring, and other negative aspects of rapid liberalization. COMCAMIN, for example, stated publicly that the "disordered and fierce" opening contributed to the recession (see *Siglo 21*, July 30, 1994, p. 21).

150. The initial demands of the Chiapan rebels called for the recognition of the EZLN as a political force, a cease-fire, the withdrawal of federal troops, the ending of the bombing, and the formation of a national mediation commission (*Mexico NewsPak* 1 (25), 1994, p. 5). The negotiating demands were economic (poor living conditions in Chiapas), social (racism, marginalization, etc.), and political (lack of political space and ability to select leaders) (*Mexico Newspak* 1 (26), 1994, p. 5).

151. At first the problem was between Manuel Camacho, the powerful mayor of Mexico City, and Luis Donaldo Colosio, the secretary of social development, following Colosio's selection as the PRI's presidential candidate. Not only did Camacho break with political tradition by indicating his frustration over the selection, but he then postured for a possible independent run at the presidency. This possibility took on more dangerous proportions when Camacho, subsequently named by Salinas as the government's negotiator with the Chiapan rebels, garnered credibility, popularity, and publicity, eclipsing that of Colosio.

152. For example, the Chiapas rebellion and the Colosio assassination combined to prompt the foreign investors to withdraw $11 billion of short-term investments from mid-January to mid-April. This represented about 9.4 percent of foreign investment. In response, interest rates rose to a seventeen-month high in April (*Mexico NewsPak* 2 (7), 1994, pp. 5–6).

153. *Mexico NewsPak* 1 (27), 1994, p. 7.

154. Cited in *Mexico NewsPak* 2 (2), 1994, p. 8.

155. According to a poll by Alianza Cívica/Observación 94 in 120 *municipios* and as reported in *Siglo 21*, August 6, 1994, p. 15.

156. The convention made the following political demands: (1) that the next government be a government of transition, be plural, and provide for widescale participation; (2) that the public vote for the candidate that best represents the demands of the CND; (3) that the public vote against the party of the state; (4) that civil resistance be used if electoral fraud occurs; (5) that the next government call for a Constituent Assembly; (6) that the EZLN be recognized as a belligerent force and that the military encirclement of the rebel holdings be ended; (7) that political trials be held against Salinas, Carpizo (head of Gobernación), and Patrocinio González Garrido (former head of Gobernación and former governor of Chiapas); (8) that the property of the PRI be expropriated; (9) that NAFTA be revised; and (10) that regional autonomy and the rights of ethnic groups be respected (see Monsivais, "Crónica de una Convención"; Alemán, "Clase Política"; and *Siglo 21*, August 10, 1994, pp. 20–21).

157. Alemán, "Clase Política."

158. *Mexico NewsPak* 2 (2), 1994, p. 8.

159. Cited in *Mexico NewsPak* 2 (3), 1994, p. 5.

160. In his speech announcing his resignation as peace commissioner, Camacho stated first that "within the PRI there exists a position of intolerance and exclusion, one contrary to the search for a reduction in the tensions that the country is suffering." He then went on to partially blame Zedillo for the failure to arrive at a negotiated solution to the Chiapan conflict (see *Siglo 21*, June 20, 1994, p. 16; and Rodríquez Castañeda, "Atrás de las declaraciones de Zedillo").

161. *Mexico NewsPak* 2 (4), 1994, p. 4.

162. It is important to note that Salinas's options were quite limited, since the law prohibits a presidential candidate from having been a government official during the previous six months. Though initially favored by José Córdoba, who was forced to resign following the assassination, Zedillo was available because he had stepped down from Education months earlier to direct Colosio's campaign.

163. See *Mexico NewsPak* 2 (3), 1994, p. 2.

164. See article by Miguel Angel Granados Chapa in *Siglo 21,* June 28, 1994, p. 18.

165. Elias Chávez, "Este sexenio, la fiebre reformadora de los lideres priístas."

166. See *Siglo 21*, August 5, 1994, p. 6.

167. *Siglo 21*, June 28, 1994, p. 16.

168. See *Siglo 21*, July 20, 1994, p. 15.

169. On Zedillo's inclusion of old politicos and others, see the series of articles by Elias Chávez: "Cambio con Zedillo," "Reunión de emergencia del Consejo Político Nacional del PRI," "La lista de candidatos del PRI al Senado," "La reforma del PRI, que debió hacerse antes, deberá hacerse después"; "Hank quiere ser el 'padrino'"; and *Mexico NewsPak* 2 (9), 1994, p. 1.

170. Under the campaign label *Bienestar para tu familia*, the PRI sold two types of baskets of goods. One basket contained a kilogram each of ham, cheese,

and wieners; the other included a kilogram of rice and beans, a bottle of oil, a can of sardines, some tuna and *chiles*, two bags of soup, and a bar of soap. The program was coordinated by the PRI but implemented by various businesses (see *Siglo 21*, July 13, 1994, p. 17).

171. Either the heightened scrutiny of the process, the greater pressures on the PRI to win, or some combination of the two resulted in a barrage of denunciations of irregularities during the campaign. A study by the Academia Mexicana de Derechos Humanos monitoring TV coverage between January and April, for example, showed that the PRI candidate had received 3.5 times more air time on the news shows than the other two candidates (Aguayo Quezada, "El Primer Tranco"). Subsequently, Alianza Cívica presented 108 cases of vote coercion, which they claimed were just the tip of the iceberg. Their report pointed to threats of withholding salary, withdrawing concessions, or forcing campaign contributions by PRI officials (32.8 percent of the cases), public officials (20 percent of the cases), and worker/peasant organizations (17.2 percent of the cases) in seventeen states. It also noted such practices as using state resources to support PRI campaigns, taking voter ID cards, pressuring people to attend PRI meetings, and offering gifts and even money in exchange for votes (*Siglo 21*, August 3, 1994, p. 4). The PRD, meanwhile, complained that it had discovered the existence of 1.21 million duplicate names on voter rolls just for the Federal District—a situation the IFE called "normal" (*Siglo 21*, August 7, 1994, p. 10). It also prepared complaints against eleven governors for providing assistance to PRI candidates (*La Jornada*, August 13, 1994, p. 5). Indeed, as of August 1, FEPADE (Fiscalia Especial para la Atención de Delitos Electorales) had received 140 complaints of irregularities (*Siglo 21*, August 2, 1994, p. 4).

172. *Siglo 21*, June 22, 1994, p. 20.

173. It was estimated prior to the vote that perhaps 70 percent of the *casillas* would be worthy of confidence because of the degree of supervision. That still left 25,000 to 30,000 *casillas* "of the past" that would not be supervised by opposition parties and where the caciques could prepare the routine vote for the PRI (see Aguayo Quezada, "Casillas Esquizofrénicas").

174. This does not mean that fraud was absent from the election. Alianza Cívica and its foreign observers, for example, found that in 39 percent of the *casillas,* the vote was not secret (51 percent in the countryside); that 25 percent of the electorate was pressured to vote by representatives of parties, caciques, or others through a range of means (again primarily in the countryside); and that in 70 percent of the *casillas* names were shaved from the voting list, an average of 4 percent per *casilla*. Meanwhile, the PRD protested 166 of the 300 districts, while the PAN requested the nullification of the results in electoral districts in the Federal District, Nuevo León, Yucatán, Tamaulipas, Coahuila, México, Guanajuato, Aguascalientes, Sonora, Veracruz, and Guerrero. Beyond electoral fraud, the PAN's postelectoral statement noted that the government used its resources to favor the PRI, greatly outspent its opponents, and manipulated and controlled information. For these and other reports see the various pieces by Monge: "Observadores, periodistas, ciudadanos y partidos," "Testimonio de observadores internacionales," and "Balance de Alianza Cívica"; Albarrán de Alba, "Análisis con cifras de las auditorías"; and "Declaración del consejo nacional del partido acción nacional."

175. See Ortega Pizarro, "Germán Carcoba y Roberto Hernández adelantan públicamente su voto por Zedillo."

176. Crespo, "¿Democracia con el PRI?"

177. The initial reports showed that two officials of the government, both from the state of Tamaulipas, were key suspects in the conspiracy to kill Ruiz Massieu. It appears that the murder may be related to conservative elements in the party that sought to cripple internal reforms (see the various reports reprinted in *Mexico NewsPak* 2 (18), 1994).

178. See Arrendondo Ramírez, "¿Apocalipsis político o parto democrático?"

179. Centeno, *Democracy Within Reason*, associates this concentration of control with the success of the economic reforms.

5

A Case Within a Case:
The PRI in Jalisco Under Salinas

As occurred in most parts of the country, in the western state of Jalisco the PRI staged a remarkable recovery following its poor showing in 1988, only to stumble once again in 1994 (see Figure 5.1). In one sense, the PRI's post-1988 recovery was dramatic in that it reversed a long-term structural pattern of decline and eased, at least momentarily, the pressures toward change. In another sense, the early recovery was less than striking. It reflected only subtle and mild changes amidst a general pattern of continuity and proved to be short-lived.

Analysis of political and electoral patterns in the state of Jalisco during the 1988–1994 period helps illustrate the reformist pattern under Salinas. Though results from one state or even one metropolitan area cannot be generalized to the national level, they nonetheless help detail the nature of the changes marking the period. Discussion begins by focusing on the general trends within the state up to 1992, followed by an examination of a series of surveys from the Guadalajara area that help document and map the initial recovery. The last section then looks at trends from 1992 to 1994 statewide.

Political Trends to 1992

Jalisco is the fourth largest entity in terms of votes (behind D.F., México, and Veracruz) and comprises one of México's largest urban-industrial areas, the city of Guadalajara. Given its people's historic ties to the church, the Cristero rebellion, the *sinarquista* movement, and opposition to *cardenismo,* Jalisco has a long history of defiance of the "center." For these reasons, opposition to the PRI in the state has always been strong, well organized, and angled from the right. Since supporting the renegade PRI candidate Juan Almazán in the 1940 election, the PAN has consistently placed candidates throughout the state and has made steady gains over the years, capturing a few mayoral seats and an occasional state and federal post along the way. In the ten federal elections stretching from

Figure 5.1   Vote Patterns in Jalisco, 1988–1994

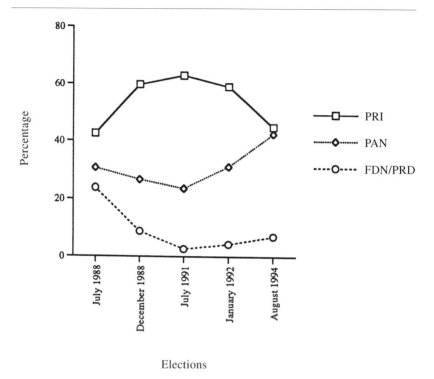

Elections

1960 to 1988, for instance, the PAN bettered its previous performance on seven of the nine occasions.[1] Moreover, the opposition, led by the PAN, long has been active in protesting fraud. In 1958, for example, the PAN even went so far as to boycott the state elections. On some occasions, such protests have actually forced the annulling of results or led to the creation of joint city administrations.[2]

As occurred in many parts of the country, the PAN's appeal and the government's reliance on fraud to maintain the PRI's hegemony increased in Jalisco under de la Madrid. In the 1985 mid-term election, the PAN's fortunes declined somewhat statewide because of fraud, but the party continued to close the gap with the PRI. Even with fraud, the PRI's share of the vote fell from 57.5 percent in 1982 to near 50 percent. And the results—which included many unlikely and illogical outcomes (like 120 percent turnout in certain districts)—triggered intense opposition protests. In the local contests that followed a few months later, the government recognized opposition victories in just three *municipios* compared to six in

1982. The level of perceived fraud, however, was again extremely high, unleashing widespread protests.[3]

The rising strength of the opposition, the growing politicization of the electoral arena, and serious rifts between the local and national levels of the PRI, all worked to weaken the PRI in 1988. First, the PAN's Clouthier marshaled support from an important segment of the state's bourgeoisie. Bending an old political rule, local business organizations like Desarrollo Humano Integral Asociacion Civil (DHIAC) publicly supported Clouthier, while some local business leaders actually joined the ranks of the PAN either to become candidates for local office or to aid, sometimes furtively, the campaign.[4] This was a critical shift. Dominated by small and medium-size family businesses, the Jalisco business sector was much less ideological and political than its counterparts in Monterrey or Mexico City and heretofore "had never rendered open and decided support" to the opposition.[5]

Second, and even more surprisingly, the left under Cárdenas, which had been insignificant in the state, was able to mobilize the support of many from the lower ranks of society, many of whom had been PRI supporters. Support ranged from local urban groups, like the Movimiento Urbano Popular in Guadalajara, to organizations in the countryside. Finally, amidst this opposition, the PRI found itself severely weakened by internal disputes. Not only had the satellite parties abandoned it to take refuge behind Cárdenas at the national level, but many of the PRI militants within Jalisco had backed one of the other precandidates in the internal party drama. As a result, they tendered only lukewarm support for Salinas.[6]

The results reflected the circumstances. Statewide, the PRI's vote dipped to 42.5 percent, as the PAN increased its share to 30.7 percent, and the FDN captured an incredible 23.8 percent of the tally. At the district level, the PAN defeated the PRI in eight of the twenty districts, all of which were located in the metropolitan area of Guadalajara. In so doing, the PAN defeated candidates from some of the PRI's main corporate organs, such as the CROC and the CTM, in districts long controlled by these organizations.[7] In December of the same year, the state held elections for governor. Amidst massive levels of abstentionism and widespread perceptions of fraud, the PRI's gubernatorial candidate, Guillermo Cosio Vidaurri, barely won with only 51 percent of the vote versus the PAN's 38 percent (see Figure 5.1).

As occurred nationally, the PRI of Jalisco in the two 1988 contests clung to its strong vote in the rural areas and relied on fraud to win. The party's leaders, however, recognized that if they could not at least weaken the tendencies or reverse them, the state would be forced to undergo some basic political changes (either a PRI loss/PAN victory, or a dangerously increasing reliance on repression and fraud to control the state). The reformist strategy that emerged was multidimensional and the results sufficient, for a time at least.

One of the reformist strategies the PRI adopted to maintain its hegemony and reverse the tide, was to shake itself up internally. It pulled in the reins on its own militants, centralized the candidate selection process, strategically picked more attractive candidates, began to organizationally emphasize territorial units as opposed to the corporate organs, and launched well-orchestrated, well-coordinated (and well-funded) electoral campaigns. Rather than *consultas a las bases,* as had been called for during the national assembly, PRI's candidates were selected from the top as so-called unity candidates, either by the president for federal elections or by Governor Cosio for state elections. In addition to handpicking its candidates, the PRI also struggled to name candidates that were more attractive electorally. To do so, they tapped candidates with strong local credentials and/or business ties, particularly in difficult areas. The gubernatorial candidate in 1988, Cosio was a local candidate with strong ties to the state's businesses, while the party's candidates for mayor and vice-mayor of Guadalajara were touted as *"priístas empanizados,"* reflecting the need to "strengthen relations with local entrepreneurs."[8] Complementing this tactic, the party's lower-profile candidates strengthened the traditional side, brandishing the names of some of the state's top political families and representing the major corporate organizations in the traditional manner.[9] This helped to reconsolidate the party and draw on its traditional bases of support.

As occurred in many parts of the country, this centralization of power within the state party unleashed the opposition of many local PRI activists. Internal factions, such as the Frente Amplio por la Democracia (FAD) and the Movimiento Democrático de Acción Partidista (MDAP) in Jalisco, emerged to protest the selection of candidates. Conflict within the ranks over the selection process marred the operations of the party in San Juan de los Lagos, Tala, Magdalena, Ayutla, Mazamitla, and Arena. Overall, some thirty-two *municipios* in the state suffered some form of internal conflict over the selection of the party's candidates in 1991 alone.[10]

With more attractive candidates selected from the top, the PRI also refocused its efforts on campaigning and mobilizing the vote. Combining new and old techniques, the party dispensed commodities during the campaign, often through Solidarity, inundated the media with its messages and "public service" ads praising the government, and put renewed pressure on teachers, bureaucrats, and union members to attend PRI rallies and vote for the tricolor. The party also went to great lengths to meticulously analyze the party's strengths and weaknesses through door-to-door canvasing and surveys, a measure that aided in designing a campaign strategy and/or strategy of alchemy. Emphasis centered on territorial units to recruit vote promoters who were charged with bringing a set number of voters to the polls.[11]

Perhaps unsurpassed in its scope, sophistication, and effectiveness was the campaign of Enrique Dau Flores for mayor of Guadalajara in 1992. With the candidate flaunting an entrepreneurial background and ties with business, the campaign featured high-profile raffles of automobiles; a massive and well-publicized survey of the wishes, fears, and desires of the local population; slick, professional TV ads; and the placement of massive amounts of propaganda throughout the city. As Alonso notes,

> During the campaign, in upper-middle-class neighborhoods, the PRI offered cheap products from trucks. In the poor neighborhoods, it used PRONASOL [Solidarity]. The candidate for mayor of Guadalajara . . . conducted an extravagant campaign. Some said that it seemed more like a campaign for President of the Republic and not mayor. Immense posters with him standing up and extending his hand invited the people to vote for the PRI. He propagated the slogan *Guadalajara tiene la palabra* [Guadalajara has the word] and pressured members of business organizations to purchase tickets at high prices for raffles of automobiles.[12]

Solidarity, Salinas's image, and Salinas himself greatly complemented these measures and echoed the messages. Solidarity dispensed goods throughout the state in conjunction with the PRI's campaign, provided important social services, financed infrastructure projects in needed areas, and generally raised the hopes of the people for a brighter future. From 1989 to 1991, CUD-PRONASOL invested some 758 billion pesos in the state, enhancing citizen participation and the government's image in the process.[13] And just days prior to the vote in 1991, Solidarity announced a program of potable water for Atotonilco, while the state government hailed in a news ad that 87 percent of the homes in Lagos de Moreno now enjoyed electricity, thanks to Solidarity. INFONAVIT also distributed housing titles with great fanfare to families in Ciudad Guzmán. On August 15—and thus in violation of the state's electoral law—the governor took out three *plegados* in the local newspapers to list the advances in public works during 1991 for every *municipio* in the state. Salinas even joined the effort, making a number of public appearances in the state to inaugurate public works projects under the Solidarity label. Just two weeks prior to local elections in 1992, for instance, Salinas toured the state, promising 202 billion pesos of Solidarity funding for Jalisco.[14]

Besides these measures, the PRI used more negative tactics to broker the precarious situation. For example, the PRI tightened its legal grip over the electoral process. The national electoral reform of 1989, as noted earlier, not only garnered some popular legitimacy for Salinas, but also ensured the overrepresentation of the PRI in monitoring elections and basically kept the electoral machinery in the hands of the pro-PRI government. The opposition in Jalisco denounced these changes, claiming on one occasion that 95 percent of the voting officials were tied to the PRI and that all of the voting officials in Guadalajara had committed prior electoral crimes.[15] The opposition similarly complained that the state law governing elections actually prevented free local contests by assuring PRI control of the machinery. Like the federal law, the state law gave PRI officials control over every step of the process and a virtual veto authority.

Fraud also figured prominently in the PRI's strategy repertoire. Indeed, fraud (or at least the widespread and very credible signs of irregularities) seemed to inform virtually every stage of the process. The new voter registration procedure in 1991 elicited a chorus of cries of wrongdoing. A report by the Academía Jalisciense de Derechos Humanos, for instance, showed that while one-third of urban residents failed to receive their voting credentials, 90 percent of rural residents did.[16] A similar report pointed out that in Districts I and XIII, traditional PAN strongholds, the level of voter credentialization reached 68.7 percent and 70.4, percent respectively, whereas in the corporate and PRI-strong Districts II and IV, the levels of credentialization were 88 percent and 90 percent. Moreover, "in many rural locations controlled by the official party there were no reports of any undelivered voting credentials, while the number of these in the city of Guadalajara and in opposition areas was high."[17]

Reports of irregularities during the voting were even more common. Claims surfaced that voter identification cards were being distributed illegally, that some voters were able to vote with altered cards, that PRI militants monitored the process from within the voting precincts, and that opposition supporters were not allowed to vote because their names failed to appear on the lists, despite the fact that they held the proper voting cards. As Alonso points out,

> In rural zones more than a few of the electoral materials arrived at the district office that were brought by persons who were not the presidents of the precincts, and some arrived already open or without having been computed. In rural as well as urban zones there were precincts that greatly exceeded the average level of turnout, to such a degree that in some the number of votes did not match the time necessary for so many votes to be placed in the ballot boxes.[18]

Through these efforts the PRI was able to turn things around. In the 1991 midterm election, not only was the economy in better shape, but the outspoken support for the PAN by many of the state's business groups evaporated, despite their general disillusionment with the performance of Governor Cosio. The PAN, moreover, lacked a solid leader or charismatic figure to motivate and lead the charge as it had enjoyed in the 1988 presidential contest. The parties that had supported Cárdenas in 1988 were also weakened by internal divisions and presented a multiple face by 1991. In a sense, the opposition was not only less than prepared to challenge the PRI, but was also caught off guard. As Alonso so eloquently concludes, "Opposition parties were incapable of discovering in time the overall design of these practices. They perceived some trees, not all, and only in the end did they realize the magnitude of the forest."[19]

Officially, the PRI garnered 63 percent of the vote in the state compared to 23.7 percent for the PAN and a mere 2.7 percent for the PRD. This couched an 80 percent increase in actual votes for the PRI and a 20.6 increase in its vote percentage over 1988. At the district level, the PRI increased its vote percentage an average of 23.1 percentage points in the districts within the metropolitan area of Guadalajara and 14 points in the other districts. As a result, the party recaptured the eight congressional districts it had lost to the PAN in 1988. The PRI's showing in the state ranked third overall among PRI gains in the 1991 national contest, making it one of the few substantial recoveries that came at the expense of the PAN. Seven months later, during the state's local elections, the PRI further solidified its electoral hold. Overall it garnered 59.2 percent of the vote compared to 31.3 percent for the PAN and 4.3 percent for the PRD, though it lost eighteen of the state's 110 *municipios* in the process.

Despite what seemed a dramatic reversal, much remained the same. First, the PAN vote really did not decline all that much. Within the metropolitan area of Guadalajara, the PAN received about the same absolute number of votes that in 1988 was sufficient to capture the eight federal posts but that in 1991 rendered none.[20] This reflected the increase in new votes for the PRI and the dramatic decline in the vote for the Cárdenas left. Indeed, the PRD failed to receive more than 10 percent of the vote in any of the state's districts. Second, the perception of fraud marred once again the 1991 and 1992 elections and triggered protests as it had been doing for over a half century. In the wake of the 1991 contest, for example, the PAN refused to acknowledge or legitimize the results, while the PRD abandoned the state's electoral offices in protest. Together with other opposition parties, they tried to place the blame for the fraud on Salinas himself. Following the 1992 local contest, thousands of PAN supporters joined the city of Guadalajara's 450-year anniversary celebration in a silent march protesting electoral fraud. At the same time, in the city of Tala, supporters of the PAN and the PRD took control of the local election offices demanding that opposition victories be respected. The group later staged a protest march to the state capital and initiated a sit-in. Though protests of fraud erupted in more than 40 percent of the state's *municipios,* the opposition lacked the capacity to overturn the fraud as occurred or would occur in the states of Guanajuato, San Luis Potosí, Tabasco, Veracruz, and Yucatán during this time.[21]

A Glimpse at Public Opinion in Guadalajara

Analysis of a series of electoral surveys conducted in the Guadalajara area by the Instituto de Estudios Económicos y Regionales (INESER), now the Centro de Opinión Pública of the University of Guadalajara, provides an opportunity to examine empirically certain dimensions of the political dynamic.[22] The four polls first show strong parallels between changes in the public's leanings toward the PRI, levels of confidence in the government, faith in the electoral process, and optimism as regards the country's economic situation. Table 5.1 shows that the percentage of respondents preferring the PRI increased as those expressing confidence in the electoral process jumped and a favorable evaluation of the government edged upward. The percentage of respondents believing that their personal economic situation over the previous five years had improved more than doubled.[23]

Cross-sectional analyses of each of the polls supported this broader tendency. In 1988, for example, 74.4 percent expressing confidence in the electoral process backed the PRI compared to only 28.5 percent of those with no such confidence; 39 percent of those expressing a favorable view of the government's anti-inflationary pact supported the PRI compared to only 25.2 percent of those holding the opposing view; and 69.3 percent of those indicating a favorable opinion of the government supported the PRI

Table 5.1   Public Opinion Shifts: Guadalajara, 1988–1992

	Year		
% of Respondents	1988 (n=492)	1991 (n=330)	1992 (n=502)
Preferring the PRI	39.5	53.8	50.7
Expressing confidence in the electoral process	8.8	28.8	26.7
With a favorable evaluation of the government or its policies	27.8	43.0	30.3
Who see their personal economic situation over the past 5 years as better	24.8	50.3	nd

Source: Arroyo, et al., "Opiniones preelectorales de la poblacion"; Morones, "Encuesta de opinion preelectoral en la zona metropolitana; and Morones and Morris, "Análisis de resultados de las encuestas."

as opposed to only 19.7 percent of those with an unfavorable view. Similarly in the 1991 survey, 74.1 percent of those expressing confidence in the electoral process noted a preference for the PRI compared to only 38.8 percent of those harboring a lack of confidence; and 69.6 percent of those with a favorable view of government's performance supported the PRI compared to 50 percent of those with a less favorable opinion. The linkage with a respondent's evaluation of his or her own economic situation (past and future) was less clear. The 1988 poll showed that those sensing an improvement in their personal economic situation were more likely to support the PRI, but only by a small margin: 43 percent as compared to 32.3 percent. A similar though stronger pattern characterized future expectations: 44.9 percent of those with an optimistic assessment of the future supported the PRI compared to 23.4 percent who saw their future in less favorable terms.

The 1991 and 1992 polls, by contrast, revealed almost no difference between the percentage of respondents with a favorable view of their personal situation during the previous few years preferring the PRI (65.8 percent) and those seeing their situation in more negative terms (62.2 percent favored the PRI). In other words, support for the opposition in 1992 came disproportionately from among those who felt their situation had not changed or chose not to express an opinion. Perhaps even more surprising, those expecting their personal situation to get worse in the near future were by 1991 actually more likely to support the PRI than another political party. The PAN actually drew more support from among those with optimistic views of the future than did the PRI. In 1991, for example, among those who felt their economic situation over the ensuing years would grow worse and expressed a political preference, 52.6 percent supported the PRI. This surpassed the percentage supporting the PRI among the ranks of those seeing the future as holding no change.

Interestingly, the data showed only a marginal and generally insignificant linkage between a respondent's confidence in the electoral process, evaluations of the government or assessments of personal economic mobility, and his or her intention to vote. Those with more positive evaluations of the government or assessments of their personal situation tended to be somewhat more likely to vote, but only by a small and generally insignificant margin: 89.7 percent expressing confidence in the electoral process in 1988 also expressed an intention to vote compared to 79.5 percent of those exhibiting a lack of confidence; 85.6 percent offering a more favorable evaluation of the government's anti-inflationary pact planned to cast their ballot compared to 79.7 percent of those harboring an unfavorable view of the program; and yet, 79.8 percent of those noting an improvement in their personal situation during the preceding five years stated an intention to vote compared to 81.9 percent of those experiencing a worsening of their personal economic fortunes. This suggests that such negative views, though generally linked to party preference, fail to inform the decision to vote. The 1992 postelectoral poll, however, did show a much stronger correlation between voting and viewing the campaign as fair. Among those having voted, 60.6 percent felt the campaign was competitive, while among those that did not cast their ballot, only 29.4 percent viewed the contest as just. Whether this represents a causal factor underlying abstentionism or simply a post facto rationalization remains open to debate.

Though the data show a negative correlation between education levels and PRI support and no linkage between education and the intention to vote—both buttressing long-noted trends—the same data indicate the PRI's support increasing most among those in the upper educational brackets who had shown the greatest increases in confidence toward the system.[24] As demonstrated in Table 5.2, in 1988, 41.1 percent of those with only a primary level of education supported the PRI compared to 23.7 percent of those with some university training; yet in 1991, the comparable figures were 55 percent versus 41 percent.[25] The PRI not only had gained most among the better educated, but had closed the gap somewhat. Moreover, the strongest portion of this shift came at the expense of the PRD. In fact, among lower educational levels, other political parties (primarily of the left) actually registered gains over the 1988–1992 period.

The 1991 poll also offered solid evidence to link the improved sentiments toward the PRI and the system to the actions and the legitimacy accruing to Salinas. Among those stating an intention to vote for the PRI in 1991, the "acts of Salinas" ranked as the reason most often cited for doing so (by 31.9 percent of the respondents). By contrast, only 4 percent cited the actions of the local government as the primary reason for casting a vote for the ruling PRI. This role of Salinas can also be seen in the growing support stemming from improved evaluations of the government's handling of elections and the economy and in the higher level of support registered for the official party in 1991, as compared to the local elections held seven months later.[26] Indeed, opinions of the local government were generally poor.

The data strongly suggest then that Salinas swayed many away from the PRD during the 1988–1991 period by restoring confidence in the electoral process and the system generally and garnering legitimacy. The vote for the left, as noted, fell statewide from 23.8 percent in 1988 to just 2.7 percent in 1991. But, since neither the 1988 nor the 1991 poll asked respondents about their previous vote, precise tracking of vote shifts is not possible. Still, the 1992 poll did tap this variable. It showed that approximately 50 percent of those planning on voting for the PRD in 1992 had previously cast their 1991 ballot for the PRI, while only about 10 percent

Table 5.2 **Changes in Party Preference by Education, Age, and Gender: Guadalajara, 1988–1991**

	Educational Levels			Age Cohorts				Gender	
	Low	Medium	High	18–24	25–34	35–44	45–64	Male	Female
PRI	+8.5	+13.9	+24.0	+5.8	+5.8	+19.5	+6.1	+8.9	+10.9
PAN	–13.5	–13.6	–13.9	–7.4	+1.6	–5.7	–5.2	–4.8	–3.8
OTHER	+4.8	–1.3	–8.5	+1.6	–8.5	–13.8	–2.2	–4.2	–7.1

Note: Without having worked with the actual data for all the polls it was impossible to calculate precise levels of significance. For numbers of respondents and classification criteria, see the orginal reports cited earlier.

of those voting for the PAN had voted for the PRI. The PAN's gain in 1992 thus came from the ranks of those who had previously voted for "other" political parties (rather than the PRI or the PRD) or among those who had failed to vote in the 1991 election.

Trends to 1994

Despite the political gains during these initial years as expressed through the polls, the government and the PRI faced severe setbacks beginning in 1992. Much of this stemmed from the precipitous loss of support for Governor Cosio owing to evidence of favoritism and corruption in the operation of the state government, a dramatic rise in violence across the state—particularly drug-related violence, the governor's hard-line policy during a teachers strike, his steadfast imposition of candidates during the 1991 and 1992 elections, the existence of electoral fraud, and the government's hard-line response to postelectoral protests. The crisis found women marching to protest the lack of security, the PAN and PRD formally requesting a state investigation of the governor's businesses, and representatives of the local private sector even asking Salinas to remove the governor.[27]

This intense anti-Cosio sentiment within the state deepened further in the wake of the April 22 explosions in Guadalajara, which killed over 300 and left thousands homeless. The explosions triggered a series of marches to the Federal District, sit-ins in front of the state palace, 1,500 official denunciations against PEMEX and the state, and a crystallization of opinion that the government was not only to blame for the tragedy, but actually covered it up. In an effort to relieve pressures, Salinas exerted federal authority and intervened to force the resignation of Cosio, jail nine state, local, and PEMEX officials, including the mayor of Guadalajara, strengthen the role of Solidarity in the state, and create a *patronato* designed to compensate those hurt by the blast.[28]

The multiple interventions to help assuage the post–April 22 situation were mildly effective. One poll in 1993 in the affected zone, for instance, suggested that the population trusted Salinas and the federal government more than the state government, and that even the newly appointed governor, Carlos Rivera, though from the same political school as Cosio, had been somewhat successful at rebuilding bridges with business and other key groups in the state.[29] Still, events continued to deteriorate for the government and the ruling PRI. The March 1993 assassination of Cardinal Juan Jesús Posadas Ocampo in the Guadalajara airport chipped at the government's image. As would occur with the car bombing at the Camino Real more than a year later, the event provided further evidence of the penetration of the drug cartels into the state and the government and its deadly impact on society.[30] In late 1993, protests and violence with agricultural interests organized in the El Barzón movement cut into the government's traditional bases of support in the countryside. Demanding a solution to their debts with the banks, the agricultural workers used tractors to occupy first the center of Ciudad Guzmán and later Guadalajara, gaining much national attention and the jailing of their leader.[31]

Coupled with the ominous national trends discussed in Chapter 4, these state and local events greatly tarnished the image of the PRI and prompted a dramatic turnaround during the 1994 election. According to early unofficial figures, the PRI barely beat the PAN statewide (see Figure 5.1), though it lost ten of the twenty federal seats to the PAN. Preliminary analysis of the data points to a number of important trends over this period and the entire *sexenio*.

First, the 1991 to 1994 pattern mirrors in certain ways the 1988 to 1991 shift. In other words, the 1994 results correlated more closely with the previous presidential election in 1988 than they did with the midterm election three years earlier. This not only suggests that the gains enjoyed by Salinas and the PRI during the first half of the *sexenio* withered during the last half, pointing to critical differences between sexenial and midterm elections, but also underscores a sexenial pattern of reformism: that the weakest reformist point in the system is during a transition (this point will be discussed in a subsequent chapter).

Second, the PRI's decline from 1991 to 1994 was not statistically different among metro Guadalajara and non-Guadalajara districts (or by level of poverty), as indicated in Table 5.3.[32] This suggests that the disillusionment with the official party during this period was generalized throughout the state despite the localized impact of the explosions or the El Barzón movement. If we look at the trend throughout the six-year period, however, the PRI actually gained slightly vis-à-vis the PAN in the metropolitan area while watching its huge edge in the countryside erode. In the nine non-metro Guadalajara districts, for example, the average decline in the PRI's vote percentage over the 1988–1994 period was –5.29 compared to an increase of 6.33 in the eleven metro districts. This indicated that the PRI's biggest decline (and the PAN's greatest gains) overall was in its traditional areas of support.

Closely related to this was the pattern of PAN gains. Mirroring the PRI, the PAN vote increased almost equally in all districts during the 1991–1994 period. Yet during the entire *sexenio*, the PAN showed its most important gains in its traditionally weakest areas: the non-Guadalajara districts and the poor districts. In fact, in its traditional strongholds in the Guadalajara area, the PAN increased its percentage by only 6.43 points, compared to more than 15 points in the non-Guadalajara area.

Finally, the 1994 results demonstrate an important shifting in the level of polarization throughout the state (best illustrated in Figure 5.1). In 1988, as noted earlier, much of the PAN victory could be attributed to the impact of Cárdenas in stealing votes from the PRI. In like manner, the 1991 recovery of the PRI was tied to the ruling party's ability to pull those votes back from the left. Though the PRD bettered its performance in 1994 by 4.5 percentage points, it still languished with only 7.2 percent statewide: more than 16 points below its strong 1988 showing. This meant not only a bipolar tendency in the 1994 vote as compared to a tripolar tendency in 1988, but that the PAN was able to challenge the PRI directly, without the help of a third party. Such a situation bode ill for the PRI facing a gubernatorial election in early 1995. [Author's note: Amidst national crisis, the PAN won the election in February 1995—a victory immediately recognized by the government.]

Table 5.3   Mean Vote Swings: Jalisco, 1988–1994
             (n = 20)

	PRI		PAN	
	1991–1994	1988–1994	1991–1994	1988–1994
Non-ZMG	–17.54	–5.29	+17.93	+15.37
ZMG	–18.16	+6.33	+17.17	+6.43
F	.1253	11.99	.4139	9.581

Note: (ZMG = Guadalajara Metropolitan Area)

Conclusion

This brief detour to a case within a case details the PRI's initial recovery from 1988 to 1992 and its decline amidst renewed crisis from 1992 to 1994 in the state of Jalisco. It reveals Salinas's early success at garnering legitimacy as a reformer and restoring confidence in elections and the economy, particularly among the more educated and urban residents, while simultaneously strengthening the PRI's hold over the traditional bases and wresting support from the left. Though the left never recovered, the PRI lost more support during the period 1992–1994 among its traditional con-stituents and among those it had brought on board over the preceding four years. In other words, reversing past secular trends, Salinas bolstered PRI support in those areas where the party long had performed poorly and lost support in those areas where the PRI traditionally had done well. As a re-sult, by 1994, the distance between the PRI's vote among rural versus urban and poor versus rich districts had eroded significantly.

In addition, the case demonstrates the coexistence of both positive with negative reforms and change amidst continuity. Despite the rise of opposition, the PRI did not totally reconstruct itself, eliminate its corporate supports from the past, or win without the use of fraud. In some cases it named better candidates with local and business credentials, promised fair contests, and used Solidarity to enhance the party and the government's image. But in other cases it continued to respect power quotas, rely on un-fair tactics, and bow to state politicians from the older school.[33] Though in the final analysis the PRI lost much of what it had gained from 1988 to 1991 and the state continued as a political difficulty for the regime, the PRI did hold on to power throughout the six-year period. True to success-ful reformism, change always seemed near.

Before looking more extensively at the pattern of change in Mexico's other states and the country's historic capacity to accomplish this reformist feat, our attention turns to a general assessment of reformism in Mexico during the contemporary period.

Notes

1. For a history of politics in Jalisco see Medina Núñez, "Fuerzas políticas y procesos electorales."

2. In response, the PRI has gone further than in most states to embrace busi-ness and the right wing. Since the 1950s, for example, the vice-mayor of Guadala-jara for the PRI has come from the private sector—a trend the party would broaden through the years.

3. The opposition won Totatiche (PAN), Encarnación (PDM) and Tizapán (PST). The PAN claimed victory in a number of cities, while in Gómez Farías and

Los Lagos, PARM and PDM supporters took over the city offices in protest. The persistent protests of the PDM in the latter eventually forced the creation of a joint city administration.

4. Sánchez Susarrey, *La transición incierta*, pp. 80–87.

5. For an overview of business in the state see Alba Vega and Kruijt, *Los empresarios y la industria de Guadalajara*. The quote is taken from page 212.

6. Alonso, "Jalisco 88: Auge y desencanto electoral," p. 86.

7. District 2, controlled by the CTM-affiliated FTJ (Frente de Trabajadores de Jalisco); District 3, led by Sindicato Nacional de Trabajadores del Seguro Social; and Districts 4 and 18, dominated by the CROC were all lost to the PAN (see "Jalisco ante las urnas"; and Sánchez Sussarey, *La transición incierta*, pp. 80–87).

8. Sánchez Sussarey, *La transición incierta*, p. 84.

9. Alonso, "Jalisco 88," p. 91.

10. See Alonso, *El rito electoral en Jalisco*, pp. 90–92.

11. On the press's handling of the elections in Jalisco see Fregoso Peralta, *Prensa regional y elecciones*; and Fregoso Peralta and Sánchez Ruíz, *Prensa y poder en Guadalajara*.

12. Alonso, *El rito electoral en Jalisco*, p. 97.

13. Figure is taken from an unpublished study of PRONASOL in the state conducted by INESER.

14. Alonso, *El rito electoral en Jalisco*, p. 98. According to a poll reported in the unpublished INESER study, the programs in the state drew heavily on PRI militants and contributed to a favorable image of Salinas.

15. Alonso, *Arrollamientos y menoscabos*, p. 6; and Alonso, *El rito electoral en Jalisco*, p. 82.

16. Cited in Fregoso Peralta, *Prensa regional y elecciones*, pp. 29–30.

17. Alonso, *Arrollamientos y menoscabos*, p. 20.

18. Alonso, *El rito electoral en Jalisco*, pp. 83–84.

19. Alonso, *Arrollamientos y menoscabos*, p. 47.

20. Fregoso Peralta, *Prensa regional y elecciones*, p. 31.

21. Alonso, *El rito electoral en Jalisco*, p. 121.

22. The 1988 poll included 492 respondents and was conducted in mid-October (less than two months prior to the 1988 state election); the 1991 poll was administered to 330 *tapatians* just four days before the midterm election; the preelectoral poll of 1992 involved 502 respondents and took place approximately three weeks prior to the municipal contest; and the postelectoral poll questioned approximately 300 individuals four days following that election. All the polls were based on a stratified sample of the population in the metropolitan area of Guadalajara. For more detailed information on the methods, see Arroyo Alejandre et al., "Opiniones preelectorales de la población económica y políticamente activa de la zona metropolitana de Guadalajara"; Morones Servín, "Encuesta de opinión preelectoral en la zona metropolitana de Guadalajara"; and Morones Servín and Morris, "Análisis de resultados de las encuestas electorales." Many of the results presented here and the discussion are taken from Arroyo Alejandre and Morris, "The Electoral Recovery of the PRI in Guadalajara."

It is important to acknowledge the possibility of problems with popular opinion polls in Mexico. As a result, it is difficult at this stage to unequivocally affirm that polls in Mexico are valid measures of popular opinion. Arguments (hypotheses) that the population may not reveal their true feelings for fear of reprisals, for example, abound. Solid proof, however, is lacking. For a sampling of these arguments see Rivera Velázquez, "Comentario a una encuesta."

23. Data from national polls conducted prior to the 1991 election revealed similar patterns. See, for instance, the pre-1991 electoral polls reported in Basañez, "Encuesta electoral 1991"; and in *Nexos* 164, 1991, pp. 27–30.

24. Public opinion polling, especially preelectoral polls, unfortunately provide a limited means of delineating the determinants of abstentionism, since more state an intention to vote than actually do. Nonetheless, data from the 1992 postelectoral poll showed that the primary reason for not voting was the lack of the requisite credentials (the most favored response given by 26.9 percent) and failure of the respondent's name from appearing on the voting list (10.1 percent). The number without such credentials fell from 29.4 percent in 1988 to 23.9 percent in 1991 and 13.5 percent in 1992. More interestingly, those without such cards tended to favor the opposition more than the PRI. Of those expressing support for the PRI in 1988, for example, 94.1 percent held the proper voting credentials compared to only 86.2 percent of those supporting the PAN. For a good treatment on abstentionism in Mexico see Pacheco Méndez, "Voter Abstentionism." For a discussion of past empirical analyses see Molinar Horcasitas, *El tiempo de la legitimidad*, 1991, p. 166.

25. For example, see Klesner, "Party System Expansion and Electoral Mobilization in Mexico"; Guillén López, "The Social Bases of the PRI"; Basañez's national polls discussed in *El pulso de los sexenios*; and Molinar Horcasitas, *El tiempo de la legitimidad*.

26. Interestingly, the 1988 data showed a clear tendency for favorable views of the government or an individual's situation to be associated with votes for the PRI, for neutral or moderate views to be tied to support for the PAN, and negative views to be linked to votes for the left. This pattern was consistent with respect to confidence in the electoral process, evaluations of the government and its programs, and evaluations of the respondent's economic mobility.

27. On the problems with Cosio in the state see, for instance, "Cosio, hombre de compadres"; and Alonso, "Sociedad y gobierno en la coyuntura de las explosiones."

28. For an overview of the political side of the explosions of April 22, see Ramírez Saiz and Regalado Santillán, "Guadalajara: La respuesta social a los desastres"; and González and Morris, "Los aspectos políticos de las explosiones."

29. One survey (unpublished) conducted by Centro de Estudios de Opinión, formerly of INESER, in the affected area in April 1993 showed a decent level of support for the new governor, Carlos Rivera, and the belief that current officials were doing better than those of the past (42.6 percent compared to just 10.5 percent who said they were doing worse). Though most blamed PEMEX and Cosio for the explosions and more than 67 percent saw a cover-up on the part of the government, 43.9 percent still cited the PRI as having the greatest political capacity.

30. For a discussion of the situation prior to the 1994 election, see "Jalisco ante las urnas."

31. See *Proceso* 931 (September 5, 1994), pp. 16–17.

32. F figures greater than 4 are considered statistically significant.

33. The coexistence of change amidst continuity makes friction. In the municipality of Tlaquepaque, for instance, conflict arose over a shifting of power away from the CROC, which had traditionally run the city, toward the leaders of the popular sector of the party, particularly those from Solidarity. When Eduardo Riverón Gámez took office in 1992 as the first non-CROC mayor in forty years, protests erupted, including the boycotting by CROC members of city council meetings. Later, conflict emerged pitting CROC against members of the local Solidarity committees (see the series of articles in *Siglo 21* dated June 28, 1994, p. 9; June 29, 1994, p. 6; and June 30, 1994, p. 6).

6

Political Reformism in Contemporary Mexico: Preliminary Conclusions

The preceding chapters outlined the dilemmas and the reformist dynamic in Mexico during the contemporary period. They highlighted the nature of the reforms under de la Madrid and Salinas and their role in surmounting or simply muddling through the political crisis. But what does the Mexican case say about the broader theoretical question? What do the reformist experiences of de la Madrid and Salinas suggest about political reformism?

This chapter takes a preliminary swipe at these questions by comparing the reformist patterns of the two leaders. It focuses first on key differences between the two and attempts to identify possible ingredients behind Salinas's somewhat more successful reformist bid. The chapter then looks at common features of the two reformist periods. The discussion then concludes by offering some tentative conclusions regarding reformism in Mexico, setting the stage for the comparative foci of Part 2.

Comparing Reformism Under de la Madrid and Salinas

As the preceding chapters have shown, the reformist experiences under de la Madrid and Salinas differed in fundamental ways. For one, Salinas enjoyed more political rewards from his economic program than did de la Madrid. Not only did he manage over an improved economic situation, but he was also able to reverse the tendency for business to enlarge the ranks of the nonsystem right progressives (Group 3) as had occurred under de la Madrid. In fact, Salinas even enlisted the support of big business or at minimum reinvigorated its traditional political acquiescence. At the same time, he succeeded in spreading his view among higher-income groups, who came to favor his brand of economic reform without being overly enthusiastic about political reforms.[1]

Salinas was also more successful at arresting the internal and electoral deterioration of the party that had hampered de la Madrid. Though the party continued to be racked by serious internal divisions, Salinas was more effective at solidifying the alliance and keeping the conservatives within the party satisfied. As a result, whereas the ranks of the nonsystem progressives grew under de la Madrid (Groups 3 and 4) and the PRI alliance suffered division, Salinas oversaw the reconsolidation of the PRI and the eruption of serious divisions within the opposition. Paralleling these trends, the PRI rebounded more effectively under Salinas than under de la Madrid, as indicated in Figure 6.1. At midterm at least, Salinas had neutralized, disarticulated, and diminished the opposition to the point of leaving it with the level of influence it had enjoyed a decade earlier.[2]

Moreover, Salinas seemed to garner more credibility as a reformer than de la Madrid. His electoral reforms of 1989, 1993, and 1994 enjoyed the approval of most of the opposition parties and restored some level of popular confidence in the process. By contrast, de la Madrid's electoral reform package of 1986 counted on the support of only the PRI's satellite parties and failed to gain much legitimacy for him or the political system. Though both faced end-of-term crises and watched the PRI draw roughly the same vote (about 50 percent), the 1994 triumph was far more credible (and sweeter) than the 1988 "victory," actually easing rather than deepening political tensions. Indeed, whereas de la Madrid fashioned a perception of enhanced reliance on fraud to maintain power, Salinas crafted an image that portrayed fraud and repression as exceptions rather than the rule.

In sum, though both were successful at forestalling fundamental political changes, Salinas was seemingly much more successful at the reformist game than his predecessor. What accounts for these different outcomes? More specifically, why was Salinas able to inspire popular confidence more effectively than de la Madrid? Why did Salinas's opponents divide while under de la Madrid the PRI split? Why did fraud and repression seem more the rule under de la Madrid and yet the exception under Salinas?

A number of factors seem critical in accounting for these differences. One centers on the nature of the crisis the two leaders faced. De la Madrid faced the worst of the conjunctural component of the crisis—economic decline—whereas Salinas ruled over a period of relative economic recovery. This made the reformist task much easier for Salinas. Besides renewing optimism among the public toward Mexico's future and the ability of the PRI to manage it, bolstering Salinas's, the PRI's, and the government's legitimacy, renewed growth also freed up needed resources that Salinas could invest politically to surmount the challenges.[3] In other words, a renewed resource base gave Salinas the leverage necessary to refashion the underlying logic of the system. Though social spending under Salinas was still below precrisis levels, enhanced state spending through Solidarity was critical in helping the PRI reestablish its base of support among the lower classes, incorporate new actors into the governing coalition, and repair the

Figure 6.1   PRI Vote, 1982–1994

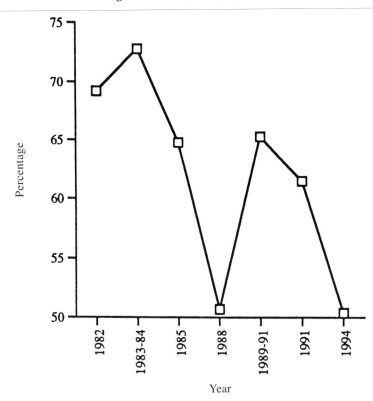

state-society links that had broken under de la Madrid. Moreover, economic recovery allowed Salinas to do this without jeopardizing his monetary goals. Even when recession hit again in late 1993, Salinas counted on
significant reserves to provide some stimulus. When de la Madrid tried to
use populist measures prior to the 1985 midterm elections to bolster PRI
support, the political gains were short-lived because of the program's inflationary impact.

Second, while the reforms of de la Madrid seemed to be highly incongruent or inconsistent, those of Salinas were the opposite. De la Madrid's
adoption of an electoral hard line toward the PAN, for instance, undermined the anticipated political impact of his economic program and the
credibility of the anticorruption campaign. His economic program (and
packaging of it) and his anticorruption campaign also tended to weaken the
president politically and undermine his control over the elite. Salinas's soft
line and mildly cooperative posture toward the PAN, by contrast, helped

the economic reforms yield more positive political results within the private sector.) This helped Salinas refashion the PRI using support from the business community and helped him play the right off against the left. Moreover, by broadening the political space for the PAN, the fraud and repression targeted selectively at the PRD could be spun and perceived as an exception or aberration to the broader democratization trend represented by the PRI-PAN "negotiated democratization" scheme. Equally striking was the multiple functions Salinas's Solidarity program played in shaping the reformist pattern. The program not only facilitated Salinas's centralization of power over the federal government, local governments, and the PRI, but also enabled him to partially refashion the clientelistic links, bolster regime legitimacy and PRI's foundations of support, and compensate the losers of the neoliberal program. Solidarity also helped the regime undermine the support and mobilizing capacity of the PRD by "stealing their thunder" and driving a wedge between the *cardenistas* and their natural constituency. As Bailey concludes, "PRONASOL reinforces Salinas's image and power much more effectively than Regional Development served de la Madrid."[4]

Critical here is temporal ordering. By the time Salinas assumed power in late 1988 the worst of the economic crisis had passed, the downward spiral had ended, and the structural and psychological foundations for recovery had been established. Salinas thus not only enjoyed the fruits of de la Madrid's labor (particularly the economic gains, which he could then invest to resolve the political crisis), but did not have to confront the problem of declining or frustrated expectations that de la Madrid faced. In a sense, the abrupt and painful process of decline challenging de la Madrid was more difficult to manage politically than the task Salinas faced.

This temporal factor may also help account for Salinas's more successful efforts at resolidifying the PRI and arresting the centrifugal tendencies that rocked the party in the late 1980s. Though the divisions between the two factions within the PRI existed prior to de la Madrid's term, it had yet to reach crisis proportions, freeing the president to devote more attention to other aspects of the crisis. As a result, de la Madrid had the fewest number of cabinet members with party experience and one of the lowest in terms of popular representation and popular origin.[5] Not only was the need to respond to this problem unclear under de la Madrid, but incorporating politicos of the conservative faction into his governing coalition at an early stage would have undermined his efforts to reestablish a working relationship with the business community. By contrast, internal division within the party was a critical and immediate issue for Salinas, one he could attend to without simultaneously having to establish his credentials with the private sector.

Besides the nature of the crisis and temporal ordering, a third factor that seemed to ease Salinas's handling of the political crisis relates to institutional changes. Throughout his term, de la Madrid faced no major threat from the left. As always, the left remained divided and inconsequential. De la Madrid therefore faced simply a one-front political battle against the emerging nonsystem right progressives of the PAN. Under Salinas, however, the PRI's opponents pinched from both sides of the spectrum, presenting Salinas with a two-front political struggle and a far more unified and dangerous opposition.

This historic difference had a significant impact on the reformist patterns. For one, the swelling of the nonsystem left progressives under the *cardenista* label and their adoption of a staunchly confrontational line enhanced business and the PAN's need to cooperate with Salinas for economic reasons. Likewise, the existence and the nature of the Cárdenas threat left Salinas few options but to strike some sort of a deal with the less threatening PAN in order to ease the pressures. This institutional shift thus informed Salinas's move to reverse de la Madrid's hard-line policy against the PAN—a policy that de la Madrid could afford to employ since, in a sense, he faced only the PAN. In the end, this helped Salinas surmount the political challenges by facilitating his efforts to convince business and other right-wing interests (including the United States, whose attacks on Mexico lessened under Salinas) to adopt a cooperative approach. Put differently, the pressures growing from the *cardenista* threat enabled Salinas to play the right off against the left to weaken the system/antisystem polarization that had racked the de la Madrid period.

A final factor underlying the different reformist outcomes centers on the leaders' accompanying rhetoric, leadership styles, abilities, and capacities. Though both promised fundamental reform, de la Madrid couched his economic reformist program in terms of "economic reality" and "sacrifice." Such a rhetorical posture, as President Jimmy Carter learned in the United States in the late 1970s, lacks in political appeal because it neither offers a positive foundation on which to garner support nor invokes any sense of nationalism, history, or culture. Even worse perhaps, it actually gives the impression that the power of the president is limited, a sentiment that further cut into the president's popularity.[6] Salinas's reformist rhetoric, by contrast, brimmed with optimism and lofty promises of change and modernization. Beginning in 1991, Salinas even attempted to package "social liberalism" as an ideological label for the country's new course, gaining acceptance for and adherents to his brand of reformism.

In addition to rhetoric, it is clear that Salinas centralized power much more effectively than de la Madrid and was perhaps far bolder in his leadership style. Within the party, for instance, Salinas exerted control through the prominent use of "unity candidates," allowing him to dispense favors and select candidates. Along with other party leaders, he carefully managed the party's fifteenth assembly to prevent broad-based participation and to rubber-stamp the selection of Borrego with virtually no input from the party's bases.[7] Salinas also reshuffled state party leaders and exerted central control over many state electoral campaigns. During the first three years of the *sexenio,* for example, there were 114 state party leaders under Colosio (an average of almost four per state in just three years).[8] This centralization of power extended beyond the party. Indeed, despite promises to the contrary, Salinas replaced more governors than any president since Cárdenas.[9] The same shuffling occurred within the president's cabinet. According to Sergio Aguayo, Salinas oversaw fifty-two cabinet changes and 130 changes in the nation's sixty-seven embassies.[10] In all these cases, the removals strengthened the hold of Salinas over the state and the party apparatus, removing any potential challengers. Salinas also intervened in elections to virtually decide when and where the opposition would win, usually thwarting local pressures to maintain the status quo.[11] Even in the congress, Salinas exerted centralized control with the percentage of congressionally initiated legislation continuing its decline to reach 9 percent.[12] PRONASOL furthered this centralizing tendency, marginalizing state and local governments, the PRI, and allowing greater centralized federal control over local budgets.[13]

By contrast, de la Madrid failed to centralize power and was seemingly more cautious, weak, and risk averse, and less willing to take on the system's entrenched interests than Salinas. Philips argues, for instance, that "de la Madrid wished to make changes but did not have the necessary confidence to stick to his guns."[14] Centeno, who also characterizes de la Madrid as weak, even suggests that during the latter half of the term, Salinas, rather than de la Madrid, was actually in charge of making economic policy.[15]

Looking beyond these key differences, however, the two reformist patterns shared a number of key similarities. One common pattern relates to the pace of political versus economic change. From de la Madrid's austerity measures in 1982 to NAFTA more than a decade later, economic transformation in Mexico was great. By the end of the period under review, the state was financially sound and running a surplus, inflation was down, and the economy had opened up to foreign investment and trade. Political change, by contrast, lagged behind.[16] In the end, elections still lacked credibility and were less than fair and open, the autonomy of social organizations continued to be limited, the PRI was tied to the state and neither operated independently of the other, and presidential power continued unchecked. Despite the reformist programs and the optimism they bred during both presidential terms, the essential features of the political system

—clientelism, corporatism, one-party hegemony, noncompetitive elections, and presidentialism—remained largely intact.

A second ingredient within both *sexenios* relates to the reformist rhythm of the *sexenio* itself. Positive reforms (like anticorruption drives and efforts to open the party or the political system) seemed to group at the beginning of the term. The truncation of the reforms and a retrenchment with the more conservative elements of the system huddled near the end. In the case of Salinas, the party reforms eased in the latter part of the term, and though significant opening occurred in 1994, Zedillo's renewed reliance on the PRI and the old guard to orchestrate victory was clear. Moreover, in both cases the final stages of the *sexenio* brought a deepening or a renewal of political crisis. The dramatic 1988 election capping the *sexenio* of de la Madrid seemed at the time a watershed, just as the events of 1994 challenged the Salinas team like never before. Figure 6.1 depicts these sexenial trends.

Finally, the two leaders pursued similar reform programs in a very pragmatic way. Both promoted neoliberal economic programs favorable to key business groups, used a divide-and-conquer strategy to maintain discipline within the labor movement, attacked corruption in some form or another, tinkered with internal reforms within the PRI that sought to weaken the corporate foundations of the party, and expanded the political space alloted to the opposition. They both made concessions when needed to maintain the integrity of the PRI and the alliance and relied on such negative reform measures as abstentionism, electoral fraud, and repression to protect the contours of the system. And they both protected and relied on corporatism to control workers and strengthen the PRI despite repeated attempts to curb the presence and power of the sectors in the party.

Preliminary Conclusions

Analysis of the differences and similarities between the two periods leads to some preliminary conclusions regarding the nature of reformism in contemporary Mexico. They range from the relationship between economic and political crisis, the congruency of reform initiatives, and the centralization of political power to the role of the *sexenio* in easing the reformist task, the coexistence of old and new institutional structures, and negative and positive reformist measures.

Relationship Between Economic and Political Crisis

The role of resolving economic crisis in easing the political crisis and the tendency for political change to lag behind economic change suggests that resolving the economic dilemmas is a precondition for resolving the political crisis. As an important component of the political crisis (the conjunctural component), surmounting the economic crisis greatly diminished the scope of the overall crisis, easing popular pressures and providing the leaders with "the economic capacity to pay for the costs of reform, including compensation of losers by winners."[17] This means that if a political system is capable of surviving a profound economic crisis (conjunctural) without undergoing fundamental political change, even if this means a temporary reliance on fraud and repression, this heightens the prospects of successful reformism, despite the changes put in place during the crisis period. The initial resort to fraud and repression, in fact, even provides a backdrop against which any positive political changes help create the appearance of progress. Likewise, the inability to recover economically augurs poorly for successful political reformism.

Congruency of Reform Initiatives

Just as resolving the economic problems seemed a major step toward easing political pressures, a tendency existed in Mexico for reformist "success" in one area to nurture perceptions of success in other areas. This tendency for success to breed success underlay the "congruence" of the reforms under Salinas and went a long way in nurturing the president's reformist credibility. Though it is extremely difficult to differentiate the sources of Salinas's popularity during the first five years of his term, it is clear that he gained crucial political capital from the economic recovery. As the polls from Guadalajara indicated, changes in evaluations of the government, the economy, elections, and Salinas, coupled with the popularity of the Solidarity program, all fed the growing vote for the PRI and declining support for the opposition. The relegitimization of the Mexican state, the PRI, and especially elections after 1988 were therefore more the result of Salinas's bold acts as president and his political style than the government's handling of elections (perhaps the true test of democratizing change). In fact, Salinas's "election" was not the source of his legitimacy, and the 1991 electoral recovery of the PRI was the result of this renewed legitimacy, not its cause. Reformist success seemingly breeds success by lending credibility to the promises of change and hence by decreasing the expected utility of a strategy of confrontation.

Centralization of Political Power

The saliency of the centralization of power under Salinas in easing the crisis suggests a negative correlation linking the strength of the president and the ebbs and flows of the political crisis. As shown, the power and prestige of the presidency declined under de la Madrid and rebounded under Salinas, paralleling the rise and decline in the dangers of fundamental political change.[18] The mechanics of this linkage seem clear: centralizing power helped Salinas manipulate the social pacts and hence the government's bases of support. In other words, Salinas's control over the PRI, elections, and Solidarity ensured flexibility and greater maneuverability.[19]

Role of the Sexenio

The *sexenio* pattern noted earlier also points to its importance in the reformist equation. Clearly the transitionary period and the election constitute the weakest link in the adaptive political system, as shown by the PRI's vote. This is due not only to the presence of an election (a plebescite on the government, the president, and his reformist credibility), but also to the temporary weakening of one of the keys to successful reformism: presidentialism. But even though the end of the *sexenio* carries the potential for renewed crisis and an intensification of the dangers of breakdown, it also seems to provide the regime a new lease on life. In a sense, the change cleanses the political system, fosters new reformist initiatives, and helps reinvigorate the public's faith in reform through cooperation rather than confrontation.[20]

Old and New Institutional Structures

In addition to the role of the *sexenio*, the Mexican case also points to the coexistence of old and new structures, the use of old tactics, and a mixture of positive and negative reforms in the reformist equation: a combination of measures designed both to protect the allegiance of the old while adding the new. As noted, despite the attacks, corporatism survived; despite the increasing importance of elections, old practices remained; and despite the antipopulist rhetoric, programs like Solidarity hammered out new clientelistic ties. As a result, a situation prevailed in which new reformist institutions were merely layered atop one another. Though recognizing the importance of the old institutions, the leaders still promoted reforms that "added" to the party's corporate foundations and coalitions. The Refundación Estructural del Partido in 1992, for example, stated explicitly that the reforms did not mean *autodesmantelamiento orgánicos* but were designed simply to extend the bases of the party. Thus, neither Salinas's new "economic" coalition rooted in the beneficiaries of the neoliberal program nor his "populist" coalition centering on the renewed state-society links in Solidarity were officially incorporated into the party or replaced it. Yet they lent critical support to the president and the PRI, easing the threat from the opposition.

The mixture of old and new structures and tactics marking the reformist process also questions the idea that these are mutually exclusive.

Rather than elections or pluralism being incompatible with corporatism, the analysis reveals that the mechanics of the linkage between old and new, is more manageable and flexible. At minimum, this suggests that perhaps other factors may influence at least the intensity if not the inherent nature of a zero-sum situation between old and new modes and alliances.

Negative and Positive Reformist Measures

The case shows not only how the process of reformism involves a strategic combination of both negative (fraud, repression) and positive (popularity, new alliances) reform measures, but that exclusive or primary reliance on negative reforms can only arrest the crisis temporarily, if not make it worse. This was clearly the pattern under de la Madrid. In other words, exclusive reliance on negative reforms to confront a crisis can protect the system in the short term but cannot surmount the crisis. Truly easing the crisis can come only through the adoption of more positive reforms. Thus, Salinas eased the crisis by translating economic recovery into a series of more positive reform measures that could refashion the Mexican state and its party to the minimal degree necessary to revitalize the system. Negative measures (fraud and repression) not only continued to survive to some extent and play an important role in the reformist equation under Salinas but, more important, the fraud and repressive machinery, though weakened by the reforms, remained at the disposal of the system's guardians if needed to protect the system during a future crisis. Though limited and insufficient to alleviate crisis, negative reforms nonetheless remain strategically significant in the broader reformist process.

The combination of liberal, even democratizing, changes (positive measures) and fraud and repression (negative measures) to diminish the pressures for greater political change and enhance authoritarian continuity in Mexico points, finally, to a seemingly contradictory view of things: that change was a key to continuity as Molinar suggests and, more specifically, that liberal, democratizing changes were important in strengthening authoritarianism as Davis and Eckstein show.[21] It suggests, furthermore, that as Mexico moved along the continuum toward greater democracy (as a result of these positive changes), such a movement actually lessened the pressures necessary to continue along that path. [The swipes at corporatism and corruption, the electoral reforms, selective opposition wins, and even Solidarity—all liberal, progressive changes—played well, earning Salinas high marks and imbuing him with a dose of reformist legitimacy which he then used to control, tame, and limit the reformist process itself.]This may have been due to the fact that such liberal changes provided inclusion without input. As Centeno notes, "Democratic planning [under Salinas] became nothing more than a series of round tables whose function was to legitimate decisions already made."[22]

* * *

But despite the importance of overcoming economic crisis, the tendency for success to breed success, the importance of the centralization of power, the turnover implied by the *sexenio*, or the tempering of change with continuity, the Mexican case also raises some important questions. For example, what factors allowed the leadership to successfully pursue economic change and restore growth without concomitant political change? Why did the presidency weaken under de la Madrid and strengthen under Salinas? And are these perhaps opposite sides of the same coin such that a crisis simply means the weakening of the presidency? In other words, did the easing of the crisis strengthen Salinas or vice versa? With regard to old and new structures, questions abound concerning the institutional factors that made it possible for the regime to avoid a zero-sum equation. Even on a much broader level we are left with the question of what historic factors shaped the adaptability demonstrated during this period. And will Zedillo be able to manage the processes set in motion and protect the political system into the next century? To help answer these and related queries, attention now shifts to a comparative context, encompassing subnational, historical, and cross-national examinations of Mexican reformism.

Notes

1. Basañez, "Is Mexico Headed Towards Its Fifth Crisis?" p. 110. The World Values Survey (cited in Camp, "Political Liberalization," p. 19) similarly found that nearly 60 percent of respondents ranked economic growth as the most important issue, compared to only 40 percent ranking greater political participation as important.

2. Beltrán del Río, "Mil días bastaron a Salinas," p. 6.

3. This optimism flourished even in areas where the facts suggested otherwise. Indeed, from 1989 to 1991, the percentage expressing the view that poverty had declined grew from 43.3 percent to 63.9 percent, though real wages continued to deteriorate and most of the economic benefits could not be felt by the majority of the population. More important, 48.3 percent of the respondents believed the economy would improve in the near future (see *Nexos* 170, 1992, pp. 83–85).

4. Bailey, "Centralism and Political Change in Mexico."

5. Basáñez, *El pulso de los sexenios*, pp. 126–127.

6. The initial point is raised by Sánchez Susarrey, *La transición incierta*, p. 42. The impact of a perception of weakness is particularly critical during a time of crisis when the perceived role of leadership becomes important.

7. The fifteenth assembly, initially touted as the Asamblea Nacional Extraor-dinaria and called merely to formalize the handpicked selection of Genaro Borrego to replace Colosio as secretary-general, was preceded by an agreement between CEN and CPN that transformed it into an Assemblea Nacional Ordinaria, thereby undermining the many demands from the party for a new assembly (see *La Jornada*, May 15, 1992, p. 9, and May 22, 1992, p. 10).

8. Beltrán del Río, "El PRI de Colosio pierde la linea y se va de la derrota a la concesión."

9. This included Enrique González Pedrero, governor of Tabasco, who was named to head the the Instituto de Estudios Politicos, Economicos, y Sociales (IEPES); Francisco Gutierrez Barrios, who moved from Veracruz to Gobernación; Enrique Alvarez del Castillo of Jalisco, who became attorney general; Luis Martínez Villicana of Michoacán, who was sacked due to the political threat of *cardenismo* in the state; Xicotencatl Leyva Mortera of Baja California, who was transferred to a "nonexistent" job at Nacional Financiera (NAFINSA) due to his reputation for corruption in a state also facing a strong electoral challenge; Mario Ramón Beteta, who left his post in the state of México; Guillermo Cosio Vidaurri of Jalisco, who fled from the scandal following the massive explosions in the city of Guadalajara in 1992; and Fausto Zapata of San Luis Potosí, Ramon Aguirre of Guanajuato, Eduardo Villaseñor of Michoacán, and Neme Castillo of Tabasco, who stepped down because of postelectoral protests.

10. Cited in Aguayo Quezada, "Hombres e Instituciones." The list includes five attorneys general (Alvarez del Castillo, Morales Lechuga, Carpizo, Valadés, and Benítez Treviño); four secretaries of Gobernación (Gutiérrez Barrios, González Garrido, and Carpizo); four secretaries of education (Bartlett Díaz, Zedillo, Solana, Pescador Osuna); and three secretaries of foreign relations (Solana Morales, Camacho Solís, and Tello Macias). Indeed, few posts were held by one individual for all six years, most notably Pedro Aspe (Hacienda) and Jaime Serra Puche in commerce. Even the second most powerful man under Salinas, José Córdoba, was removed in 1994 as coordinador de asesores de la presidencia.

11. Roett, "At the Crossroads: Liberalization in Mexico," p. 11.

12. Cited in Camp, "Political Liberalization," p. 27.

13. See Bailey, "Centralism and Political Change in Mexico."

14. Philips, *The Mexican Presidency*, p. 144.

15. Centeno, *Democracy Within Reason*, p. 95. Though such factors may indeed be important in understanding reformism, explanations of this sort remain problematic. It is not only difficult to operationalize such variables as bold or cautious, but it is even more difficult to define them apart from what they purportedly explain. In other words, Salinas was generally perceived as risk averse for what he had done, so explaining his behavior based on this trait becomes a tautological somersault. To be sure, many of the terms used to describe Salinas were lavished on de la Madrid during the initial years of his term when optimism toward change ran high.

16. This was not only clear with respect to the pattern of change, but statements by both leaders suggest that this was in fact their intention. For example, in one interview (cited in Aguayo Quezada "The Inevitability of Democracy in Mexico," p. 125), de la Madrid stated that "Mexico was not ready for a bipartisan or pluralistic political system in which the opposition could win." Salinas, in "A New Hope for the Hemisphere?" (cited in Camp, "Political Liberalization," p. 18) shared this view: "When you are introducing such a strong economic reform, you

must make sure that you build the political consensus around it. If you are at the same time introducing additional drastic political reform, you may end up with no reform at all. And we want to have reform, not a disintegrated country."

17. Reynolds, "Power, Value and Distribution in the NAFTA," p. 86, refers to this as an "adjustment dividend."

18. Aguilar Camín, *Después del milagro*, p. 121, even suggests that under de la Madrid the presidency "lost a large dose of . . . symbolic power."

19. In his comparative analysis, Huntington, *Political Order in Changing Societies*, 1968, pp. 346–364, highlights centralization of power as a factor accompanying both processes of reformism and revolution.

20. Knight, "Solidarity: Historical Continuities and Contemporary Implications," makes a similar point when he mentions "the reverential cult of 'the new'," which, he argues, Solidarity effectively tapped.

21. Molinar Horcasitas, *El tiempo de la legitimidad*; Davis, "Divided over Democracy"; and Eckstein, "Formal Versus Substantive Democracy."

22. Centeno, *Democracy Within Reason*, p. 217.

2

Comparative Perspectives

7

The Subnational Perspective

Mexico cradles vast cultural, geographic, ideological, political, and socio-economic diversity. Electoral analyses and public opinion polls, for instance, consistently have shown the PRI enjoying its highest levels of support among the lower socioeconomic sectors and in the more rural and marginalized portions of the country, particularly in the center and southern states. The opposition, meantime, tends to attract its support among the more urbanized and educated segments of society, particularly in the more industrialized and culturally independent states of the north (the Baja Californias, Chihuahua, Coahuila, Durango, and Sonora), in the historically antirevolutionary states of the Bajio region (Guanajuato, Jalisco, and Michoacán), and in Mexico City.

Such subnational or regional variations provide a laboratory to explore in greater detail some of the mechanics of political reformism in Mexico. Attention to the state and regional levels not only helps disaggregate factors linked to reformism, but also facilitates an analysis of the role of state and local politics in shaping the challenges to the regime and future direction. This chapter provides both quantitative and qualitative analysis of the subnational units. It first presents an empirical analysis of federal election results by state and region with particular attention to the various vote swings during the period. This is followed by a general analysis of reformism at the state and local levels. Stressing trends at these levels over the period, the chapter concludes by briefly addressing the issue of the regime's future and whether state and local elections truly represent, as Guillén López suggests, "the first steps of a new era in the Mexican political system."[2]

State and Regional Analysis of Federal Elections

To empirically tap the dynamic nature of reformism, the percentage change of the PRI's vote during the five federal elections spanning the 1982–1994 period was calculated for the thirty-one states and the Federal District.[3] This rendered four vote shifts within the *sexenios* (1982–1985, 1985–1988, 1988–1991, and 1991–1994) and two spanning the presidential terms (1982–1988 and 1988–1994). As might be expected, the states boasted a wide range of variation along this scale. During the 1985–1988 period, for example, the PRI's vote fell by as much as 53.6 percentage points in Michoacán while increasing 5.6 in Sonora. From 1988 to 1991, similarly, the change in the PRI's vote ranged from an increase of over 30 points in Morelos to a decline of more than 13 points in Chiapas.

A number of factors were hypothesized as possibly shaping the PRI's changing electoral fortunes. They included a state's initial level of support for the PRI (in 1982 and 1988), the presence and weight of opposition parties in the area, previous vote swings, a state's level of socioeconomic development, its rate of economic growth, the recent removal of a governor, federal spending (like Solidarity), and simply geographical region.[4] Measures for some of these independent variables related only to specific time periods or were omitted because of lack of data. Figures on economic growth by state were available only for the 1982–1988 period, while the removal of governors was calculated just for the Salinas period. Data on Solidarity were not collected, largely because of the availability of a similar type of analysis of this important program.

Table 7.1 presents regression coefficients for the data. The results show, first, that the PRI's initial strength in a state was wholly unrelated to the vote swings under de la Madrid but significantly and strongly linked to the changes under Salinas. As indicated, the PRI's vote improved under Salinas overwhelmingly in those states where he had done poorly. While this somewhat taps the presence and strength of opposition within a state, other measures for the opposition were also found to be unrelated to the vote swing under de la Madrid but linked to the early change, 1989–1991, under Salinas. As expected, the PRI's recovery during the period 1988–1991 was most dramatic in those states where Cárdenas had done well in 1988.

Beyond the relative strength of the PRI and the opposition, analysis shows no significant correlation between the within-*sexenio* shifts. In other words, swings in either direction during the first half of each *sexenio* had little or no relationship to the shift during the second half. Even the PRI's electoral stumble from 1991 to 1994 under Salinas was not simply an erosion of its remarkable 1988–1991 recovery as seemed to be the case in the state of Jalisco. Still, the two sexenial shifts were inversely related such that the PRI's gains under Salinas encompassed to a certain degree the losses under de la Madrid and vice versa. Analysis of level of development and economic growth during 1982–1988, in turn, shows generally no linkages or very weak ones. Economic growth over the 1982–1988 period had no direct impact on the vote shift during this or the subsequent time period, while the vote change during the latter half of the Salinas era tended to be positively tied to a state's level of socioeconomic development.[5]

Table 7.1   Correlation Matrix of State-Level Changes in PRI Vote,
             1982–1994
             (n=32)

	1982–85	1985–88	1982–88	1988–91	1991–94	1988–94
PRI vote during prior presidential election	.0404	–.1690	–.1405	–.8441[a]	–.5354[a]	–.9366[a]
Prior vote swings	—	.2061 (82–85)	—	—	.1404 (88–91)	–.7181[a] (82–88)
Opposition strength	—	—	.2524	.8335[a]	.1980	.7434[a]
Level of development	–.1194	.1658	.1026	.2192	.3389	.3523[b]
Growth 1982–1988	na	na	–.1631	.2549	na	na

1–tailed significance
a. level of significance less than .01
b. level of significance less than .05

Given the apparent influence of the various factors linked to the 1988–1994 shift, a multiple regression test was performed. It demonstrated clearly that the shift could be accounted for by the initial level of PRI support (1988), with the earlier vote shift—from 1982 to 1988—weakly related. In other words, the link with the vote for Cárdenas and level of development disappeared when controlling for these factors.

Gauging the impact of the removal of the state governor and geographic region required a comparison of means. Though on average the share of the PRI vote fell somewhat less over the 1988–1994 period in those states where the governors were removed, (–6 versus –1), the difference was only weakly significant. Differences among regions, however, were more robust. As Table 7.2 indicates, the shift in the PRI's electoral fortunes varied by region and at increasingly more statistically significant levels over time. During the 1982–1988 period, the center states suffered the strongest decline, followed by the south and finally the north. This pattern paralleled the shifts in party identification and opinions toward the government over the 1983–1987 period, uncovered by Basañez.[6] Then, during the first half of the Salinas period, the PRI staged its strongest comeback in the central region, followed by the north. Despite the incredible comeback in these regions, the PRI failed to register significant gains in its traditionally strongest region, the south. During the second half of

Table 7.2   Mean Changes in PRI Vote by Region, 1982–1994
             (n = 32)

	1982–88	1988–91	1991–94	1988–94
North	–11.4	6.4	–8.0	–1.6
Central	–21.5	12.0	–12.3	–.3
South	–17.3	1.2	–18.1	–17.0
F =	1.93	3.60	3.71	5.30

the term, the PRI lost more ground in the southern states and watched its recovery in the central region disappear.

A closer look at each of the two reformist periods shows that the data are generally unable to account for the PRI's erosion of support during the de la Madrid period. The fact that the PRI's decline from 1982 to 1988 was strongly associated with the vote for Cárdenas in 1988 suggests that the discontent associated with the crisis reached its fullest expression in the vote for the renegade PRI candidate, but it still fails to explain a state's vote for Cárdenas (and hence the PRI's fall). The regional comparisons showed that the PRI lost more ground in the central and southern regions and that this shift even paralleled the decline in support and confidence found in public opinion polls, but again this finding fails to explain the decline. The regional decline was not related to the direct impact of the economic crisis, nor to the original level of support for the PRI or the opposition. A simple means comparison, for example, revealed that the central region actually did better economically than the northern or southern states during the period. Perhaps being most closely associated with the old political and economic model, these states were most affected by the programmatic changes and/or were simply closer ideologically to the ideas expressed by Cárdenas. Though this did not translate directly into economic decline, the state reforms of de la Madrid seemed to undermine the PRI's solid bases of support in this region, spawning a dissatisfaction and demobilization that Cárdenas successfully capitalized on in 1988.

By the same token, data indicate that the dramatic vote for Cárdenas in 1988 undermined the impact of other variables that might otherwise have influenced the vote change—variables such as socioeconomic development, past PRI performance, and economic crisis. Hence, Cárdenas pulled votes away from the PRI in some of the nation's more developed areas (e.g., Baja California and the Federal District) as well as its less developed states (e.g., Michoacán and Guerrero), and stripped votes in states where the PRI had consistently done well (e.g., Guerrero, Morelos) and some where the opposition had long done well (e.g., Baja California, Federal

District). Countering past patterns linking the opposition to the urban, educated, and industrial centers of the country, "the left did better in 1988 in
districts with higher concentrations of the poorly educated and peasants
than it has ever done before."[7] Even economic crisis, though a causal determinant of the political crisis, failed to assert a direct impact on the
PRI's vote.

During the Salinas period, the PRI improved its vote percentage most
in those states registering the lowest vote for the PRI in 1988 and vice
versa, and to a lesser degree where the PRI had lost ground during the de
la Madrid period. This was particularly true for the 1988–1991 period. But
as with the vote swing under de la Madrid, these factors identify where the
subsequent shifts occurred, but really fail to explain it. The data indicate
that the PRI rebounded precisely in those states where it most needed to
recover and lost ground in the areas where it could afford to, and that this
weighed more heavily on the more developed states. But the mechanics of
that linkage are not evident.

One possible mechanism would be federal spending, particularly Solidarity. This can be seen most dramatically in the case of Chalco, the site
of Salinas's pet project for Solidarity, located in the state of México. Here
(District 15) in 1991 the PRI increased the absolute number of its vote by
312.86 percent. Of the 300 federal districts, this ranked as the third largest
percentage gain for the ruling party.

However, more rigorous analysis seems to raise doubts about the role
of such factors, suggesting that the linkage is probably due more to the nature of Salinas's policies and reforms. Changing state proportions of federal investments from de la Madrid's to Salinas's term, employed, for example, as a statistical proxy of the government's reformist strategy of
targeting key states to aid the PRI's electoral recovery, was unrelated to
the change in the PRI vote during the 1988–1991 period.[8] Regional levels
of support for the Solidarity program as measured by one opinion poll also
failed to even parallel in the anticipated direction the PRI's regional gains
during the first half of the Salinas term. Contrary to expectations, the most
pronounced gains for the PRI in 1991 were actually located in those areas
of the country expressing the lowest levels of support for the program.
This suggests that either favorable views of the program did not translate
into political support for the PRI and/or that political support as a result of
the program (if such existed), perhaps through renewed clientelism, did
not necessarily forge a favorable opinion toward it.[9]

Perhaps more telling, empirical analysis of Solidarity spending by
Molinar Horcasitas and Weldon found that rather than spending in states
with the highest level of poverty or where Cárdenas did well in 1988, the program generally spent more in states where the PRI did well in 1988, except
in those states where gubernatorial elections were held in 1991. This suggests, as Molinar Horcasitas and Weldon note, that in states where no

gubernatorial elections were held, increased spending through Solidarity yielded no political gains, while in those with gubernatorial elections where Cárdenas had done well in 1988, the increased spending was effective in reversing the tide.[10]

Overall, the weak linkage between the vote swings under de la Madrid and initial support, the negligible impact of level of development, and the regional shifts all suggest an underlying trend drawing us away from the patterns of the past. As presented in Table 7.3, the PRI's vote in one election

Table 7.3   Correlation Matrix of State-Level Vote for PRI and Level of Development, 1982–1994 (n=32)

	1985	1988	1991	1994	Level of Dev.
1982	.9141	.6521	.7943	.5635	−.7189
1985		.6839	.7764	.4870	−.6933
1988			.7626	.4716	−.4664
1991				.5067	−.5686
1994					−.4345

1–tailed significance: level of significance less than .01 for all figures

Figure 7.1   PRI Vote by Region, 1982–1994

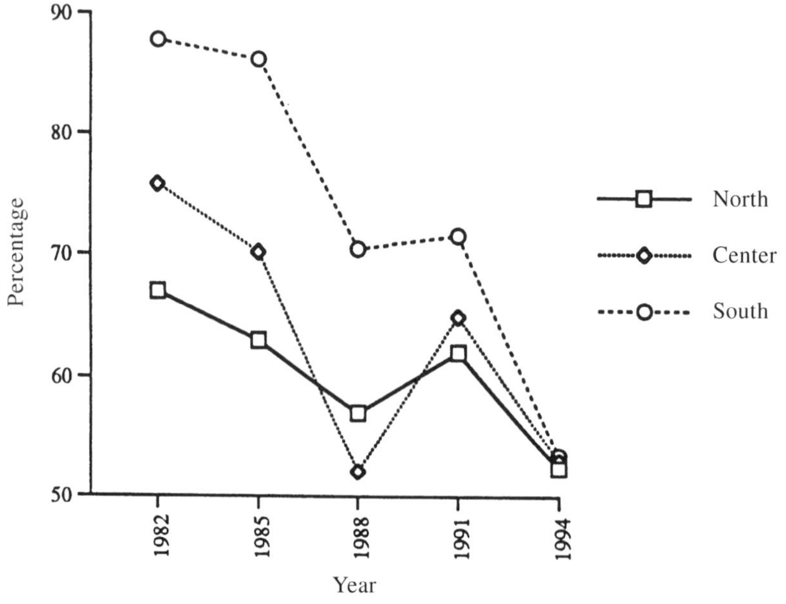

could be accounted for in large measure by its past vote as the PRI continued to draw its highest levels of support from among the less developed
states. Regionally, as well, the PRI continued to perform best in the southern and central states as it always had. Yet the strength of these associations tended to decrease with time such that the impact of level of development on the vote reached its lowest point in 1994.[11] Indeed, the
historical regional differences, as shown in Figure 7.1, had deteriorated to
such a point that by 1994 they were no longer statistically important.[12]

State and Local Elections

Though revolving around states and regions, the above analysis focused on
federal elections. A brief review of state and local elections during the period provides a further means to assess the nature of reformism and Mexico's likely political futures. Attention centers on the reformist patterns at
the state level and their outcome during both the de la Madrid and Salinas
eras.

State and Local Dynamics Under de la Madrid and Salinas

State and local elections under de la Madrid featured the PRI facing stiff
challenge from the PAN (electorally through the vote and politically
through protests and mobilization) in a select number of states while generally maintaining its electoral/political hegemony in most parts of the
country. The ruling party captured all the seats at stake in 1983 in Aguascalientes, Campeche, Oaxaca, Veracruz, and Zacatecas and won 227 of
230 municipalities in Guerrero, Tamaulipas, and Michoacán; yet it lost the
capital city of Durango and all the important cities in the state of Chihuahua (Camargo, Casas Grandes, Chihuahua, Delicias, Juárez, Meoqui,
Parral, and Saucillo) to the PAN. In 1984, similarly, the PRI won all the
local legislative seats in Hidalgo, México, Nayarit, Quintana Roo, San
Luis Potosí, and Yucatán, and all but a small number of the 335 municipalities; yet in Piedras Negras, Coahuila, PAN-led violence erupted following the announcement of the PRI's win. Similar campaigns of civil disobedience and violence followed gubernatorial elections in 1985 and 1986
in Sonora, Durango, Nuevo León, and San Luis Potosí.

   A range of reformist strategies characterized the handling of state and
local matters under de la Madrid. They included, as noted in Chapter 3, the
strategy of respecting election results and allowing the opposition to win
at the local level and the use of fraud to prevent it from winning. Another
strategy involved the introduction of internal party reforms. As noted earlier, such reforms were attempted in Tamaulipas, San Luis Potosí, Nayarit,
and Hidalgo. Under the name Sistema Hidalgo, for example, the PRI of

Hidalgo in 1984 and 1987 established preliminary elections in thirty-five of the state's *municipios*.[13]

In other settings, the government and the PRI employed a perplexing mixture of soft-line and hard-line reformist tactics to counter the opposition and the PRI's decline. In Juchitán, Oaxaca, for example, the government faced a strong leftist coalition known as COCEI which had been in power since the 1980 special election. Yet in 1983, the PRI-controlled state government threw the COCEI local government out of office, using federal troops to take control of the streets and repress opponents. With a new election placing a PRI mayor in power, the government then gradually softened its line by negotiating to establish a joint PRI-COCEI city government, pouring infrastructure money into the town and curbing repression. Meanwhile, the PRI tried to polish its image by regrouping and selecting more progressive candidates for local and state offices.[14]

A similar mix of reformist techniques were employed in the northern state of Chihuahua.[15] An initial soft-line reformist touch found the government allowing local election results to stand—a move that swept the PAN into power in the state's major municipalities. But by midterm this approach gave way to a much harder line as de la Madrid forced the resignation of the state's governor, Oscar Ornelas, in September 1985 because, according to one observer, of the governor's "willingness to make space for the opposition" and work gracefully and fairly with the local PAN administrations.[16] The president then appointed hard-liner Saul González Herrera. During the subsequent gubernatorial election the following year, the government and/or the PRI employed massive vote fraud to ensure a PRI win. The depth of the fraud was so great and conspicuous that it triggered massive protests. Following the installation of the PRI governor, however, the government and the PRI again softened its line in an effort to adapt. The new governor, Fernando Baeza, struggled to cater to the local business community and to mend fences with the church. He even reached out to the PAN, passing what some have characterized as the "most advanced electoral law in the country."[17]

At the same time, the PRI in Chihuahua altered its campaign/electoral strategy, making Chihuahua a major reformist test for the nation. It shifted away from the corporate-based structure that was producing ever diminishing electoral returns to rely more heavily on territorial-based units targeted more specifically at "getting out the PRI vote." It introduced a dose of local autonomy into the political machine, allowing local militants to select their district representatives in charge of mobilizing the PRI vote and in some cases used *mesas receptoras* to select local PRI candidates with greater appeal within the state. The party even adopted a more modern strategy of carefully identifying key precincts, registering the voters, and getting them to the polls. This strategy dovetailed nicely with a more careful and selective orchestration of vote fraud in key voting districts through the manipulation of registration lists. Both tactics, of course, responded to the new need and obligation for the PRI to "put on a better show of vote counting."[18]

Under Salinas, similar reformist techniques were employed. The government, for instance, recognized opposition victories in certain locations, manipulated personnel, intervened to ease popular protests by overturning election results, used federal authority to make governing by the opposition difficult, and used both repressive and conciliatory means to ease tensions. Meanwhile, the PRI struggled to reinvigorate its electoral efficiency by concentrating its efforts on getting out the vote and imbuing the party with resources, including internal reforms and the selection of more attractive candidates.

One of the more important developments in state and local elections under Salinas was the tendency toward holding postelectoral negotiations. Forced by the intensity of protests, the related violence, and the perceived level of ingovernability, Salinas intervened frequently to force the resignation of newly "elected" state governors and the elaboration of joint municipal governments or similar types of arrangements in a host of states, including Guanajuato, Jalisco, Michoacán, Oaxaca, San Luis Potosí, Tabasco, Veracruz, and Yucatán, among others. In Guanajuato, for instance, PAN-led protests in response to fraud during the gubernatorial election in 1991 forced Salinas to call for the removal of the PRI governor-elect, Ramón Aguirre, and actually arrange for the appointment of an interim PAN governor.[19] Massive protests in San Luis Potosí, from women blocking the passage to the state house to the massive *éxodo a la democracia* march to Mexico City led by PRD–PAN–Frente Cívico gubernatorial candidate Salvador Nava, similarly forced the resignation of that state's newly elected governor, Fausto Zapata.[20] In like manner, the *éxodo para la democracia* protest march from Tabasco and Veracruz in 1991 produced an agreement between the secretary of Gobernación, the PRD, and Tabasco governments calling for mixed city governments in a number of the state's *municipios*.[21]

Critical to this reformist strategy was the direct and assertive involvement of Salinas—a tactic that went beyond postelectoral negotiations to include the selection of candidates at the state level, the removal and appointment of state party leaders, the removal and appointment of governors, and more centralized control over spending. As noted in Chapter 4, over 90 percent of the candidates for the 1991 election were selected from the top, while Salinas intervened to remove more governors than any president since Cárdenas. Moreover, at a time when local governments were increasingly controlled by the opposition, the federal government exerted more control over local funds and maintained greater ties to local groups through Solidarity.

In Baja California, for example, a state Salinas lost in 1988, the state executive, Xicotencatl Leyva, was removed in an effort to revive the image of the government and to exert more centralized control over the state party. The new governor, Oscar Baylón Chacón, then tried to instill a new political style based on federal moneys (1.5 billion pesos in urban infrastructure) and public demonstrations of support from the federal government. Later, in preparation for state elections, the PRI marginalized the sectors to select a well-known local businessman as its candidate.[22]

But not all interventions were to oust hard-liners and replace them with progressives: they were simply designed for political survival. In the state of México, for instance, a state Salinas also lost to the FDN in 1988, the removal of Governor Rámon Beteta brought the appointment of Ignacio Pichardo Pagaza and the reempowerment of the old Atlacomulco group led by conservative Hank González. As in Baja California, the new group used Solidarity and strong federal support—*"Votar por el PRI es votar por la solidaridad"* was the campaign slogan in 1991—coupled with 1,200 vote promoters, gifts, and irregularities, to revive the PRI's fortunes in the state.[23]

Causes and Consequences

The various examples of reformism at the state level raise two important questions: What accounts for the adoption of a given reformist strategy, and what determines its outcome? First, it seems clear that reformist changes took place primarily in those locations where the opposition threatened and instability prevailed. The two, of course, go hand in hand since a strong opposition will be capable of either competing electorally against the PRI or mobilizing strong protests to perceived fraud. In Chihuahua during the early 1980s, for example, the PAN enjoyed not only a solid base of support, but also spectacular growth as a result of increased participation by the business community and the church and popular discontent over the nation's declining economy, while the many postelectoral conflicts under Salinas and Salinas's intervention were clearly due to the strength of the opposition and the nature of the protests. Generally, only where the opposition threatened and instability existed would the center intervene to overturn local autonomy, remove governors, impose its candidates, marginalize the role of the sectors in the process, and promote reforms designed to enhance centralized control. By contrast, in states where conditions were relatively stable (nonthreatening) and/or the local political forces were strong and cohesive, the center tended to abide the autonomy of local forces or use such states to reward corporate leaders with gubernatorial positions.[24]

But this is not always the case, as the example from Hidalgo demonstrates. Though the PRI vote had decreased dramatically from 75 percent in 1976 to 65 percent in 1982, while at the local level opposition had spread throughout the state, Hidalgo was still a solid PRI state. The Hidalgo reforms in 1984 and 1987 resulted not from opposition strength, but from the fact that Hidalgo hosted one of the early elections under the new *sexenio* and that the PRI's national leader, Lugo Verduzco, hailed from the state.

Though reforms generally took place in states where instability or change threatened, the type of the reformist response varied. One factor shaping the response was the nature of the opposition. In 1983, when the government was respecting PAN wins in the north, it was repressing the COCEI in the south. Similarly under Salinas, the government's reformist reactions differed in cases where the opposition centered on the PAN as compared to the PRD or other groups. This could reflect the PAN's superior ability to monitor elections, its ties abroad, and/or its degree of ideological agreement with or cooperative posture toward the national government.[25] This point should not be overdrawn: despite the recognition of important PAN victories, the party continued to allege fraud in such states as Sinaloa, Coahuila, Yucatán, and Nayarit.[26]

Besides the nature of the opposition, reformist response also shifted within states, combining both hard line and soft-line remedies. The hard line revolved around the elections (what politically could be considered the bottom line), including legislative efforts to block coalition candidates; the use of the military on election day, which (advertently or not) helped bolster levels of abstentionism; fraud to control the outcome; and repression.[27] The soft-line stance, by contrast, involved efforts at reconciliation or improving the image of the party or the government. It included efforts at reconciliation, the removal of hard-line governors, the selection of candidates with local roots and popularity, the implementation of social programs to assuage the demands of the population and reincorporate the PRI's bases of support, and partial capitulation to the demands of the opposition through the creation of joint local governments, the negotiation of opposition victories, or the removal of state governors or PRI gubernatorial candidates popularly perceived as imposed through fraud. These measures were orchestrated not only to alleviate the ramifications of the negative reforms, but more important, to reduce the objective need for them in the future.

A final factor shaping the nature of the reformist response may be something called timing. This refers to the particular political stage a state finds itself in and the existence of parallel events. In states where widespread fraud had already been used to impose a PRI candidate, future elections heighten the political stakes and lessen the ability and utility of further fraud. The Chihuahua contest of 1992, for example, took place within the shadow of the 1986 contest. Not only was the PAN bolstered by the memory, but the world was watching. Another massive vote manipulation would have perhaps pushed instability far beyond the levels attained in 1986. Put differently, there may be a learning curve that makes a state's second time around distinct from its first.

Timing also refers to the existence of parallel elections or events. The Baja California contest in 1989, for example, took place at the same time as elections in Michoacán. As a result, the credibility costs of massive fraud in both cases would have been extremely high for the regime, prompting the Baja contest to be sacrificed in a sense to the PAN in order to shadow the fraudulent elections in Michoacán.

Turning to reformist outcome, the evidence suggests that reforms of the party and even strong intervention by the center in local affairs had the effect of fostering intense instability in the ranks. In Hidalgo, not only was the emergence of 15,000 precandidates in 1984 and over 500 in 1987 unmanageable, but irregularities, fraud, and the imposition of candidates prompted *desplegados* (demonstrations), marches, meetings, occupation of city halls, desertions from the party, vandalism, and kidnappings. Though the PRI continued to dominate the state electorally, the internal clashes of intraparty competition meshed with external clashes of interparty competition. In 1991 in Tabasco, where the attempt at a local, primary-style vote prompted so many irregularities that state leadership merely announced the names of the winners without providing the numbers, PRI militants installed a *plantón permanente* in front of the PRI offices in Mexico City. Many fled to the PRD, while others broke off to form the Movimiento Popular Priísta.[28] Here too, the state became problematic for the PRI as the ranks of the PRD swelled. Finally, in Nayarit in 1993, the selection of gubernatorial candidate Rigoberto Ochoa Zaragoza similarly unleashed massive protests, with PRI militants in the municipalities of Jala and in Santa María del Oro taking control of the party offices.[29]

As occurred with reforms or impositions, postelectoral negotiations with the opposition also ignited intraparty conflict. For instance, the decision to force Aguirre to resign his gubernatorial seat, coupled with the appointment of a PAN governor in 1991, set off a minirevolt within the PRI in Guanajuato. Accusing Salinas of treason against his own party, local PRI militants staged a protest march to León, the state capital, vowing to continue their struggle for democracy but outside the party.[30] Similar signs of discontent accompanied the postelectoral accords reached in Michoacán, San Luis Potosí, Sinaloa, Tabasco, and Veracruz, again bolstering the ranks of the opposition and weakening the party.

Beyond the impact on the PRI, however, overall success of the reformist efforts varied widely. In Chihuahua, the PRI's strategy was successful, but only for a time. Fraud put Baeza in office, and his strategy of reconciliation helped depoliticize the climate and enhance the PRI's reformist image in the state.[31] For example, mildly satisfied that the new governor had delivered on his economic and political promises, business, which had opposed Baeza in 1986, adopted a more quiescent stance. Coupled with the rebooting of the PRI machine and electoral fatigue, the PRI rebounded politically in the local elections in 1989. Though cries of fraud rang out and manipulation of voting lists was apparent, the situation was much less politicized than in 1986. In other words, not only did the PRI win, but political hell did not break loose. Yet in the subsequent gubernatorial election in 1992, the PAN, which by now had developed a working relationship with the PRI, rallied behind its charismatic candidate from 1986, Francisco Barrio, and won—an outcome this time recognized immediately by the Salinas government perhaps even before the results were in.

In large measure, as suggested by the Chihuahan case and the earlier empirical analysis, the primary factor shaping reform success may have been the nature and organization of the opposition. In contrast to the Cárdenas vote, the vote and appeal for the PAN, particularly in the northern states, was more solid and stable, making reformist success less pronounced and shorter-lived in those states. This suggests that the more institutionalized the opposition, the greater the difficulty of staging a PRI reformist comeback.

More specifically, reformist success depended on the organizational strength of the opposition or the PRI. Even where the PAN was strong, the PRI proved successful at recovery when the PAN found itself struggling with internal problems. Manuel Reynosos, for instance, attributes the inability of the PAN to increase its support in the state of Sonora to conflict between PAN leader Casimiro Navarro and the party's gubernatorial candidate.[32] A similar situation aided the PRI's ability to control Aguascalientes, Puebla, and Nuevo León. One report noted the existence of at least five separate currents within the PAN in Aguascalientes, while in Puebla the PAN was so deeply divided in 1988 that business members argued that the party had been taken over by ultrarightists.[33] In Baja California, by contrast, the absence of internal conflict within the party seemed a critical factor behind its win.[34]

The same was true for the PRI. Its reformist success reflected in many ways its internal problems, particularly the divisions between local and national forces. The imposition of candidates from the center, in other words, proved to be a double-edged sword for the party, attracting support from key sectors in the state while at the same time disillusioning many of the party's more traditional sectors. In a highly competitive state, this rupture often proved dangerous given the option available to former militants and voters of abandoning the party. In Tabasco in 1988, for instance, the former state president of the PRI, Andrés Manuel López Obrador, broke with the party to run on the FDN ticket. Later during state/local elections, he capitalized on the PRI's souring of relations with the petroleum workers union, turning this traditionally PRI state into one of the PRD's more important states. In Nayarit as well, the PRI's capitulation to the candidate of the state's (and the country's) most powerful cacique as the party's gubernatorial candidate, unleashed an electoral backlash against the party, forcing the widespread use of fraud to protect the PRI's hegemony and setting off a wave of protest.

Regionalism in the Prognostic Equation

Regardless of where or how the PRI held on to its power, one underlying trend at the state and local level is evident: with time, local elections became more important, more competitive, and more problematic. In the words of Vargas, they became the "privileged space" of political struggle and social conflict.[35] This can be seen in three distinct areas. First, the opposition increasingly won more posts and in more states than ever before. Whereas at the beginning of 1983 the opposition controlled only thirty-five municipalities in the country, a figure climbing to slightly more than fifty at the height of the *sexenio,* the opposition won 256 municipalities during the initial forty-seven months under Salinas. Among these, the opposition ruled in fourteen of the forty-three major cities in the country by 1992.[36] Beginning in 1989, the PRI even relinquished control of three gubernatorial seats to the PAN for the first time in history: in Baja California in 1989 via an election; in Guanajuato in 1991 via appointment; and in Chihuahua in 1992 via election.

Second, and closely related, the number of what could be classified as problem or competitive states for the PRI increased dramatically during the period. In addition to the PAN's continuing threat in the north and *bajío* region, threats flowered from the PRD and various coalitions in what were once states solidly under PRI domination, like Chiapas, Michoacán, Oaxaca, and Tabasco. Indeed, the decline of the PRI's bases of support in the southern states under Salinas essentially made all the regions equally competitive.

Finally, the scope and intensity of instability over perceived electoral fraud increased, affecting more and more states and gaining ever more attention nationally and abroad. After 1988, virtually every election in the country generated official charges of vote fraud and protests, often unleashing repression and violent clashes between partisans. While the PAN led protests and civil disobedience campaigns in certain states, the *cardenistas,* the PRD, and others spearheaded the move in others. Even in such historically PRI strongholds as Campeche, protests and violence over elections erupted during the 1991 contest as the PARM, the second strongest force in the state, backed by the PAN and PRD, declared fraud and demanded the annulment of the results in eight of the nine electoral districts.[37]

In sum, the trends suggest not only that the opposition will continue to grow as expressed either at the polls or through postelectoral protests, but that the PRI will continue to suffer defeats at the state level. They also underscore the critical problems the PRI faces at the state level as well as the tendency for negative reforms to politicize local contests, spark violence, and perhaps only delay rather than block the rise of the opposition. But interpreting the significance of these trends is not easy. At what point will such local trends threaten the PRI's national success? How important are local loses to the PRI and the political system? More generally, are the two indeed related?

A number of factors should be taken into account in answering these questions. For one, in a strong presidential system, the power of local government remains minimal, allowing the federal government to use its resources to tame and coopt the opposition even when they are in power at the local level.[38] To a large degree, this was what the Solidarity program did, sidestepping the role of local authorities. Most important, this marginalizing of local governments by the federal government occurred at precisely the historic moment when the opposition had begun to make significant inroads into state and local governments. In a sense, local PRI control was sacrificed and yet the damage was contained through renewed presidentialism. Presidentialism also played a critical role at election time. Even with local machines in turmoil, the national machine can continue to operate and provide patronage benefits.

But despite the reformist role of the president, the critical issue may hinge on the PRI's ability to mobilize the vote (locally and nationally) in states actually controlled by the opposition. To be sure, the loss of a state to the opposition means a stripping of the local PRI of its special and privileged ties to the state and local governments, undermining a portion of its traditional reliance on the government to protect its hegemony. As Gómez Tagle spells out, "Local elections are putting the state-party regime at risk . . . [in part] because an adversarial local congress could force the removal of the governor and/or set the stage for a non-PRI majority in congress."[39]

In Baja California, for example, the PAN governor altered the political game by developing voter ID cards with the voter's photograph (a move that forced the federal government to do the same nationally in order to enhance its credibility) and by inviting in foreign election observers. Moreover, relegated to the role of opposition, the PRI faced severe difficulties in mustering support from among its corporate organs, with CROC, CNC, and Central Compesino Independiente (CCI) either declaring their independence or, as with the taxi drivers affiliated with the CROC, actually backing PAN candidates. The PRI reacted by trying to democratize its candidate selection process, an attempt that proved relatively peaceful and somewhat successful.

The earlier means comparison showed a weak tendency for the PRI's vote to gain more in those states where governors were removed, suggesting a degree of reformist success. Yet it appears that it is more difficult for the PRI to recapture a state it has lost and allowed the opposition to govern, than when it loses a state and, through fraud, does not allow the opposition to take office. In Baja California, where the government allowed the PAN to take office, the PRI lost three of the six state seats in the national Chamber of Deputies and one senate seat to the PAN in the 1991 midterm election, suggesting that recovery in such places is difficult. Yet from 1991 to 1994, the PRI actually increased its vote in Baja California by 4.8 percentage points, a 13.7 point increase over its 1988 showing. In PAN-ruled Chihuahua, the PRI also enjoyed a 1.4 point increase during the 1991–1994 period with a 5.5 jump during the *sexenio,* while in Guanajuato it increased its vote by a mere .6 of a point. By contrast, in Michoacán, San Luis Potosí, and Yucatán, three states where fraud prevented the opposition from winning the gubernatorial post, the PRI's share of the vote fell 9.1, 3.1, and 7.8 points from 1991 to 1994.

Conclusion

The foregoing treatment of the subnational level echoes on the nature of reformism in three ways. First, it points to the incredible reformist success of Salinas in reversing, if not simply freezing, the threat of fundamental political change. With survival challenged, Salinas was successful at gaining ground in those states where the party needed it the most, though how or why he was able to do this is not quite clear. In accomplishing this reformist task, however, the PRI lost ground among its more solid bases, something with which reformism in the future will have to contend. Second, the analysis points to the volatility of the reformist game. Nationally, the PRI's political gains from 1988 to 1991 were just as dramatic as Cárdenas's rise from 1985 to 1988 and just as short-lived; the PRI's recovery in the state of Chihuahua was equally volatile. Such is sufficient, of course, to ease tensions and surmount the crisis.

Finally, the analysis points to the dynamic nature of the game. As the low correlation between the PRI's vote at the beginning of the de la Madrid era and the end of the Salinas era (r=.5635) indicates, substantial change occurred during the period. In fact, the trends showed that by the end of the period the PRI was in as bad if not worse shape and closer to the brink of change than at any time throughout the period. The PRI's margin of victory was much narrower and in more states in 1994 than in any of the previous elections.[40] Yet this too seems to be part of reformism: approaching the brink, making it appear that change is imminent, but not taking the plunge.

While the recent experience suggests that these trends bode poorly for the regime and that the PRI may be approaching a point of "increasingly diminishing reformist returns," interpreting the future requires perhaps even greater attention to the past. Discussion thus turns to a comparative historical perspective on Mexican reformism: its ability to adapt to crisis.

Notes

1. See, among others, Aziz Nassif, "Regional Dimensions of Democratization"; Klesner, "Party System Expansion and Electoral Mobilization"; and Molinar Horcasitas, *El tiempo de la legitimidad*.

2. Guillén López, "Elecciones de 1989 en Baja California," p. 177.

3. Official electoral data from the Electoral Commission for the 1982 and 1985 elections were graciously provided by Joséph Klesner; data for the 1988 and 1991 elections were taken from *Nexos* 164, 1991, pp. 34–40. Preliminary data for 1994 were taken from Baez Rodríguez, "Elecciones: El fin de los zapatos y los cienpiés."

4. Opposition presence under the de la Madrid period represents the percentage of *municipios* within each state in which the PRI ran unopposed, as presented in Horcasitas Molinar, *El tiempo de la legitimidad*, pp. 116–117. The measure for the Salinas period was the state's vote for Cárdenas in 1988, taken from *The Mexico Journal* 1 (41), 1988, pp. 16–17. The level of socioeconomic development was taken from a composite measure incorporating urbanization, portion of the economically active population (EAP) engaged in industry, gross state product per capita, proportion of the EAP earning more than three times the minimum wage, agricultural productivity, number of telephones and automobiles per capita, literacy, percentage of homes with electricity and water, and per capita consumption of gasoline and sugar, as presented in Palacios, *La política regional*, p. 141. A state's economic growth was calculated based on figures provided by INEGI in *Anuario Estadística de los Estados Unidos Mexicanos*, p. 32. The regional-based measures of the vote were tabulated following Basañez's regional classification in *El pulso de los sexenios*: north (Baja California, Baja California Sur, Chihuahua, Coahuila, Nuevo León, Sonora, and Tamaulipas); center (Aguascalientes, Colima, Federal District, Durango, Guanajuato, Hidalgo, Jalisco, México, Michoacán, Morelos, Nayarit, Puebla, Querétaro, San Luis Potosí, Sinaloa, Tlaxcala, Veracruz, and Zacatecas); and south (Campeche, Chiapas, Guerrero, Oaxaca, Quintana Roo, Tabasco, Yucatán).

5. State changes in income/expenditures from 1982 to 1988, a proxy indicator of the economic situation for the states, was also unrelated to the vote shift. Data were taken from *Finanzas Públicas Estatales y Municipales*.

6. See Basañez, *El pulso de los sexenios*, pp. 218–219.

7. Klesner, "Modernization, Economic Crisis, and Electoral Alignment in Mexico."

8. The data were provided by John Bailey during a presentation at Tulane University, New Orleans, in September 1993.

9. The poll was presented in *Este País* 7 (October 1991), p. 11.

10. Molinar Horcasitas and Weldon, "Electoral Determinants and Consequences of National Solidarity," pp. 123–142.

11. This delinking of the vote for the PRI from level of development duplicates the findings of Klesner, "Realignment or Dealignment?"

12. The regional means of the PRI vote as depicted in the graph had the following significance (F) levels: 9.55 (1982), 10.7 (1985), 4.28 (1988), 3.03 (1991), and .035 (1994). An F greater than 4 is considered statistically significant.

13. Vargas, "La insurgencia en las elecciones municipales," provides an excellent overview of the reform experiment "Sistema Hidalgo" and its impact on politics in Hidalgo.

14. For an overview of the Juchitán case see Rubin, "State Policies, Leftist Oppositions, and Municipal Elections."

15. For a discussion of the Chihuahua case see Aziz Nassif, "Electoral Practices and Democracy in Chihuahua" and "Chihuahua: La fatiga electoral"; and Rodríguez and Ward, *Policymaking, Politics, and Urban Governance in Chihuahua*.

16. Rodríguez and Ward, *Policymaking, Politics, and Urban Governance in Chihuahua*, p. 38.

17. Ibid., p. 41.

18. Ibid.

19. See, for instance, Ortiz Pinchetti, "Salinas, en reunión privada con Gutierrez Barrios y Colosio."

20. See *Cuadernos de Nexos* 41, 1991, pp. i–v; Galárza, "Sacerdotes, empresarios y ciudadanos de San Luis"; Galárza, "Advertencia a Zapata"; and Granados Chapa, *Nava Sí, Zapata No*.

21. See Guzmán, "Neme Castillo dió 'madruguete'."

22. See Guillén López, "Elecciones de 1989 en Baja California."

23. See Aguirre M. "Mago electoral en el estado de México."

24. In Chiapas, for example, where the PRI faced no electoral threat, it maintained its alliance with local caciques, employing a repressive and hard-line stance against the indigenous population. It was only after the Xi'Nich' march to Mexico City in April 1992 over land disputes that the government began to negotiate with these groups. However, this traditionally repressive stance coupled with deep social problems exploded in January 1994 with the violent attacks of the Zapatista guerrillas (see Correa, "Documenta el centro 'Bartolome de las Casas'"; and Vera, "Caciques del PRI."

25. There were contrasting explanations (not necessarily mutually exclusive) for the election in Baja California. Some interpreted it as basically clean (see, for instance, Beltrán del Río, "El centro no va a soltar el poder"), while others pointed to the direct intervention of Colosio and Salinas in preventing the culmination of fraud (*Latin American Weekly Review* 89–34 (August 31, 1989), p. 8). Gómez Tagle, "La violencia y la normatividad en las elecciones mexicanas," p. 8, associates the PAN victory with the supervisory and computing capacity of the party. Just one day after the election, for example, Ruffo claimed victory based on the results of 989 of the 1,168 precincts. A report in *Latin American Weekly Review* 89–30 (August 3, 1989), p. 10) suggested that the concession may have been due to the degree of media attention in the United States.

26. In state elections in Coahuila in 1990, for instance, widescale accusations of fraud abounded. According to a state PAN leader and federal deputy, cited in

Proceso 731 (November 5, 1990), p. 12, "The promise of Carlos Salinas to respect the vote in Coahuila was not kept." It was during this contest that the PRI developed the operation *ratón loco*, where people are forced to run around trying to find their name on electoral lists. PAN proposed an investigation of the charges of fraud, which were backed by PRD, PARM, and even PFCRN but turned down by the government (see *Proceso* 732 [November 12, 1990], pp. 12–13). The 1993 elections in the state were similarly haunted by accusations and the widespread perception of fraud.

27. As did the federal government, state governments placed legal obstacles in the way of the opposition. In Tabasco, for instance, the state electoral commission prevented candidates from running for more than one political party in 1988, while in Oaxaca the local legislature prohibited coalitions and the state electoral commission denied permission for common candidates in 1989. Abstentionism was high during local races, reaching an estimated 70 percent in Tabasco in 1988; 85 percent in Oaxaca and 70 percent in Chihuahua in 1989; and 75–85 percent in Hidalgo in 1990. Vargas, "La insurgencia en las elecciones municipales," found the rate to be higher in the more competitive areas—an indication of the role of fraud. See the various chapters in Alonso and Gómez Tagle, eds., *Insurgencia democrática: Las elecciones locales.*

28. See Beltrán del Río, "El repudio a candidates de Nemé."

29. The selection or imposition bowed to the power of cacique Emilio M. González in the state, and the old school allied with the CTM (see Chávez, "Totalmente dividio, el PRI espera en Nayarit").

30. Ortiz Pinchetti, "Salinas, en reunión privada con Gutierrez Barrios y Colosio."

31. Ortiz Pinchetti, "Pruebas del fraude en gestión."

32. Reynoso, "Sonora: Tres piezas para armar."

33. See Beltrán del Río, "Desarraigado y desconocido en Puebla"; Chávez, "Muchos aspirantes en Aguascalientes"; and Garza, "En Nuevo León, empresarios contra empresarios."

34. Guillén López, "Elecciones de 1989 en Baja California."

35. Vargas, "La insurgencia en las elecciones municipales," p. 47.

36. See Presidencia de la República, *Las Razones y las obras*, p. 65; and Beltrán del Río, "Con Salinas, cuatro años de una conducción política coyuntural y arbitraria."

37. Beltrán del Río, "19 días de protesta, que seguirá hasta enero"; and *La Jornada*, November 26, 1991, p. 14.

38. Guillén López, "Elecciones en 1989 en Baja California," suggests that the Baja election marked a critical turning point in that it demonstrated a new stage of presidentialism involving the forging of official relations with opposition parties.

39. Gómez Tagle, "La violencia y la normatividad en las elecciones mexicanas," p. 20.

40. Molinar Horcasitas, *El tiempo de la legitimidad*, for example, finds that the number of hegemonic or safe districts for the PRI declined significantly during the 1980s.

8

The Historical Perspective

Levy and Szekely correctly cite stability as the most "striking feature" of the Mexican political system.[1] But stability should not be taken to imply the absence of political conflict, rather the capacity to surmount it. Indeed, Mexico's adaptive authoritarian regime has weathered a string of political crises, each threatening key components of the system, encapsuling innovative forms of "antisystem behavior," and heightening the possibility and promise of political change.[2] Yet none were capable of stimulating fundamental change.

This chapter provides a historical comparative perspective on crisis and reformism in Mexico. It first explores past crisis/reform periods, culls the common aspects of reformism, and highlights the important systemic features contributing to this pattern. It then compares past crisis/reform patterns with those marking the contemporary period to help assess the probable direction of political change.

Past Crises/Reforms

Crisis or reform has been the primary feature of scholarly analysis of Mexican politics since the revolution. The following traces just some of the more critical political crises and the government's reformist responses.[3]

Elite Division in the Forties and Fifties

Given the importance of controlling interelite conflict, internal divisions within the official party have often been the trigger of political crisis.[4] Generally, shunned presidential hopefuls pull the trigger, abandoning the official party to mobilize those similarly disillusioned by the regime and its policies. The historic ranks of such internal "dissidents" include Vicente Lombardo Toledano, the former labor leader who challenged the regime in the 1930s and 1940s; General Juán Andrew Almazán, who broke from the ruling PRM to attract support from the business community and oppose Avila Camacho in the 1940 presidential contest; General Ezequiel Padilla, Avila Camacho's secretary of foreign relations, who broke from the newly formed PRI in 1946 to challenge Miguel Alemán under the banner of the Partido Renovación Político-Social; General Miguel Henríquez Guzmán, who opposed the PRI's Ruíz Cortines in the 1952 election; and, of course, Cárdenas in 1988.

For example, the *henriquista* movement in 1952, which proved to be the strongest internal challenge to the regime (until Cárdenas in 1988), was triggered by the expulsion of Henríquez from the PRI in 1951 for attempting to open up the presidential selection process and for criticizing the government's probusiness policies.[5] The Henríquez faction within the party had been active and vocal at least since the mid-1940s. Following his expulsion, though, the charismatic figure united groups frustrated by the policies of Alemán into the Federación de Partidos del Pueblo (FPP). He garnered strong support in the countryside among those upset over the reversals of the *cardenista* agrarian program, in the factory among those hurt by Alemán's policy of wage restraints and the purging of union leaders, and in the military among those irked by the selection of a civilian president (Alemán), his elimination of the military sector within the party, and his limited reliance on the military.[6] Among the ruling elite, the movement drew support from *cardenistas* and *avilacamachistas*, including some major officials within the regime such as Bartolomé Vargas Lugo (ex-governor of Hidalgo), Ernesto Soto Reyes (ex-leader of the senate), Antonio Espinosa (Mexico's ambassador to the United States), the former governor of the state of Mexico, and even members of the Cárdenas family.[7] Efforts were even made to unite all the opposition behind Henríquez, though these failed.

The threat posed by elite divisions, like the *henriquista* movement, is partially revealed by the "official" electoral outcomes. In both the 1946 and 1952 elections, for instance, the PRI's share of the vote dipped below the 80 percent mark: Padilla garnered 19.3 percent and Henríquez 15.87 percent of the "official" vote. Even discounting the widespread fraud involved, the relative level of the PRI's vote and those of the two opposition candidates would go unmatched until the 1980s. But the electoral threat provided just a glimpse of the larger threat: the ability of the dissident elites to mobilize the population and raise questions about the regime's legitimacy, particularly its centralized means of selecting a successor (imposition). The fact that the ranks of the "out group" expanded every six years further compounded the inherent risk.

The government responded to these internal threats in a variety of ways. To counter the immediate political/electoral danger, the government combined secret negotiations and cooptation with fraud and repression. It reached a secret accord with the Monterrey elite and the Unión Nacional Sinarquista in 1940, for example, to block the growing support for the right-wing dissident Almazán.[8] In 1946, it headed off the swelling of the *henriquista* movement within the party by offering important governmental posts to his supporters. Following Henríquez's subsequent bid for the presidency in the 1952 election, the government again split the movement by adopting many of their ideas and offering important positions in the government to *henriquista* supporters.[9]

Fraud and repression were also used to contain the challenge. Various historical accounts, for instance, note the widespread use of fraud during the presidential contests of 1940, 1946, and 1952, ensuring "victory" for the "official" candidates. Claims that Almazán, or Padilla, or Henríquez actually won the presidential elections can still be heard. Like fraud, repression also played a critical role. The massacre at León, Guanajuato, in January 1946, for example, pitted *padillistas* against *alemanistas*, resulting in the dissolution of state power.[10] Clashes between *henriquistas* and the government and the mass arrests of the former significantly marred the 1952 campaign trail. As Rodríguez Araujo notes, "The repression against *henriquismo* did not stop. . . . Throughout the year 1952 they pursued them and jailed them, accusing them of subversion and criminal acts."[11] Two years later, the FPP was stripped of its party registration on the grounds it fomented violence in the state of México and attempted to stir rebellion in Chihuahua.[12]

Combined, these measures defused the immediate crises. According to Contreras, "The *almazanistas* were seen to be involved in a most grotesque and hapless tentative rebellion in history"—and the movement faded.[13] Similarly Padilla left the country "without announcing a rebellion as many had speculated."[14] And *henriquismo,* divided and organizationally proscribed as noted, reportedly disappeared gradually from the national political scene.

But the government faced more than the immediate threat; it also faced declining confidence in the system and the possibility of having to overcome such divisions in future successions. To assuage these problems, President Alemán experimented with an internal reform of the party based on a party primary system. The initiative ran into internal opposition, however, and was abandoned by 1953.[15] Legal reforms of the party and electoral system proved a more successful method at containing the problem. Legal reforms in 1946, 1949, 1951, and 1954 centralized the federal government's control over the electoral process, prohibited the participation of independent candidates, and tightened the requirements for political parties.[16] This closed the window through which "dissident" candidates entered and eliminated the periodic rise of "electoral" parties. This enabled the PRI not only to rebound in future successions and elections, but it effectively blocked the reoccurrence of dangerous elite divisions and eased electoral opposition to the official candidate. As noted, Padilla's 19 percent performance in 1946 remained a record for an opposition presidential candidate for over three decades—until Cárdenas in 1988.

Labor Unrest: Crises of Corporatist Control and Reformism

In addition to internal splits, labor conflict has also unleashed periods of political crises. During the late 1940s, late 1950s, and mid-1970s, for instance, labor unrest threatened the regime's corporatist controls and the inclusive nature of the PRI itself.[17] Throughout the 1940s and 1950s, for example, important segments of the industrial working class mobilized to demand wage increases and improved working conditions. Many such movements, however, ended up struggling for labor autonomy and union democracy, attacking the PRI-affiliated labor confederation in the process. In the late 1940s alone, telegraph workers struck to demand recognition of their decision to abandon the Sindicato Nacional de Trabajadores de la Secretaría de Comunicaciones y Obras Públicas (SCOP). Teachers from section 9 of the union (in the Federal District), under the leadership of the Movimiento Revolucionario Magisterio (MRM), protested to demand the right to freely elect their representatives. And railroad workers mobilized across the nation to demand recognition of their "elected" leaders.

Perhaps the stiffest resistance and challenge to the regime during the period emerged from railroad workers organized within the Sindicato de Trabajadores Ferrocarrileros de la Republica Mexicana (STFRM). Spawned in part by the prior purging of the union's officials (*charrazo*) by President Alemán, the union first struggled with the CTM for hegemony over the labor movement only to abandon the CTM in 1947 and form the independent Central Unica de Trabajadores (CUT). The new organization, in turn, attracted the support and affiliation of airline workers, cement workers, and metal workers, and staged a series of public demonstrations against the high cost of living and the government's right-wing economic policies. The government responded to these demands by intervening in the internal operations of the union and using repression. The slightest dissidence within the union was quelled, the exclusionary clause as well as police and the army were frequently used, and arbitrary systems to enforce discipline were developed. After jailing the dissident leaders in the early 1950s, the government manipulated the internal elections to place a more pliable labor leader, Jesús Díaz de León, in charge.[18] By 1952 the government had snuffed out the independent movement and had regained control of the railroad workers movement.[19]

But by the late 1950s the movement resurfaced, culminating in the creation of the Gran Comisión Pro-Aumento General de Salarios, led by famed labor leader Valentin Campa. The workers set up a series of parallel organizations within their own "official" union and demanded not only salary increases, but also the right to freely select their leaders. Once again the movement attracted the solidarity of a wide range of unions across the country, including the SME, the MRM, and sections 34 and 35 of the

STPRM. Strikes and work stoppages were widespread. As one observer recalled, "Anyone who had lived in the D.F. during this period will remember 1958 as a year of protests, hunger strikes, the occupation of public buildings, the hijacking of buses, and also the use of tear gas and billy clubs."[20]

Repression met the labor challenge head on. The government imprisoned the leaders of the railroad workers movement, parlayed concessions to various other labor organizations and other opponents to cripple the momentum of the workers, launched a campaign to discredit dissident unions, and reasserted control over the internal operations of their organizations. The lead group, the railroad workers, was crushed, though protests and violence lingered into the early 1960s with the police being used periodically to "disperse students, workers, and the unemployed who had taken to the streets."[21]

With repression easing the immediate threats, the government launched a series of reforms in the following years to help contain the opposition and restore legitimacy to the party, the government, and the electoral process. Noting the lack of participation by the public and opposition parties in elections, coupled with destabilizing protests by such opposition parties as the PAN, the government garnered the support of all opposition parties to reform the electoral system in 1963. Among other features, the measure established a minority block of proportional representation seats in congress for the opposition and eased the requirements for the formation of political parties. This helped contain the pressures and ensured at least the appearance of competitive and legitimate elections.[22] At the same time, the reform strengthened the government's control over the electoral process, banned much of the antisystem behavior the PAN had engaged in during the 1950s, and was implemented in such a way as to discourage the emergence of a biparty system.[23] Such moves helped the regime keep the opposition divided and at bay while enhancing its own legitimacy and participation.

Complementing the 1963 electoral reform, the PRI once again experimented with a series of internal reforms. Citing the need to attract youthful leadership and be more responsive to local demands, PRI president Carlos Madrazo sent the party leadership out to consult with local officials and establish mechanisms by which they could elect their own leaders in local assemblies. Such elections were then to be followed by primary elections to select candidates for municipal president and council.[24] Madrazo also supported the establishment of a Commission for Honor and Justice "to expel racketeers from the party."[25] But despite the efforts, the reforms generally stopped far short of their pronounced objectives. Threatening the interests of state and local officials, the reforms of Madrazo died in a showdown with Leopoldo Sánchez Celis, the governor of Sinaloa, prompting Madrazo's resignation in 1965.[26]

Finally, the government eased the popular pressures of the times by responding to the material demands. Embracing the leftist symbols of the revolutionary ideology, López Mateos reinvigorated the land reform program, redistributing more land than any president since Cárdenas; instituted the long-neglected profit-sharing provision within the constitution, giving workers within the official organizations material benefits and a say in the implementation of the program; and increased and extended a range of government programs, including social security and subsidies to the urban poor through CONASUPO.[27] Such moves helped relieve the pressures for change and enabled the regime to recover lost legitimacy.

The Crises of 1968 and 1976

Perhaps the most spectacular and best known of Mexico's political crises centered on the 1968 student movement and Tlaltelolco. Though triggered initially by the intervention of *granaderos* (riot police) to break up a fight among rival student groups, the student movement mushroomed to encompass a massive protest against the authoritarian regime and its right-leaning model of stabilizing development.[28] At one point the students rallied an estimated half a million in the Zocalo demanding political and economic change. With the Olympic Games just weeks away, the government of Gustavo Díaz Ordaz responded ruthlessly to the students. During a massive demonstration at the Plaza of the Three Cultures on October 2, 1968, the government killed more than 300 and arrested over 2,000.[29]

The government's response disarticulated the student movement and restored order, but the cost was great. The act altered the government's image and undermined "the official 'myth' of the Mexican Revolution."[30] As faith in the PRI and the regime slid, the urgency for change grew. Some abstained from elections and withdrew; others took up arms. Guerrilla activity by the Liga Comunista 23 de Septiembre, the Frente Revolucionario Armado del Pueblo, the Asociación Cívica Nacional Revolucionario, the Partido de los Pobres, and the Movimiento de Acción Revolucionario shocked the nation. Many such groups enjoyed the support and sympathy of the nation's students and leftist intellectuals.

The need for change was equally clear to the ruling elite and analysts of the system. As PRI leader of the time Jesús Reyes Heroles argued, "Without profound changes that improve and augment participation, stability will be endangered."[31] Analysts, meantime, saw the regime at a critical juncture between dictatorship and democracy. Martin Needler, for example, stated in the early 1970s that "if political liberalism is not to be permitted to flower into a thoroughly competitive democratic regime, then force will increasingly have to be used."[32]

But in the end, it proved to be neither dictatorship nor democracy. Instead, the regime embraced political and economic reforms to ease the tensions and pressures that seemingly created this "false" choice. The reformist process extended over a number of years and encompassed a range of initiatives. Generally, the reformist process involved incorporating and taming the leftist opposition that had been mobilized and radicalized by the events of 1968 while restoring popular faith in the party, elections, and the government.

The post-1968 reforms included, first, Echeverría's *apertura democrática,* or an opening of the channels of communication between the government and burgeoning social organizations. Through a variety of means, new political and social space was opened to the rising middle class, intellectuals, universities, and the left. The state itself even sponsored new organizations, such as the Comité Nacional de Auscultación y Consulta (CNAC), to tie middle sectors, workers, and intellectuals to the government. The opening also included the promotion of independent unionism by the government to curb the control exerted by the old union bosses,[33] a broadening of press freedoms,[34] efforts by Porfirio Múñoz Ledo and Reyes Heroles to reform the PRI internally, and an electoral reform in 1973 that legalized the Communist Party and lowered the voting age.

Second, Echeverría adopted a leftist discourse and used it for the government's purpose. Openly criticizing the stabilizing model of his predecessors, Echeverría offered a program of "shared development" that coupled the popular demands for redistribution voiced by the students with a strong dose of nationalism.[35] Concomitantly, state spending increased, government control over the economy grew, and government employment skyrocketed.[36] As government agencies proliferated through everything from new social programs and *fideocomisos* to governmental scholarship programs, the expanding bureaucracy crafted clientelistic ties between the state and the society that bypassed or at least complemented the role of the PRI in incorporating opposition and containing conflict.[37]

But while successful at tempering the situation in the short term, crisis returned by the mid-1970s. Labor unrest, spearheaded this time by the Tendencia Democrática within the electrician workers union, again challenged the regime's corporatist controls. Unidad Obrera Independiente (UOI), Frente Auténtico del Trabajo, Federación de Sinidactos de Trabajadores Universitarios, SPAUNAM, STUNAM (university workers), and others flourished, raising the percentage of total strike actions motivated by democratic principles from 14 percent to 53 percent between 1970 and 1975.[38] In October 1975, the Tendencia Democrática alone mobilized more than 100,000 in a mass demonstration in Mexico City, where the dissident leadership equated *charrismo syndical* with imperialism. This act prompted Echeverría to backtrack on his earlier policy and throw official support to the traditional labor groups such as the CTM. And again the regime relied on repression to contain the threat. As Basurto relates: "The complete disintegration of the movement became evident on September 28, 1977, when its leaders installed an encampment beside the presidential residency . . . [and] on November 5 a group of *granaderos* and firemen rounded them up and returned them to their places of origin."[39]

But the 1976 crisis was spurred in large part by economic crisis and the estrangement of the private sector from the state, both consequences of Echeverría's shared development program. Uncontrolled spending triggered deficits, inflationary pressures, and balance of payments difficulties, forcing the government to devalue the peso and sign a standby agreement with the IMF.[40] Moreover, Echeverría's proleftist policies raised the opposition of the right. Concerned about the government's apparent shift toward "socialism" and suffering attacks from the violent left, most notably the guerrilla kidnapping and assassination of industrialist Eugenio Garza Sada in 1973, the private sector used its strength to mobilize its opposition to the regime, including capital flight. By 1975, the newly created and independent CCE, made up of the private sector's major organizations, such as CONCAMIN, CONCANACO, COMPARMEX, and the Bankers Association, bitterly attacked the government's economic programs and questioned the regime's political credentials. Echeverría's expropriation of lands in Sonora in 1976 further polarized the situation, leaving the government facing a severe deficit of confidence and support in the private sector.

To ease the 1976 crisis, incoming president López Portillo consciously and strategically reached out to the business community while abiding the requirements set down by the International Monetary Fund (IMF). He launched Alianza Popular para la Producción, increased private sector participation in his government (e.g., the appointment of Santiago Roel of Monterrey to foreign relations), consulted directly with the private sector concerning key policy decisions, released some of the more outspoken leftists in the previous cabinet (Múñoz Ledo and Reyes Heroles), and toned down the government's leftist rhetoric.

In addition, López Portillo sponsored yet another installment of political reform. Known by its acronym LOPPE (Ley Federal de Organizaciónes Políticos y Procesos Electorales), the reform completed the government's reconciliation with the left begun under Echeverría. It pried open political space by lowering registration requirements for political parties, increasing the number of proportional representation seats in the Chamber of Deputies while lowering the threshold for obtaining them, and providing public financial subsidies to opposition parties. The measure not only succeeded in enhancing the government's electoral legitimacy and channeling participation into the electoral arena and away from guerrilla activity, but also effectively divided the opposition and forestalled polarization. Within a few years after the initiative, the left claimed about a dozen political parties and political organizations, participation in the electoral process increased, and legitimacy levels climbed. Meanwhile, the government protected its control over the voting process and the PRI maintained its hegemony.

Largely overshadowing or easing López Portillo's policy toward the business community and his political reforms was the political bonanza generated by the 1978–1981 oil boom and the influx of cheap foreign loans. With economic growth averaging 8.4 percent and public debt growing at an average rate of $35.7 billion from 1978 to 1981, Mexico shifted from IMF beggar to renewed economic miracle. Oil flowed and growth soared. Again populist subsidies and programs mushroomed, this time without destroying the good relations with the private sector. Public expenditures increased from 34 percent of GDP in 1979 to almost 42 percent by 1981.[41] This period of prosperity greatly facilitated political stability and eased pressure on the regime for change, though such good times would evaporate when the 1981–1982 economic downturn forced the regime to nationalize the banking industry in a desperate move to garner popular legitimacy and halt capital flight.[42]

Historical Patterns

This brief historic sampling highlights some of the basic dimensions of Mexican reformism. First, crises have been common. With the exception of the three elite divisions—a problem the regime effectively avoided for over three decades—labor conflict, popular demands for political and economic change, and electoral disputes seemed to ebb and flow. Second, crises generally resulted from the contradictions or dilemmas set in motion by early reformist efforts.[43] The resolution of the electoral parties through reforms in the 1940s and 1950s, for example, led to the problem of declining electoral participation and legitimacy in the 1960s.[44] The reforms of Echeverría in response to the 1968 crisis similarly created the conditions that would rebound to forge the economic crisis of 1976. As Newell and Rubio eloquently note, "By robbing the left of its 'progressive' rhetoric, the government avoided dealing with leftist radicalism; but by so doing it triggered radicalism from the right."[45]

Third, crises also seemed to occur around the end of a sexenial cycle. *almazanismo, padillismo,* and *henriquismo* all haunted the end of one term and the beginning of the next. The railroad workers movement coupled with economic downturn capped the term of Ruiz Cortines. The 1968 movement took place during the penultimate year of the Díaz Ordaz administration. And the terms of Echeverría, López Portillo (de la Madrid and Salinas) all ended with the nation's economy or polity marred in crisis. In many cases, as with the elite divisions and the electoral challenges, the reasons for this pattern are obvious: the electoral setting provides the opposition the institutional opportunity to openly challenge the PRI's hold on power. But it also seems that the PRI and the government may be at their weakest reformist point during the transition process. Whatever the cause, the pattern is clear.

As with crisis, the regime's response also exhibited certain common ingredients. Each of the periods reviewed here, for instance, featured the critical use of negative reforms like repression and fraud to disarticulate and divide the regime's opponents. As Pereyra correctly pointed out in referring to the decade of the 1950s, "Bureaucratic control could only be maintained because railroad workers, teachers, telegraphers and petroleum workers were violently contained and their leaders jailed."[46] The regime also relied on electoral fraud to help maintain its grip. Fraud was reportedly widespread during the electoral threats posed by the dissidents in the 1940s and 1950s, and even more common in maintaining the PRI's hold over local and state offices in the ensuing years.

But while crucial in dealing with the immediate threats to the regime, in a sense halting the momentum, such negative measures were usually tempered by some form of controlled political opening or liberalization. This refers to a broadening (both rhetorical and real) of the inclusiveness of the PRI as well as the political system to accommodate opposition voices, opposition parties, social organizations, and the demands of the middle class. On a very real level, by incorporating new actors and interests into the system, it softened the organizations' demands and facilitated the government's response. New actors not only won real benefits in the process, but were usually granted "institutional recognition" and hence a means to express their demands and continue the struggle for change in the future.[47] Though ceding a degree of autonomy in the process,[48] the organizations nonetheless developed an institutional stake in the system. Actors would constantly try to stretch the boundaries of behavior or press the regime for a further amplification of the political space or the distribution of spoils, particularly during the ensuing crisis; but most abided by the rules of the system.

Political opening, moreover, allowed the government to embrace the ideas of its opponents and incorporate them as their own. This type of symbolic cooptation enabled the regime to steal the opposition's thunder and use it to actually mobilize support for the regime.[49] The fact that labor movements usually won material concessions only to have their demand for autonomy blocked testifies to this tendency of the government to be partially responsive to popular demands. Avila Camacho adopted much of the reformist rhetoric of Henríquez Guzmán just as Echeverría did with the student/leftist demands of the late sixties. As Hansen states, "The regime has responded to Mexico's cycles of discontent with piecemeal measures designed to ease mounting pressures without significantly altering existing government policies."[50] The once popular pendulum theory of Mexican presidential politics indeed reflects this responsive reaction of incoming presidents to "end-of-sexenio" crises.[51]

On a more symbolic though equally important level, controlled opening also enhanced the government's reformist credibility. An opening provided solid "proof" of the government's sincerity in its promises for political change, allowing the regime to increase the legitimizing function of elections as demonstrated by the rise of participation following the 1963 and 1977 reforms. This garnered support for the president's "controlled" and tempered program of change, thereby easing pressures and the reformist process. As Gómez Tagle notes, "Only the wider participation of opposition parties has been able to give gradually . . . an image of legitimacy to the Mexican elections, which up to now have been suspect."[52]

The overall pattern suggests a tendency then for controlled political openings in Mexico to weaken rather than strengthen the attractiveness of a strategy of confrontation. It reduces the level and likelihood of antisystem polarization and as a result diminishes the dangers for the further buildup of political pressures for change. But what were clearly steps in the right political direction (liberalization), and therefore interpreted as progress, merely delayed rather than encouraged fundamental change. Put differently, hints at democratization, rather than undermining the regime, actually strengthened authoritarian survival.[53] This has been true only to the extent that the state has been able to craft the opening to channel participation into nonthreatening avenues (electoral arena or state agencies), or been able subsequently to weaken those avenues, thereby controlling the pace and direction of change from above—or structure the benefits in such a way as to explicitly reduce antisystem behavior and the likelihood of a unified opposition.

The substantive elements of the 1963 electoral reforms, for instance, prohibited much of the protest activity of the PAN, while the 1977 political reforms ensured a proliferation of opposition parties that would help dilute the growing appeal of the PAN. De facto implementation of the election laws over the years went even further by favoring those parties more closely allied with the PRI to the detriment of the more independent opposition parties such as the PAN, guarding against the development of a biparty system. This pattern suggests then that while repression may facilitate maintaining control and reestablishing the rules of the game, it is the subsequent opening that aids in legitimizing and institutionalizing this level of control. The lack of opposition in Mexico is due more to the state's influence over workers' organizations and the state's ability to "control the attitudes of all political organizations" than to repression.[54]

This historic pattern of crisis and reform, in turn, has over the years crafted a unique "adaptive authoritarian" system notable for three factors: its blending of old and new institutional mechanisms, its incorporation or cooptation of change, and its record of "failed" reformist measures. First, as a consequence of the periodic strategic openings, Mexico has tended to graft new reformist institutions onto the old. Beginning with the PRI as the primary mechanism to contain political conflict and maintain the revolutionary elite in power (and a series of attempted reforms to revitalize it over the years), the government subsequently opened and altered the party system to channel opposition into the electoral arena, a move that enhanced its own credibility.[55]

Under Echeverría and López Portillo, the government subsequently strengthened its credibility and legitimacy by using the state to create bureaucratic links with key segments of society. Intellectuals enjoyed stipends and grants, workers received subsidies and loans, and farmers enjoyed controlled markets, easy credit, and guaranteed purchase agreements. The PRI could then use these links to help mobilize electoral support. As Foweraker and Foley note, López Portillo shifted political control away from rural caciques and the PRI toward the Secretaría de la Reforma Agraria (SRA) and the Secretaría de Agricultura y Recursos Hidraulicos (SARH).[56] In a similar manner, Salinas grafted another layer of reformist institutions through Solidarity. Though disparate and overlapping, this combination of party, state, Solidarity, personal, and corporatist mechanisms provided a patchwork of institutions designed to support the existing regime; to divide, undermine, and weaken opposition; and to arrest the danger of fundamental political change.

A second and perhaps the most outstanding feature of the adaptive authoritarian regime is its incorporation or cooptation of change itself. Indeed, each administration has touted the need for fundamental change, set in motion a range of reform initiatives, and denounced the policies and practices of the past. As a result, past crises all seemed to signify a decisive political showdown with continuity viewed as a virtual impossibility. Measured change further fed this liberal expectation that change was on the political horizon, giving the appearance that the reformers were sincere in their desires to bring change. But this credibility enhanced the system's resiliency to surmount the crisis and contain the threats inherent in the political openings. Just as Salinas prompted an avalanche of praise by those sensing true political change on the horizon, so too did the earlier reforms of Avila Camacho, Luis Echeverría, López Portillo, and de la Madrid. As Molinar Horcasitas so brilliantly suggests, "Party hegemonic systems, behind their apparent stability, live at the edge of crisis: either they increase the repression of mobilized groups and social sectors or they constantly renew themselves to survive with democratizing."[57]

A final feature of Mexico's "adaptive authoritarianism" is the abundance of "failed" reforms. As numerous analysts of the various internal reforms of the PRI have shown, none of the attempted reforms fundamentally

altered the nature, structure, or operation of the hegemonic party. The reforms launched with great fanfare by Madrazo, Reyes Heroles, Sansores,
and others were all discontinued following decisive political showdowns
that threatened the more entrenched interests within the party. In like manner, none of the countless anticorruption campaigns effectively reduced the
presence of corruption; and none of the electoral/political reforms conclu-
sively ushered in democracy, despite the stated intent of their authors and
predictions by the analysts. Indeed, many of the complaints about electoral
fraud and irregularities heard a half century ago continue to be voiced today.

To be sure, such reform efforts can be considered failures only if
judged by the rhetorical criteria accompanying them. If the survivability of
the regime is used as the sole criterion, however, then their introduction
and subsequent discontinuance is a sign of their success at surmounting
the political dilemmas that produced them. Upon reducing the pressures
for change (their primary objective), reforms tend to weaken and fade,
leaving the underlying problems intact. This reflects in part the tendency
noted by Hirschman for the reformer to "extrapolate progress to the point
where the problem is considered to be wholly liquidated and no longer in
need of public attention."[58]

The Components of Adaptive Authoritarianism

Before comparing past and present and exploring implications for Mexico's political future, it is important to first ask about the systemic features
that have facilitated the government's adaptive success over the years.
Based on the foregoing review, five factors seem prominent, echoing some
of the conclusions from Part 1: strong presidentialism, the prohibition on
reelection, the existence of institutional vehicles that can incorporate the
opposition, an expanding resource base, and ideological flexibility.

First, past reformism centered primarily on the president and presidential initiative. In each period described, the president played the central
role in maneuvering and bargaining to ease political tensions. The extreme
power of the Mexican presidency allowed the president to unilaterally
offer and withhold governmental benefits to select groups in a cooptive
spirit. The president could, at times, take from the PRI (or from key segments within it) and, despite opposition from within the ranks, enforce a
level of discipline necessary to effectively open space for the opposition or
other non-PRI groups while keeping the alliance together.[59] As Monsivais
contends, the government often "sacrifices some of the impunity of
caciques and business" to save its integrity.[60] Extreme presidential power,
moreover, enabled the president to change the direction of public policy
and alter the political agenda unencumbered by the party or the elite,

including denouncing the past and rhetorically recasting the ideological tint of the regime. The president controlled enough of the key political levers to give and take as the crisis demanded, thereby helping the system escape the dangers of intransigence and ossification.[61]

An important ingredient supporting presidential flexibility, besides the relative weakness of the party or other actors, has been the institutionalized turnover of the Mexican governing elite. Rooted in the principles of the Madero revolution, this guaranteed turnover supports two important components of the regime's reformist success. One, it prevents the entrenchment of one group of elites and hence discourages their adoption of antisystemic means of gaining power and privilege. As many have alluded to in the past, the "out-group" simply waits in the wings until they have a shot at influencing policy and enjoying the spoils. Two, it enables the incoming government to distance itself from prior governments. Sexenial changes in Mexico give the government the opportunity to regenerate a sense of hope and renew legitimacy in large part by denouncing past policies and promising change. This sense of renewal wrapped up in the charisma of the presidency helps lavish the regime with reformist and nationalist credibility, which provides a reservoir of support to confront and respond to popular demands. Virtually all presidents have done this, perhaps none better than Presidents López Mateos and Echeverría, who insisted on reexamining the policies of the past and returning the government to its revolutionary origins.

In addition to the power of the presidency, the successful management of liberalization in Mexico also seems to have centered on the existence of a range of organizational divisions in society that can incorporate, capture, and divide regime opponents. Similar to a strategy of divide and conquer, the Mexican example shows the reformist benefits of taking advantage of existing divisions within society and the political landscape to successfully coopt opponents. Divisions within the labor movement (CTM, CROM, CROC), among various organizations competing for governmental favor, among different sectors within the PRI, and among opposition parties— many in large part the result of past reformist moves—facilitated the ability of the president to effectively manipulate, offer, and withhold resources while balancing the competing forces. In the end, these divisions both enabled the government to play competing groups off against one another as a means to help guard against a unification of the opposition, and provided opponents with an outlet to express their political grievances. This not only helped temper their demands and contain the level of conflict, but also enabled the regime to coopt its opponents' ideas. Indeed, with no means to express new ideas or bring new leaders to the fore, such demands can fester and explode. Institutional escapes are hence necessary to dilute pressures and foster communication between the state and society.

Another element crucial to reformist success appears to have been an expanding resource base. The enhanced governmental role in the economy, particularly under Echeverría and López Portillo, provided the elite the spoils that anchored loyalty within its ranks, the material rewards that made their political arrangements palpable, the profit opportunities for the business community that bought acquiesence, and the plethora of subsidies needed to coopt a range of social organizations.

A final ingredient associated with the regime's historic ability to coopt change was ideological flexibility. Encapsuling strands of syndicalism, Marxism, Anglo-Saxon democracy, indigenous communalism, and even French egalitarianism, the ideology of the Mexican Revolution has been highly malleable over the years and open to interpretation. As Ross explains: "The doctrine of the Mexican Revolution is noteworthy for its complex, even contradictory character. . . . The essentially contradictory nature of various aspects of the Constitution of 1917 made possible an amazing flexibility."[62] This flexibility, in turn, enabled presidents to bend the ideology as the crisis demanded without undermining the legitimacy the ideology nurtures. Thus, emphasis shifted periodically in Mexico from social justice to economic growth to nationalism to stability to democracy, as the period and the crisis demanded.[63]

Comparing Past and Present

Examining this reformist past provides one means of interpreting the current crisis/reform period and speculating on Mexico's political future. The outcome of past reformist measures is clear; hence, if the current period is to support a different outcome (say democratization or authoritarian crackdown as opposed to adaptive authoritarianism), then this should stem from the presence of one of three determining factors: fundamental differences in the nature of the current crisis, differences in the nature of the reforms, or some type of underlying cumulative dimension to reformism.

As demonstrated here, the contemporary crisis and reforms were strikingly similar to those of the past. The emergence of the Corriente Democrática within the ranks of the PRI and the dissident candidacy of Cárdenas in 1988 were reminiscent of the crises brought on by Almazán, Padilla, and Henríquez. The rise of labor and popular movements in the mid-1980s in protest over the economic crisis similarly paralleled the independent labor movements of the 1940s, 1950s, and 1970s. And the economic crisis of the contemporary period was similar to the economic downturns recorded in earlier times. Likewise, the reform efforts of de la Madrid and Salinas paralleled those of the past. Both assailed the policies of their predecessors, embraced the need for fundamental political and economic change, attempted to reform the internal operations of the PRI to enhance its electoral appeal, attacked institutionalized corruption, pursued selected political and electoral openings, engaged in various populist measures to enhance their popularity, and relied on fraud and repression to maintain power. By the same token, neither truly resolved any of the nation's political problems or "completed" their political reformist tasks, and neither crafted a democratic transition or reverted to dictatorial control as had been predicted 20 years earlier and repeated ad nauseam during the intervening years. As demonstrated under Salinas particularly, strengthened presidentialism coupled with renewed clientelism through Solidarity and a partial (divide-and-conquer) political opening crafted the slightest renewal of legitimacy and faith needed to defuse the tendency toward antisystem polarization and protect the basic contours of the political system.

Despite these similarities, the crisis of the contemporary period was clearly much broader in scope and deeper than crises of the past. None of the protest movements from 1958 to 1968 achieved national, multiclass standing.[64] In fact, the contemporary crisis combined the most dangerous threat to the system—internal party scission—with deep-seated economic crisis and the lingering problems of the previous crises. Moreover, the reformist options available to the government during the contemporary period were more limited. The depletion of the government's resource base during much of the period prevented the immediate use of populist government spending to resolve the dilemmas, particularly under de la Madrid. The option of using repression also seemed much less viable. Though the levels of repression rose dramatically during the late 1980s and was an important factor—particularly in the countryside among *perredistas*, teachers, Indians, and independent labor—its role had diminished somewhat because of the presence of human rights organizations and the critical role of international public opinion. In contrast to the role of repression in crippling the postelectoral threats of Almazán, Padilla, and Henríquez, for example, Salinas had to contend with the *cardenista* movement in other ways. The availability of repression and even electoral fraud to cripple the PAN in the north also seemed of limited utility by the 1980s, forcing the regime to abide a number of local electoral setbacks.

The uniqueness of Mexico's adaptive authoritarian regime and the similarities of current and past reformist patterns complicate any assessment of Mexico's possible future exceptionalism. On the one hand, the saliency of constant change, political opening, and reform within the adaptive authoritarian model suggests that real change in Mexico may flow more from political rupture (via confrontation) than political continuity (via cooperation). In other words, if concessions to the opposition have historically revitalized and enhanced the staying power of the authoritarian system, then continued concessions, even in a democratic direction, could continue to forestall change rather than encourage it. If anything, history suggests that the adaptive authoritarian regime will continue to survive into the foreseeable future.

But despite this historic implication, it is equally plausible that adaptive authoritarianism contains inherent limits and that rather than preventing fundamental change, reforms merely delay it. This suggests a certain underlying cumulative dimension to reformism, as alluded to earlier. Concessions to shore up legitimacy and coopt the opposition, for example, however functional in adding to the longevity of the system, are limited to the extent that they do not threaten "real" political power. But each concession strengthens the long-term capacity of the opposition to press for more changes and may eventually lead to the big prize, when piecemeal concessions are no longer plausible. For example, although the government can offer seats in the congress or local offices to its opponents without undermining its real power base, the PRI cannot allow the opposition even the smallest part of the presidency to garner legitimacy and hence prolong the system.

Supporting this view is the fact that each reformist period has bought the regime less time, has reduced the range of subsequent maneuverability, and has spawned a countercrisis. Not only did Echeverría's adaptation to the crisis of 1968 unleash the crisis of 1976, but the political manueverings of both Echeverría and López Portillo contributed to the crisis of the 1980s. The López Portillo reforms of 1977 survived only until the de la Madrid reforms of 1985, which were then revised four times under Salinas. Because the PRI is forced by each crisis period to cede more political space, it is conceivable that finite limits exist, that the loopholes through which the PRI escapes will eventually be closed. Moreover, as the time separating crises diminishes to virtually nothing and each reform breeds a countercrisis, the regime's range of action is reduced. If the regime is unable to revitalize and regenerate the authoritarian system, democratic breakthrough or authoritarian breakdown then emerges as a likely alternative.

If we divorce the conjunctural and programmatic dimensions of the current and past crises, there is a clear underlying secular pattern that points to a gradual erosion of the PRI system and a slow march toward liberalization. Under this perspective it is conceivable that Mexico is embarked on a steady yet slow progressive shift toward democratization via reformism, with small quantitative changes eventually producing some type of qualitative change.[65] In other words, rather than stopping this erosion of the system's foundations, reformism has only been able to delay it.

If so, when will the system reach this limit? And will the final "crisis" that provokes fundamental change entail rupture or negotiated solution? Moreover, how will the reforms during this phase differ from those of the past? Will confrontation or cooperation work to produce this crisis?

Though each crisis has raised these questions and the expectations that change resides around the corner, history suggests that the pressures for change have grown, the opportunities to confront the regime have multiplied, and the adaptive potential of the regime has lessened. Much of this erosion of the system is taking place at the local level, as indicated in Chapter 7. Though this too delays the breakdown of the system, the rise of opposition in the states could eventually undermine the PRI's ability to control national elections and their results. Even nationally, the regime's adaptive capacity seems to have deteriorated somewhat. The dramatic reforms of the early years under Salinas though successful proved to be amazingly short-lived. Indeed, rather than authoritarian breakdown or democratic breakthrough, any "final" crisis within the adaptive authoritarian regime will probably fuse the two in some unrecognizable and debatable mix.

Conclusion

Just as stability does not imply the absence of crisis as noted at the outset, stability in Mexico cannot be equated with the periodic resolution of crisis and a return to equilibrium. Adaptive authoritarianism, as we have seen, is a type of political balancing act, a Machiavellian juggle featuring the minimum degree of change needed to survive without threatening the basic contours of the system. Reform, in other words, has been managed effectively in Mexico to prevent rather than trigger fundamental change. While the foregoing helps place the contemporary period in historical context, attention now turns to a cross-national comparative perspective to help uncover the key ingredients of the regime's historic and contemporary reformist successes and the role of international factors in shaping them.

Notes

1. Levy and Szekely, *Mexico: Paradoxes of Stability and Change*, p. 1.
2. The reasons for the constant occurrence of crisis in Mexico vary, though most tend to associate it with some inherent contradictions within the development model or the authoritarian system. With no true measure of crisis, it is appropriate to ask (as suggested by an anonymous reviewer) whether these were really crises or just called that by politicians and analysts.
3. The historical review provided here implicitly adopts around 1940 as the beginning of Mexico's contemporary political system. This does not mean, of course, that crisis was not present prior to this time.
4. Hansen, *The Politics of Mexican Development*, emphasizes the system's ability to contain elite conflict as one of the key ingredients behind regime stability. On the problems of presidential succession generally see Martínez Assad, ed., *Sucesión presidencial en México*. For more specific treatment of the problems

during this period see Medina, *Del cardenismo al avilacamachismo*. On the Almazán movement see Almazán, *Memorias*; and Meno Brito, *El PRUN, Almazán y el desastre final*. On the *henriquista* movement see Pellicer, "La oposición electoral en México, el caso del henriquismo"; Eisenberg "The Mexican Election of 1952"; and Rodríguez Araujo, "El henriquismo."

5. Officially, Henríquez was ousted for futurism or premature posturing for the presidential nomination (see Rodríguez Araujo, "La disidencia política organizada," p. 149).

6. Pellicer, "La oposición electoral en México," pp. 477–478.

7. Ibid., p. 478; Meyer "La encrucijada," p. 1329; and statement by Daniel Cosio Villegas in *Excelsior*, April 30, 1975, cited in Rodríguez Araujo "La disidencia política organizada,", p. 153.

8. Contreras, "Estado y sociedad civil en el proceso electoral de 1940," p. 116.

9. Pellicer, "La oposición electoral," pp. 480, 485.

10. Macotela, "El PRI y la elección del primer presidente civil," p. 132.

11. Rodríguez Araujo, "La disidencia política organizada," p. 166.

12. Molinar Horcasitas, *El tiempo de la legitimidad*, p. 36.

13. Contreras, "Estado y sociedad civil," p. 119.

14. Macotela, "El PRI y la elección," p. 134.

15. Padgett, *The Mexican Political System*, p. 50; and Bailey, *Governing Mexico*. For a general overview of early reforms in the PRI see Garrido, *El partido de la revolución institucionalizada;* and Story, *The Mexican Ruling Party*.

16. See Molinar Horcasitas, *El tiempo de la legitimidad*, pp. 17–60, for a discussion of the political/electoral reforms during this period.

17. See de la Garza Toledo, "Independent Trade Unionism in Mexico."

18. Jesús Díaz de León had accused Valentín Campa and Luis Gómez Z. of robbing union funds. Valentín Campa was accused of robbing 206,000 pesos from the CUT as well as committing an act of sabotage in Guadalajara (see Ortega, *Estado y movimiento ferrocarrilero*).

19. Topete, *Terror en el Riel*, p. 21, cited in Ortega, *Estado y movimiento ferrocarrilero*, p. 18.

20. Loyo, "La movilización syndical," p. 174.

21. MacLachlan and Beezley, *El Gran Pueblo*, p. 365.

22. The PRI faced three problems in legitimizing itself through elections. One related to the lack of coverage by opposition parties: the PRI often ran either unopposed or facing nominal opposition (see Molinar Horcasitas, *El tiempo de la legitimidad*, p. 71). Abstentionism was a second problem. With limited choices and the widespread belief that voting meant little, the citizenry often stayed home. The third problem centered on opposition protests of electoral fraud.

23. See Molinar Horcasitas, *El tiempo de la legitimidad*, p. 85; Middlebrook, *Political Liberalization;* and Bailey, *Governing Mexico*.

24. Bailey, *Governing Mexico*, p. 109.

25. MacLachlan and Beezley, *El Gran Pueblo*, p. 368.

26. Padgett, *The Mexican Political System*, p. 50.

27. MacLachlan and Beezley, *El Gran Pueblo*, p. 365. On the profit-sharing program see Purcell, *The Mexican Profit-Sharing Decision*.

28. The students demanded the release of political prisoners, the removal of the leaders of the police department, the disbanding of the *granaderos,* the elimination of the crime of *"disolución social,"* indemnization for the victims of repression, and punishment for those responsible. The demands of the students were

not revolutionary but rather democratic in context; however, as Sánchez Susarrey, *El debate político*, pp. 17–20, contends, the leaders of the movement were more revolutionary than the participants, perhaps even using democratic demands as a means rather than an end. For a complete analysis of the 1968 movement see Sergio Zermeño, *México: Una democracia utópica*.

29. There continues to be substantial debate as to who ordered the military to fire on the student demonstrators. One of the best accounts that suggest that the military itself took the decision is provided by Camp, *Generals in the Palacio*.

30. Sánchez Susarrey, *El debate político*, p. 20; and Middlebrook, *Political Liberalization*, p. 6.

31. Molinar Horcasitas, *El tiempo de la legitimidad*, p. 38.

32. Needler, *Politics and Society in Mexico*, p. 36. Most works, like Johnson's, *Mexican Democracy: A Critical View*, echoed this view. Perhaps one of the few to recognize the regime's capacity to overcome the crisis without fundamental political change was Hansen, "PRI Politics in the 1970s."

33. This policy of the government swelled the ranks of such independent movements as COR and the Tendencia Democrática within the electrical and railroad sectors (see Franco, "Labor Law and the Labor Movement," p. 114).

34. On such changes see Basáñez, *El pulso de los sexenios*; and Pereyra, "México: Los límites del reformismo."

35. Pereyra, "México: Los límites del reformismo," p. 31.

36. Much of the increased spending was targeted at the university. Between 1970 and 1975, matriculation at the Universidad Nacional Autónoma de México (UNAM) increased 108 percent and the budget increased 350 percent. At the same time, the university became a "privileged space" for the left and social organizations (Sánchez Susarrey, *El debate político*, p. 42).

37. Bailey, *Governing Mexico*, p. 21.

38. De la Garza Toledo, "Independent Trade Unionism in Mexico," p. 160.

39. Basurto, *La clase obrera en la historia de México*, pp. 274–275.

40. As the public sector deficit climbed from 2 percent of GDP in 1971 to 10 percent by 1975, inflation jumped from slightly higher than 5 percent in 1971 and 1972 to an average of almost 20 percent from 1973 to 1976, and the current accounts deficit rose from 2.7 percent of GDP to over 5 percent in 1974.

41. Figures are taken from Lustig, *Mexico: The Remaking of an Economy*, pp. 23, 100–101.

42. On the 1976 economic-political crisis see Basáñez, *El pulso de los sexenios*; and the articles in Maxfield and Anzaldua, eds., *Government and Private Sector in Contemporary Mexico*.

43. As noted earlier, this is the principal thesis developed in Basáñez's, *El pulso de los sexenios*.

44. Molinar Horcasitas's *El tiempo de la legitimidad* makes this point.

45. Newell and Rubio, *Mexico's Dilemma*, p. 123.

46. Pereyra, "México: Los límites del reformismo," p. 37. Alcocer V. "Fidel, sobreviviente," echoes the point, noting that the survival of Fidel Velázquez in the CTM is due to a history of "purges and internal repression, of the crushing of any dissidence or complicity with the repression used by the government."

47. Foweraker, "Popular Movements and Political Change," p. 11.

48. Knight, "Historical Continuities in Social Movements," p. 99.

49. The notion of symbolic cooptation was suggested to me by John T Passé-Smith.

50. Hansen, *The Politics of Mexican Development*, p. 203.

51. The pendulum theory was developed by Needler in his *Politics and Society in Mexico*, pp. 41–47.

52. Gómez Tagle, "Democracy and Power in Mexico," p. 162.

53. In her analysis of politics within the Federal District, Eckstein, "Formal Versus Substantive Democracy," arrives at a similar conclusion.

54. Pellicer. "La oposición en México," p. 477.

55. As Peschard,"PRI: Los desafíos de la recuperación," p. ii, suggests, it generally has been easier politically to change the party and electoral system than the internal operations of the PRI. This is because officials within the party have and can mobilize an important constituency. Given the absence of reelection, however, it is more difficult for government officials to build a territorial-centered base of support. Where they do, the national government can allow them autonomy in their region in exchange for national control.

56. See Foweraker, "Popular Movements and the Transformation of the System," p. 113; and Foley, "Agenda for Mobilization: The Agrarian Question and Popular Mobilization in Contemporary Mexico."

57. Molinar Horcasitas, *El tiempo de la legitimidad*, p. 81.

58. Hirschman, *Journeys Toward Progress*, p. 246.

59. On the resistance from the sectoral leaders within the PRI to the 1977 LOPPE reforms see Middlebrook, *Political Liberalization*.

60. Cited in Ortiz P., *La democracia que viene*, p. 132.

61. In characterizing the regime's stability, Meyer, *La segunda muerte de la Revolución Mexicana*, p. 70, points to the historic flexibility of the PRI, which he subsequently relates to the party's subordination to the presidency.

62. Ross, ed., *Is the Mexican Revolution Dead?* p. 11.

63. On the revolutionary ideology and its role in contributing to the stability of the regime see, for instance, Benjamin, "The Leviathan on the Zocalo"; Calvert, "The Mexican Revolution: Theory or Fact?"; Foley, "Agenda for Mobilization"; Hansen, *The Politics of Mexican Development*; and Ross, ed., *Is the Mexican Revolution Dead?*.

64. Meyer, "Democratization of the PRI," p. 338.

65. Hellman, "Continuity and Change in Mexico," suggests this conceptualization. Interestingly, this continuity view of Mexican democratization seems to assume that democracy and authoritarianism are situated along a continuum in such a way that democracy can actually be one small quantitative step away from authoritarianism rather than a giant qualitative leap.

9

The Cross-National Perspective

As noted at the outset, many authoritarian regimes besides Mexico's struggled with economic and political crises during the 1980s. This simple temporal fact points a priori to the role of international factors in shaping crisis and reformist options. Yet despite this common thread, reformist processes and outcomes differed. Generally, the military regimes of Latin America and the one-party, communist regimes of Eastern Europe failed to weather the political storm, undergoing fundamental change. Some changed in more abrupt, violent, and chaotic fashion than others, and many continue to face extreme difficulties in consolidating their new regimes, but virtually all transited from authoritarian rule to some form of civilian, democratic rule. Mexico, by contrast, exhibited a much higher degree of political continuity, maintaining its basic authoritarian structures and forestalling fundamental change. This difference suggests the presence of factors that work to condition an authoritarian regime's response to common external stimuli.

In an effort to place Mexican reformism within a broader context, this chapter offers a cross-national comparative perspective. Its purpose is to identify and differentiate the role of international versus national factors in shaping reformist patterns and the critical ingredients in Mexico's reformist experience. The first section of the chapter traces the common international factors behind the intense pressures for change and the resulting crisis of authoritarianism marking the 1980s. The second section contrasts Mexico's relative success at adapting to these pressures (reform preventing change) with the failure of authoritarian regimes in Eastern Europe and Latin America to do so (reform provoking change).

The International Dimension of Crisis/Reformism

Because all countries operate within a global political economy, international developments condition domestic crises and shape reformist alternatives. Briefly, it is posited here that the strong pressures for change (the crisis) marking the 1980s reflected a confluence of global trends that weakened the foundations of many authoritarian regimes. The scope of the crisis was largely the result of reformist measures adopted during the preceding decade. The nature of the crisis, however, was such that no easy reformist alternatives were available.

The Authoritarian State of the 1970s

Global trends during the 1970s were generally favorable to authoritarian states at medium levels of development or in the semiperiphery of the world economy. These states exerted a growing influence not only over international affairs—as manifested through their participation in OPEC, the nonaligned movement, the NIEO (New International Economic Order), UNCTAD (UN Conference on Trade and Development), and even the global diffusion of dependency thought—but also vis-à-vis transnational forces, core states, and their own societies. The period was characterized by national and regional policies detrimental to the global interests of multinational corporations (MNCs) and the incredible expansion of the state itself.[1] The state enjoyed the highest rate of growth during that time, becoming the major producer, employer, buyer, and seller within the nation.[2]

A confluence of global trends contributed to this pattern, ranging from the particular phase of MNC penetration into the periphery[3] and heightened competition and economic recession among core states,[4] to the declining hegemony of the United States[5] and cooperation among Third World countries.[6] But perhaps the most important factor shaping this trend was the massive transfer of capital from core countries to the semiperiphery, choreographed by commercial banks.[7] According to Frieden, this was "the most rapid, most concentrated, most massive flow of investment capital to the Third World in history."[8]

Among less developed countries (LDCs), external debt climbed from $63.9 billion in 1970 to $313.5 billion by 1978. In Eastern Europe, it skyrocketed from $6.5 billion in 1970 to $88 billion by 1981.[9] The flood of financial resources favored certain countries over others. Larger, more developed economies, particularly those with major growth potential (e.g., Mexico due to oil and market size; Brazil due to market size; Korea due to export potential) seemed to enjoy the bulk of these loans. Though some have attempted to associate the loans inversely to the level of state strength, it appears that the states that could take advantage of this opportunity did.[10] Despite cross-regional differences in levels of state autonomy or the nature of economic policies, the debt profile of major Latin American, Eastern European, and even East Asian countries followed strikingly similar patterns. Even the East Asian newly industrializing countries (NICs) generally touted as the "stronger" and more "autonomous" states in the periphery, relied on foreign debt to help finance their export-oriented development projects.[11]

The massive inflow of foreign capital enhanced not only the relative autonomy of these states in the world system, but also their power, size, and autonomy internally. With as much as 80–90 percent of the debt going to the public sector and the rest guaranteed by the state, the state garnered the financial wherewithal to underwrite its expansive domestic and international role.[12] Moreover, by freeing the state from relying on the domestic bourgeoisie for financial support or complying with the conditions and restrictions normally attached to foreign investments and foreign aid, the flow bolstered the state's level of autonomy.[13] Put differently, the state possessed abundant resources it could use in accordance with its own political criteria. Funds could therefore be used to promote national industry, exports, or the national ownership of the means of production; to purchase expensive military hardware, inappropriate foreign technologies, or lavish vacations for the political elite; or to shore up weak foundations of political stability and "buy" precious political time for their authoritarian regimes regardless of the long-term economic or political consequences.

The availability of loans during the period represented, in a sense, an easy reformist option. It helped support successful reformism and stabilize authoritarian rule in much of the semiperiphery. Thus, throughout Eastern Europe and Latin America, authoritarian regimes dominated the period, facing only limited opposition or threats of political breakdown. In Eastern Europe, the Stalinist regimes of Ceausescu, Honecker, Kadar, and Zhivkovan survived a third decade of rule—this time without relying on the deployment of Soviet tanks to do so.[14] And in Latin America, technocrats, the military, and the private sector came together to forge what O'Donnell termed bureaucratic authoritarian regimes.[15]

This debt-led swelling of the state bolstered the stability of these authoritarian regimes in three important ways. First, it enabled these regimes to sustain a high level of economic growth, which constituted the primary basis of their legitimacy. Both developing market and socialist economies registered slightly higher average annual rates of growth during the 1970s than they did during the 1960s. From 1973 to 1980, for example, Eastern Europe enjoyed a per capita growth of 5.3 percent per year, while Latin American countries showed a 2.6 percent increase. Overall, LDCs' share of world manufacturing output increased from 11.75 percent in 1970 to 15.5 percent in 1980, an increase greater than during the previous twenty years (from 8.4 percent in 1950). What is most significant about this economic record, of course, is that it was accomplished *despite* the international economic instability of the times, the lower rates of growth registered in the core countries, the high costs of imported oil, global inflation, and the inherent "problems" associated with the highly skewed distribution of income in Latin America, the "exhaustion" of import substitution industrialization (ISI), or the inefficiencies associated with "then-existing socialism."[16]

Second, the enhanced economic role of the state during the period contributed to authoritarian stability by augmenting the state's capacity to satisfy popular demands, guarantee obedience, and even coopt opponents. By freeing the state to pursue purely "political" investments over economic ones, it parlayed its economic omnipresence into programs and initiatives designed to keep the bourgeoisie politically at bay; coopt intellectuals, lower-level bureaucrats, and others; or make "preemptive" concessions to the middle class or the popular sectors. The expansion of the state's role for primarily political reasons under Presidents Echeverría and López Portillo in Mexico, for instance, was a typical response facilitated by the times. Even when relying on repression, as in the Southern Cone countries of Latin America, the regimes seemed to enjoy the support of the elite and middle classes, who benefited from the economic growth, and a type of international impunity, given their level of relative autonomy from international political forces.[17]

Finally, the shift toward state power aided authoritarian stability by forging the opportunity to postpone difficult economic and political reforms. Economically, Latin American and Eastern European states availed themselves of existing international opportunities (primarily debt) to breathe new life into their particular "state capitalist" and "inward-oriented" models of economic development. This they could do with little regard for the strategy's short-term or long-term impact on economic efficiency. Unlike the states of the core, moreover, they did this without making structural adjustments to the increased costs of imported oil. As one World Bank study summed it up, "During the 1970s external funds were often used to postpone adjustment to an altered international environment and to support the continuing pursuit of economic policies unsustainable in the long run."[18]

In Eastern Europe, more specifically, governments overcame their serious shortfalls and bottlenecks in the area of technology and consumer goods by opening trade with the West. Financed by cheap loans, trade with the West jumped more than 800 percent during the decade.[19] In Poland, foreign financing for the purchase of Western technology became "the cornerstone of Gierek's program."[20] Hungary followed a similar path to help "paper over" the failures of the socialist sector, a situation Phillips called "goulash/communism."[21] As Bunce observes, such external subsidies had a clear political function:

> Trade with the West offered the Soviets and the Eastern Europeans a way out of the dilemmas posed by too little growth and too many claimants of the surplus, by growing pressures for political and economic reforms that would necessarily undercut "Planner" and Party sovereignty, and by the necessity of moving toward capital-intensive growth and the provision of more consumer goods.[22]

Referring to Hungary, this is what Kis called the "the fatal policy of postponement."[23]

Though hardly facing socialist bottlenecks, Latin America nonetheless pursued a similar strategy. Alleviating the necessity to adjust the policies of ISI, foreign loans enabled Latin America to survive without increasing its export capacity, adjust overvalued exchange rates, improve economic efficiency of local industry, or ease the balance of payments disequilibria—problems associated with ISI that had arisen during the 1960s. Latin America's balance of payments difficulties, in fact, became manageable in the 1970s only in the face of cheap foreign lending.

Just as these trends made economic problems less pressing, so too with respect to the countries' political problems. The need to build stable political institutions, contain growing pressures, or even adapt to long-building secular changes of the postwar period all seemed to fade behind the facade of economic growth and prosperity that foreign loans helped fashion. In the Soviet Union, for instance, society had clearly changed:

> The social and demographic changes from the mid-1950s to the mid-1980s transformed the passive and inarticulate peasant society of the era of Stalin into an urban industrial society with a highly differentiated social structure and an increasingly articulate and assertive middle class.[24]

But rather than respond politically to these changes or adjust the economic model, Brezhnev, like other leaders in Eastern Europe, availed himself of the existing global opportunities to simply muddle through. Becoming a more active participant in the world economy, the Soviet Union used Western credits and foreign investments to augment its supply of needed capital and consumer goods.[25] Politically this enabled the regime not only to temper one of the major demands of the population, but also to avoid major dilemmas associated with the economic costs of its political system, the political costs of its economic model, or the costs of change.[26]

This was not a conscious policy of postponement, of course. Regimes did tinker with structural reforms, many of which resembled those of the 1980s; but the reforms were normally postponed or watered down once their perceived costs surpassed need. In fact, the "failure" of the reforms attempted during this or preceding periods provides just one indication of the authoritarian regimes' tendency to postpone hard reforms and yet survive. As Barkey demonstrates, efforts to adjust ISI in Latin America during the period ended up being only half measures.[27] The Kosygin reforms in the Soviet Union also "fell into disuse or were abandoned." Though such reforms "failed," as one observer notes, "because they threatened the interests of influential sectors of the bureaucracy and . . . they clashed with rigid administrative procedures of the established planning system,"[28] it is equally clear that they failed merely because the regimes and their leaders could "survive" politically and economically for the moment without them. Or as Barkey so aptly puts it, ISI in Latin America was not dismantled because, thanks to foreign lending, "the necessity never arose."[29]

A similar pattern, of course, characterized Mexican economic and political reforms during this period, as highlighted earlier. Though being challenged to incorporate the democratic demands of the rising middle classes following the 1968 crisis and deal with underlying structural economic problems, Presidents Echeverría (1970–1976) and López Portillo (1976–1982) employed available resources to greatly expand the role of the state, and then used the political spoils thus generated to help shore up political stability. The populist state of the 1970s subsidized an array of important groups in society, linking them to either the PRI or the state in corporatist fashion. Though many subsequently found Echeverría's program economically questionable, the point is that it was politically driven and, at the time, economically feasible.

Given the economic growth and the power of the authoritarian regimes during the 1970s, it would seem that this would have been an opportune time to make the long-term reforms that were needed. But politically such a course was not the path of least resistance. Most of the reforms elaborated during the period, as noted, were either eliminated or watered down because of the restraints. Thus, availing themselves of the existing international opportunities proved the most viable solution to their pressing economic woes and was far more palatable politically than more difficult reforms.

But while international trends in the 1970s crafted a successful short-term reformist strategy, it deepened many of these nations' problems in the long term. Indeed, neglecting problems and postponing difficult reform for a decade can hardly do otherwise. This meant that the reforms needed to resolve these problems would have to be much deeper and more painful than had they been made earlier. Latin America's continuation of ISI during the period, for example, deepened entrenched interests and became "transformed into self-serving policies." Agriculture further underdeveloped and the inefficiencies of certain national industries intensified.[30] In Eastern Europe as well, the inefficiencies associated with socialism grew worse, while bureaucratic and party elites became more deeply entrenched as society lost faith in the "socialist experiment." Along with their populations, the elites grew intensely cynical.

The 1980s' Decline of the Peripheral State

In politically reacting to the trends of the 1970s and pursuing their own interests, core states, transnational capitalist forces, and semiperipheral societies eventually reasserted their power, influence, and autonomy during the 1980s to the detriment of the authoritarian semiperipheral state. Core states (particularly the United States and Britain) engaged in a "competitive deregulation of national capital markets,"[31] restructured their fiscal policies, weakened their own labor movements, and increased global interest rates to reverse the flow of capital.[32] The jump in real interest rates from .97 percent average during 1974–1979 to 5.85 percent during 1980–1989, for instance, not only abetted this resurgence of bourgeois hegemony in the world arena,[33] but also threw large parts of the periphery into deep economic depression. This turn undermined the peripheral state's strength; its state-led, inward-oriented economies; and, consequently, its authoritarian polities.[34]

These unfavorable global trends brought precipitous decline to the economies of the semiperiphery throughout the 1980s. Debt servicing requirements, as a percentage of exports, increased dramatically, reaching 33.3 percent in Brazil, 36.8 percent in Mexico, 52.2 percent in Argentina, 23.3 percent in Hungary and 17 percent in Yugoslavia.[35] Coupled with a cutoff of foreign credit, this triggered negative capital flows, a precipitous fall in imports, and economic decline. In 1988 alone, developing countries suffered a net negative capital outflow of $43 billion.[36] In the period 1980–1988, as annual gross domestic investments throughout Latin America dipped 3.2 percent, in Hungary 1.0 percent, and in Poland 1.6 percent, economic growth plummeted.[37] The average annual growth for "severely indebted countries" fell from 6.0 percent during the period 1965–1980 to 1.5 percent from 1980 to 1988, while in per capita terms, Latin America averaged an annual rate of –.06 percent and Eastern Europe .8 percent during the decade.[38]

The trends had critical political effects. First, the economic plunge undermined the political legitimacy of the authoritarian regimes, precipitating an onslaught of demands on the state for change. Because an authoritarian regime's primary (if not sole) source of legitimacy rests with delivering the goods, such a turn of events is usually politically catastrophic. Dietz adequately depicts the causal chain in describing regime change in Peru: "There can be little doubt that the principal reason for the decision by the military to relinquish its power derived from its poor performance in economic affairs, which led, in turn, to a dramatic loss of confidence by the people in its ability to rule, and hence to its claim to legitimacy."[39]

Second, the financial-cum-economic crisis enhanced the objective need for capital and thereby empowered those with it: the IMF, the banks, the MNCs, the core states, and even the domestic bourgeoisie, where one existed. With enhanced bargaining power, these groups could thus condition their participation on extensive economic reforms.[40] With governments forced to adjust their economic policies to create an environment more hospitable to the global and domestic capital, the role of the political thus gave way to the economic as Latin American and Eastern European governments embraced strikingly similar economic reforms: fiscal austerity, the elimination of consumption subsidies, devaluations (or convertability schemes) of national currencies to enhance export potential (competitiveness), the privatization of public-owned firms, deregulations, and numerous incentives to encourage private domestic and international investments.

Since the state itself had acquired the debts or guaranteed them during the preceding period, the greatest burden of fiscal adaptation fell on the state. The state thus had few alternatives but to scale back its involvement in the economy and its use (or misuse) of society's resources. Such a move drastically eroded the state's capacity to mobilize support or coopt its opponents as it had done in the past and thus functioned to greatly expand the relative political space offered to society.[41]

In many ways, the economic reforms were incompatible with the existing political structures. Not only were those with capital explicitly demanding a reduction in the size and role of the state for ideological and practical reasons (the IMF; the local bourgeois), but the new economic course made continued investments of large sums in political directions unsustainable. In sum, it was no longer possible to maintain the economic or the political system. The economic crisis even made it difficult for the state to use repression to respond to the growing pressures. Though always a reformist option to maintain an authoritarian regime, repression would have seriously jeopardized the international and domestic support the state needed to deal with the economic crisis. Thus, with the authoritarian regime's means of sustenance removed and its alternatives greatly limited, the need for political change peaked.

In the Soviet Union, for example, Gorbachev, like other leaders, originally embraced a series of "perfecting" changes of the economic system in an effort to stop the nation's economic decline. This included such measures as a decentralization of decisionmaking power to the enterprise level. That his efforts were unsuccessful in the short term, however, led not only to the adoption of more radical economic reforms, but also to the view that the problem was largely political. As Gorbachev himself argued, the problem centered on "the repressive political system, the strategy of economic development, an over-centralized and cumbersome planning apparatus, above all a deeply entrenched bureaucracy jealously guarding its turf to protect jobs and privileges."[42] Political changes were needed both to garner legitimacy for Gorbachev and support for his economic program and to strengthen his political control over the bureaucracy.

In sum, the shifting of international conditions made political survival difficult. Just as debts had subsidized domestic economies and authoritarian states in the 1970s, domestic economies and the states were squeezed to service it during the 1980s. This not only eliminated the 1970s means of "papering over" the structural problems that had festered during the previous decade, but also exacerbated those problems and unleashed new ones. Coupled with the direct impact on the state apparatus itself, these changes challenged the existing economic and political institutions with a force unmatched in history, creating a volatile reformist dynamic.

The Paths of Crisis/Reformism

Though the international factors roughly outlined here played an important role in shaping the pressures for change in the authoritarian regimes of Latin America and Eastern Europe, the reformist processes differed. Essentially all the regimes were forced to embrace reforms in the face of these growing pressures in order to "relax social tension." But in most cases, this process of reformism led to further pressures that generated additional reforms, eventually bringing down the authoritarian regimes. In Mexico, however, the regime was able to contain the liberalization process, using such reforms to prevent rather than provoke further change.[43]

According to Przeworski's model of political reform, growing pressures on authoritarian regimes lead to a process of liberalization.[44] This involves the decision within the ruling elite to allow or tolerate autonomous organizations in society. In Eastern Europe, this usually occurred after repressive crackdowns were attempted. In Poland, for example, a repressive period that began with the December 31, 1981, military coup that outlawed Solidarity eventually gave way to "roundtable talks" in February 1988 that dealt with the dissident labor union. This was followed by the regime of Jaruzelski passing an amnesty law that signaled the de facto legalization of the opposition. In Hungary in 1989, growing popular pressures similarly led the regime of Karoly Grosz to legalize noncommunist organizations. In Czechoslovakia in December 1989, following the rise of the New Civic Forum and the massive rally of 250,000 in the streets of Prague demanding the resignation of the government, the new prime minister, Ladislav Adamec, named a cabinet that incorporated five noncommunists. In the Soviet Union, Gorbachev launched glasnost (the relaxation of press controls, an opening of social space to the church, criticism of the past, etc.), which led to the formation of groups independent of the state.

In most of Eastern Europe, the decision to liberalize stemmed in part from the removal of the major restraint on change that had undermined reforms in the 1960s: the threat of Soviet intervention. Reflecting the Soviet Union's own economic problems, Gorbachev indicated during 1988 and 1989 that the Soviet Union would not interfere "in the internal affairs of other states under any pretext" and that "there are no universal models of socialism."[45] This decision undermined the position of the hard-liners within Europe and hence helped shift power to the more moderate elements. The moderates not only favored basic economic and political changes, but had much less of a stake in the existing regime to protect.

(Initial liberalizations were intended, of course, to contain the pressures and alleviate the need for change rather than provoke change. This can be accomplished, as in Mexico, by incorporating the "new groups" into the regime. This was tried in most cases. In Poland, for example, the strategy initially was to create democratic institutions at the lower administrative levels. Later the regime allowed Solidarity to compete in elections but limited its presence to 35 percent of the legislature. In East Germany and Czechoslovakia, similar piecemeal measures to incorporate dissents included the naming of noncommunists to the cabinet. The Soviet Union also attempted to tame the crisis by creating new "democratic" political institutions. In March 1989, Gorbachev, before allowing opposition parties to form, created the Congress of People's Deputies, or People's Congress (PC). This opened political space for a host of noncommunists, including such longtime dissidents as Sakharov and Shevardnadze, in an attempt to dissipate the pressures.)

But liberalization, as Przeworski argues, is "inherently unstable" because the lessening of repression opens the way for more and more opposition.[46] This, the "de Tocqueville principle," was clearly the pattern in Eastern Europe and Latin America. Within less than a year, for example, glasnost resulted in the establishment of over 30,000 independent organizations in the Soviet Union. In Hungary, the legalization of noncommunist parties gave way to a march of 75,000 in Budapest demanding free elections and the withdrawal of Soviet troops. In Poland, the new elections in 1989 that allowed Solidarity to participate first prompted a "partnerlike cooperation" with the communists but eventually gave way to the naming of noncommunist Tadeusz Mazowiecki as prime minister and the election of Lech Walesa as president.

As liberalization failed to contain the growing pressures, the ruling elites were forced to democratize. A period of extrication ensued in which moderates within the regime basically attempted to trade political change for some level of continuity. Continuity ranged from allowing the hegemonic party to compete in elections (and perhaps win, as occurred in Bulgaria); to allowing the military to remain intact (throughout Eastern Europe and Latin America) and enjoy important checks on the exercise of political power (Brazil, Chile); to allowing a continuity of leadership (Soviet Union). Even following the eventual disintegration of the Soviet Union, former members of the Communist Party (CPSU), like Russian president Boris Yeltsin, remained as the new republic leaders.

The timing and sequences differed greatly among countries. What took years in Poland, for instance, took just weeks and days in East Germany and Czechoslovakia. The Soviet Union, for reasons to be examined shortly, delayed final breakdown through a series of reforms until late 1991, almost two years after most of Eastern Europe had completed the task. In Latin America, similarly, the process was more rapid in Argentina than Brazil, owing to the military's humiliation during the Malvinas war. In Chile, the military seemed to stave off political change longer than the Brazilian regime.[47] In all these cases, hard-liners and reformists proved capable of resisting breakdown, but only for a short time. Where hard-liners ruled, as in East Germany and Czechoslovakia, the regime resisted liberalization longer than in Poland or Hungary. But even in these cases, the process could not be contained. In the end, hard-liners such as Ceauşescu as well as soft-liners like Gorbachev were unable to strategically deploy negative or positive reforms to stem the tide.

Mexico, of course, followed in many ways the same sequence as the other authoritarian regimes. Growing pressures (popular and objective) for change during the 1980s led to a series of economic reforms and to political opening, but the regime was more successful at incorporating the pressures and withstanding them. Consequently, the degree of political continuity in Mexico (reformist success) surpasses that of any other authoritarian regime under analysis. Not only was Mexico able to tame the dangers of liberalization during the 1980s but, as indicated in Chapter 8, it has consistently done this in the past.

Soviet and Mexican Reformism

The similarities and differences between the reformist process in Mexico and the Soviet Union are illustrative. First, in both cases reformist leaders concentrated political power. Early on in his term, Gorbachev, like Salinas, used his power to remove both conservatives and liberals opposed to his gradual reformist program. During Gorbachev's first year, for example, fourteen of twenty-three department heads in the Central Committee were replaced and four of fourteen leaders of republic parties. In November 1987, even Yeltsin was demoted from head of Moscow party organization and then removed from the Politburo three months later. In September 1988, Gorbachev removed Ligachev from secretary of ideology and placed himself as chair of the Presidium of the Supreme Soviet. At the same time, he reorganized the CPSU, transferring control from individual secretariats to six policy commissions led by his own supporters. In April 1989, seventy-two full members and twenty-four candidate members of the Central Committee were forced to step down. In July 1990, Gorbachev had the rules of the CPSU altered to allow the full congress the right to select the Politburo and the general secretary instead of the Central Committee. Finally, in September 1990, Gorbachev obtained emergency powers from the Supreme Soviet to rule by decree. Much of this concentration entailed a consequent erosion of the power of the hegemonic political party.

Second, both leaders used political openings to try to garner popular support and harness the pressures of society for political change. In both cases, this included a denunciation of past policies and practices. In the Soviet Union, the opening involved glasnost and the creation in early 1989 of the PC, based in large part on competitive elections, though no opposition parties. A crucial part of Gorbachev's political opening, glasnost or disclosure, involved a relaxation of state censorship, a denunciation of the policies of the past, the release of political prisoners, and a freeing of the church. This supplement to the process of de-Stalinization that had stalled during the Brezhnev years found Gorbachev distancing himself from the policies and practices of the past and exerting pressure on the more deeply entrenched conservatives within the party and the bureaucracy. The creation of the PC was designed to incorporate popular demands, garner legitimacy, and strengthen Gorbachev's push for reforms. Though many of the CPSU lost in the elections, the congress itself was supportive of Gorbachev, electing him as president by a wide margin.

Finally, both leaders attempted to play the middle to stave off polarization. But Gorbachev was unable to protect his centrist position and keep the system intact as Salinas did. Instead, a polarization of the republics emerged. Beginning with anti-Russian protests in Kazakhstan in late 1986, glasnost unleashed pent-up national sentiments, uniting political movements at the republic level and prompting the republics to usurp federal political authority. As one observer notes, the reforms "brought to the surface long-simmering resentments among Russians and non-Russians alike that exploded with stunning force from Alma Ata to the Baltic to Armenia and Azerbaijan."[48]

This process moved in a rapid step-by-step process. Initially, popular protests erupted, marking key historic dates. In August 1987, for instance, people in the Baltics protested their incorporation into the Soviet Union. In February 1989, a similar demonstration in Tiblisi marked the sixty-eighth anniversary of the annexation of Georgia. Subsequently, the governments of the republics recognized the existence of nationalist fronts, thereby breaking the monopoly of the Communist Party. These soon become important political forces and vehicles for independence. By 1989, the popular fronts in Estonia, Latvia, and Lithuania won a majority of the seats in the Congress of People's Deputies. Just months later, the Ukrainian nationalist front was created. Later, in March 1990, the popular front Sajudia won the Lithuanian Supreme Soviet and formed the republic's first noncommunist government. Finally, the republics began to break their ties to the Soviet Union through legal means. Beginning with legislation making local language the official language (instead of Russian) adopted by Estonia, Lithuania, Latvia, Kirghizia, Moldavia, Uzbekistan, and Ukraine during 1989, the republics went one step further by granting themselves the legal right to ignore Soviet law. Beginning with the November 1989 decision by the Estonian government to ignore Soviet laws that conflict with those of Estonia, the government of Lithuania voted to declare its independence from the Soviet Union. Later, the Russian government declared its sovereignty over its own territory and resources and implemented a "shock therapy" reform of the economy. In April 1991, Armenia and Georgia also declared their independence.

To an extent, the nationalist movements revolved not only around repressed nationalist sentiment. In Russia, for example, the "nationalist" context merely provided a vehicle for liberals ousted by Gorbachev to challenge the national leader. Thus, in March 1990, Yeltsin and other liberals won the Russian Supreme Soviet and took control of the major cities. Three months later, Yeltsin, Popov (mayor of Moscow), and Sobchak (mayor of Leningrad) resigned from the CPSU. By June 1991, Yeltsin was elected as the executive president of Russia, a position that would enable him to effectively challenge the power of Gorbachev.

The growing centrifugal pressures provoked even more extensive political change at the national level. In February 1990, Gorbachev called for the elimination of the party's constitutional monopoly on power as well as sweeping economic reforms (again to salvage what might be saved, rather than destroy the system). By the end of the year, however, the situation had deteriorated even further. By this time the reform process clearly had developed a life of its own and had gone "far beyond what the leadership envisioned."[49]

A final, almost poetic, contrast between Mexico and the Soviet Union: On August 19, 1991, the conservative forces in the Soviet Union made one last reformist attempt to keep the system from crumbling. The coup failed. Although Gorbachev returned to power, the central government had lost all authority and within a few months Gorbachev himself resigned and the country dissolved. On this same day in Mexico, midterm elections were held in which Salinas staged a credible recovery for the PRI. Though conflict continued, the regime was clearly far more successful than the Soviet regime in using reforms to forestall change.

Contrasts and Determinants

Comparing Mexico to these other cases highlights a range of factors shaping a regime's ability to use reforms to prevent change. Many echo the conclusions of prior chapters. One important ingredient was economic recovery.

Though requiring a substantial period of time, Mexico's fiscal and structural reforms eventually attracted sufficient foreign capital to help stage a mild recovery, as shown. This not only brought a degree of reformist legitimacy to Salinas, but also provided the regime with the economic wherewithal to address many of its political problems. In Eastern Europe, most Latin American countries, and the Soviet Union, however, economic recovery was elusive during the critical years. Gorbachev, for instance, faced a deteriorating economy, which further undermined his own support and prompted the various republics to view independence as economically more feasible than unity.

Much of this reflected different starting points and a critical international dimension. The state-dominated socialist economies of Eastern Europe clearly had farther to travel to restore growth than did the Mexican economy. By the same token, Mexico enjoyed a level of international support that was absent in most other cases. On the one hand, Mexico received economic and financial assistance from the U.S. government. In bilateral terms, Mexico enjoyed a handful of emergency loans to stabilize the currency and prevent a run on the peso, including a multibillion-dollar package following the 1988 election and the 1994 assassination of Colosio; it was the first to enjoy debt relief under the Baker Plan in the mid-1980s and the Brady Plan in 1989, and the first developing country to sign a free trade agreement under Bush's Enterprise for the Americas Initiative. More specifically, it was the largest recipient of assistance under the General Sales Management (GSM) program of the Department of Agriculture ($1.2 billion in 1988), accounting for a fifth of the entire GSM-102 program in 1992; it stood as the largest benefactor of Export-Import Bank finances, accounting for more than 25 percent of the loans financed in 1992, with almost 20 percent of those loans going to PEMEX; and it received economic and food aid from the U.S. Agency for International Development (USAID), including $40.6 million in economic assistance and $27 million in food aid in 1992 alone. Moreover, it was the largest recipient of drug-related assistance, receiving $150.3 million in aid from 1978 to 1990, with over half of that since 1986. This special treatment also came through in international forums where the United States exercised considerable influence. Under Salinas, for example, Mexico ranked first in total non-poverty lending by the World Bank, becoming the bank's largest recipient in 1992.[50]

On the other hand, the United States provided such assistance without mounting significant pressures for political change or making political change a prerequisite for these concessions. As Russell notes, a "lack of any visible concern for democratic process in Mexico was one of the most highly criticized aspects of the Bush-Salinas relationship."[51] This was particularly notable following the 1988 rise of Cárdenas. Reagan, after all, had resented Mexico's position on Central America, lashed out against official corruption, and even developed a certain affinity for the PAN. Poor relations, along with the strident calls for free elections in 1985–1986, however, ended after 1988. The Mexican government, struggling to enhance its political image, conceded to many of the economic demands that the United States had long backed.[52]

This pattern of international assistance contributed directly and indirectly to easing the economic crisis and the social costs of economic restructuring, both of which had critical political consequences for the regime. Besides providing the wherewithal for Mexico to address its economic problems, the United States' seal of approval legitimized Salinas in the eyes of foreign and domestic actors, bringing in foreign investment and sparking renewed economic activity. As Cárdenas once complained, "The economy of Mexico is being saved thanks to a political decision of the U.S."[53]

More specifically, this pattern contrasts remarkably the U.S. response to Soviet reformism and that of the international community. Though enjoying some trade and financial benefits from Europe and some humanitarian aid from the United States, such assistance remained quite limited. Despite the effort, for example, Gorbachev was unsuccessful at having the Soviet Union removed from the export control limits in the United States and the multilateral Coordinating Committee for Multilateral Export Controls. He was also unable to obtain IMF or World Bank funding.[54] Generally, international support for reform came after political breakdown in Eastern Europe, not before (or instead of).

Besides international differences, the differing reformist patterns also reflected differences in the nature of the ruling institutions. The military regimes of Latin America and the communist regimes of Eastern Europe lacked strong historical, nationalistic, and organizational ties to their societies. Both were relatively young—the military regimes of Latin America traced their origins back to the 1960s and 1970s, the communist regimes of Eastern Europe to the post–World War II era—and neither emerged from popular national struggles. Indeed, the Eastern European regimes had come to rely almost exclusively on support from the Soviet Union and on economic well-being to keep their regimes afloat.

This lack of social grounding impacted on the ruling elites' political alternatives. In other words, the crisis of the 1980s found these regimes with no institutional mechanisms with which to mobilize popular support or deep-seated feelings of allegiance to mobilize. Neither the military regimes of Latin America nor the communist regimes of Eastern Europe could appeal to historic goals, ride the wave of nationalism, or mobilize their supporting institutions to help overcome the crisis. Isolated, the communist parties of Eastern Europe virtually disintegrated once the support from the Soviet Union evaporated. The internal divisions within the ruling alliance (many since the 1960s had shown a preference for fundamental economic and political change) prompted reformers to ride the wave of popular uprising to turn the tables on the hard-line conservatives. With the economy deteriorating further, the old elite had virtually no option but to negotiate with reform. Such reforms, of course, opened the door for total breakdown.

The military, which dominated the authoritarian regimes of Latin America, also faced an option that neither the Mexican PRI nor the CPSU enjoyed: to relinquish political control without undermining its own institutional integrity. Not only could the military broker its return to the barracks and still be the military, but relinquishing political power became a prudent means to protect the military and its privileges. As one observer notes,

> Military regimes and their allies are willing to cede authority to conservative or moderate civilians only because they fear a more radical, popular upsurge, which would threaten not only their political position but their positions of social and economic privileges as well . . . if there is no popular struggle, no threat to move to more radical goals, the military will have no incentive to budge.[55]

As a result, the military effectively "preserved their autonomy" in Latin America and "continued to exercise tutelage over the political system."[56]

In Mexico and the Soviet Union, by contrast, the PRI and the CPSU had no such reformist option. Being something akin to a political party (civilian), relinquishing power would have clearly undermined the nature and operation of the PRI or the CPSU as political institutions. More important, relinquishing power would have stripped the parties of their only means of surmounting the crisis: their privileged relationship with the state. The parties were therefore less inclined to opt for the type of negotiated pact that prevailed in most Latin American countries and more likely to struggle in a reformist bid to hang on to power.

Variations in the existing institutional mechanisms within society that could contain the opposition and control liberalization also were important. In Mexico, the regime had tolerated semiautonomous actors long before the 1980s crisis, whereas most communist regimes, with the exception of Poland, had not. This limited level of social pluralism found Mexico with a range of labor confederations (CTM, CROC, CROM, among others), peasant groups, and popular organizations that competed against one another for the favors of the regime. In Mexico at the same time were a number of ideologically diverse political parties that were allotted some political space and representation in the government and a semiautonomous business class, intellectual groups, and an autonomous church and press.

Such pluralism not only allowed outlets for opposition and dissidence, but also facilitated the efforts of the regime to employ a divide-and-conquer strategy to stave off polarization.

As shown in our historical review, such a reformist response was crucial to the survival and continuity of the Mexican regime. The Soviet Union, however, supported virtually no outlets for the dissipation of opposition. The CPSU's monopoly on power, though in a sense equal to the PRI's in Mexico, included a complete ban on competing political parties. Hence it was forced to liberalize but did not enjoy the institutional mechanisms needed to contain it. As a result, this released many pent-up pressures, which intensified because of the widespread fear that the gates could close at any minute. This also fomented higher levels of social polarization and encouraged a strategy of confrontation rather than cooperation. Thus, as controls eased, the onslaught led rapidly to the conclusion by the new actors that change was more important than continuity. As it was, they had little institutional stake in the existing system.

Two caveats arise from this difference: one involving the linkage between political and economic institutions; the other, the political experience of the ruling parties. In the Soviet Union, the political elite held both the political and the economic reins. This complicated the task of economic reform. As one observer notes, "It proved impossible to reform them [socialist economies] largely because the managers were so closely tied to the ruling political machinery."[57] More important, this meant that economic reforms to restore growth would require extensive political reforms, a conclusion Gorbachev arrived at in 1987: "There was no way out of the [economic] crisis within the existing political and economic arrangements."[58] The political option of satisfying party and government bureaucrats with spoils and the population with consumer goods, both paid for by an economic opening to the West—the prevailing strategy during the Brezhnev years—was no longer viable and had to be replaced. The pillars of Soviet political stability marking the 1970s thus became the fetters of economic change for the 1980s. Glasnost was aimed at paving the way for economic restructuring. The separation of an economic and political elite in Mexico, by contrast, meant that economic reforms could be pursued more easily and with only limited political changes. Indeed, such reforms could be undertaken while leaving many of the political privileges of the PRI-based elite intact.

The second caveat relates to the relative inexperience of the CPSU in mobilizing for elections or controlling their outcome. During the critical March 1989 election of the Congress of People's Deputies, for instance, the CPSU did not effectively control the levers necessary to guarantee the victory of entrenched communists or the defeat of liberal reformists. This inexperience contributed to their failure to control the political opening.

Mexico's PRI, however, had years of experience at manipulating the electoral machinery to its own advantage, allowing it to hold elections without necessarily ceding the upper hand.

A further factor shaping the reformist pattern in Mexico goes beyond institutional setting to the state's ideology and its flexibility, again echoing the conclusions from Chapter 8. The Mexican ideology encapsules the ideas of democracy, property, and pluralism. Though limited in practice, this meant that democratic reforms (rhetorical and real) were fully consistent with the regime's ideology and could therefore be used strategically (or coopted) to gain reformist credibility. This was important in convincing people that cooperation with the regime for a gradual process was more appropriate than confrontation, despite the common goals. In the Soviet Union, however, where democratic opening was tried but failed, the effort itself ran contrary to the state's dominant ideology. The ideas of legitimate conflict and political competition were totally absent from the writings of Marx, Lenin, and the Soviet constitution.

But besides its mere content, the Mexican ideology exhibited a much higher degree of ideological flexibility than did the Soviets'. "Communist economies were based on a very coherent world view."[59] Gorbachev recognized that the "theoretical concepts of socialism had remained in many respects at the level of the 1930s–1940s."[60] Such ideological rigidity had not only alienated the populace over the years, but even the elite had come to hold a limited respect for it. Much of this rigidity stemmed from the fact that the Soviet revolutionary movement was better defined and more tightly and rigorously organized than the Mexican Revolution.

As a result of ideology and ideological rigidity, economic, democratic, and opening reforms in the Soviet Union, although necessary to generate the political and economic reforms to ease the crisis, produced a clear ideological rupture. With policies and positions totally contrary to its ideological foundations, the CPSU, in an effort to save itself, produced an important and irreparable break with the past—a fissure that reformist events subsequently tore further apart. Mexico, by contrast, did not suffer an ideological rupture or historic break. Though pursuing policies contrary to the spirit of the ideology, Salinas not only continued to enjoy and mobilize the "capital of the Mexican Revolution," but also effectively manipulated it and redefined it in accordance with his own reformist agenda. This was crucial in enhancing the continuity for the regime.

A final domestic factor in the case of the Soviet Union was multinationalism. This played a critical role in the eventual breakup of the Soviet Union and reflected in large part the vacuum occasioned by the ideological rupture. With no historically or nationally based ideology with which to unite supporters (indeed due to the ideological rupture, many saw the reformers as traitors) and continued economic decline, renewed nationalism among the republics emerged as the sole ideological framework toward which the various opposition political movements gravitated. Nationalism, in a sense, became the dominant channel through which pent-up political demands could be expressed. This proved perhaps impossible for the authoritarian regime to deal with without occasioning an outright revolutionary situation.

Though rival nationalisms were not present in the case of Mexico, the process of change during the 1980s clearly had a regional dimension, as described in Chapter 7. Just as centrifugal tendencies spurred by nationalism proved the major disintegrative force in the Soviet Union, regionalism could be the key force undermining Mexico's adaptive authoritarian regime.

Conclusion

Any exploration of crisis and reformism would be incomplete without focusing on the international component. Because a state participates in a global economy and a competitive state system, its capacity to achieve its objectives (including reformist survival) is shaped by a combination of international and domestic variables. The analysis developed here suggests first a dialectical pattern among political-economic forces wherein global shifts engender a process of adaptation feeding a subsequent reversal. In a sense, it is precisely the reeling from defeat that becomes the necessary condition for future triumphs. Thus, the rise of the MNC in the 1960s, which put "sovereignty at bay," played an important role in creating the conditions for the rise of the peripheral state vis-à-vis the MNC in subsequent years. The rising power of the peripheral state in the 1970s likewise eventually gave way to a reassertion of core state power and a new "hegemony of global capital" in the 1980s. And the expansion of state power in the periphery in the 1970s fed the proliferation of social organizations and the informal sector, which eventually triggered a shift in decisionmaking authority in the 1980s. This dialectic view of change among both political (nation-state) and economic (capitalist) forces underlies a continuous interactive learning process and parallels the world system's emphasis on the nature of capitalist development and class struggle on both global and domestic levels.

But the patterns described here suggest not a continuous, smooth, adaptive process of institutional adjustment, but rather a disjointed course involving rapid and distorted adaptation. Krasner borrows the notion of "punctuated equilibrium" from natural scientists to describe this type of change.[61] It envisions long periods of stasis broken by a moment of rapid change and adjustment. This pattern arises from the tendency of authoritarian institutions toward maintenance, inertia, and path dependency.

Rather than slowly adjusting to changing realties, forces linger and institutions stagnate until an abrupt change forces a political-economic reaction.

Finally, the foregoing demonstrates the interaction of both international and domestic components in the reformist process. Though the pressures necessary to bring about the downfall of deeply entrenched authoritarian regimes such as in the Soviet Union are historically rare and shaped by international factors, only under certain circumstances can reforms ease the pressures and forestall change. As the Mexican case demonstrates, however, those conditions are unique and in large part a reflection of Mexico's exceptional institutional and historical configuration and perhaps even its geographical "curse/blessing."

Notes

1. On the global pattern see, for instance, Becker et al., eds., *Postimperialism: International Capitalism and Development in the Twentieth Century*; Evans, *Dependent Development*; Frieden, "Third World Indebted Industrialization"; Krasner, *Structural Conflict: The Third World Against Global Liberalism;* Lake, "Power and the Third World"; and Rothgeb, "Compensation or Opportunity."

2. Duvall and Freeman, "The State and Dependent Capitalism," p. 99. For a review of the role of the state during the period see, for instance, Bennet and Sharpe, "The State as Banker and Entrepreneur"; Evans et al., eds., *Bringing the State Back In*; Haggard, "Newly Industrializing Countries in the International System"; Stepan, *The State and Society;* and Trimberger, *Revolution from Above.*

3. According to Evans, *Dependent Development,* pp. 197 and 202, the peripheral state enjoyed a unique position during the 1970s to exert greater control over and extract greater rewards from international enterprises. This was due, in part, to the tendency for the "diminishing need for inputs of the transnational firm," particularly in extractive industries, and the general development and maturity of state bureaucracies to enhance the bargaining power of host states. On this changing balance see also Becker et al., *Postimperialism: International Capitalism and Development in the Twentieth Century.*

4. The heightened competition of the core states also eroded the bargaining power and influence of the core states and MNCs during the period. See, for instance, Bergsten, "The Threat from the Third World"; Gilpin, "Three Models of the Future"; Gill and Law, "Global Hegemony and the Structural Power of Capital"; MacEwan and Tabb, *Instability and Change in the World Economy;* and Pfister and Suter, "International Financial Relations as Part of the World-System."

5. This includes, but is not limited to, the United State's dismantling of the Bretton Woods system, the devaluation of its currency, and its growing trade and budget deficits during the decade.

6. On this factor see Krasner, *Structural Conflict.*

7. The transfer of capital through loans during the 1970s reflected changes in international banking operations, the development and growth of the Euromarket, the glut of U.S. dollars in the world market, sluggish growth rates, and the lack of investment opportunities in the core.

8. Frieden, "Third World Indebted Industrialization," p. 407.

9. Ibid., pp. 408–409; and Bunce, "The Empire Strikes Back," p. 38.

10. See Mastanduno et al., "Toward a Realist Theory of State Action"; and Snider, "Political Strength, Economic Structure and the Debt Servicing Potential of Developing Countries." Note that most of the poorer Third World countries were unable to take advantage of the global liquidity surplus, though they did benefit from increased capital flows from official agencies. It is important to recall that at substantial points during the decade, real interest rates actually dipped into the negative range. Given the world economic downturn, few alternatives other than debt were available to maintain growth (and political stability)—at least few as appealing as those based on debt.

11. See Frieden, "Third World Indebted Industrialization"; Gonick and Roth, "The Structural Location of Third World States"; and Haggard, "Newly Industrializing Countries."

12. Frieden, "Third World Indebted Industrialization," p. 411.

13. Evans, "Transnational Linkages and the Economic Role of the State," p. 205.

14. See Korbonski, "The Politics of Economic Reform in Eastern Europe."

15. See in particular Collier and Collier, eds., *The New Authoritarianism in Latin America*; Evans, *Dependent Development;* O'Donnell, *Modernization and Bureaucratic-Authoritarianism;* and Stepan, *The State and Society.*

16. Much of this growth, it should also be noted, was clearly linked to the debt. In fact, among the peripheral nations that took the greatest advantage of the available foreign capital, growth and development proceeded at astounding rates. For selected semiperipheral countries, for example, growth averaged 7.4 percent from 1965 to 1980, exactly double that of the industrialized nations for the same period. Brazil registered an annual growth rate of 9 percent, Mexico 6.5 percent, Korea 9.5 percent, Singapore 10.2 percent, and Yugoslavia 6.1 percent (see Gonick and Roth, "The Structural Location of Third World States").

17. Haggard, "Newly Industrializing Countries," for example, demonstrates clearly the leverage that loan capital gave the Korean state to dictate to local business groups.

18. Quoted in Pfister and Suter, "International Financial Relations," p. 250.

19. Bunce, "The Empire Strikes Back," pp. 36–38.

20. Gentleman and Zubek, "Economic Crisis and the Movement Toward Pluralism."

21. Phillips, "The Debt Crisis and Change in Eastern Europe," p. 23.

22. Bunce, "The Empire Strikes Back," p. 31. Also see Clark and Bahry, "Dependent Development: A Socialist Variant"; and Kis, "Turning Point in Hungary."

23. Kis, "Turning Point in Hungary," pp. 235–237.

24. Lapidus, "State and Society: Toward the Emergence of Civil Society in the Soviet Union."

25. Kaiser, "The End of the Soviet Empire."

26. Chase-Dunn, "Socialist States in the Capitalist World Economy," p. 518.

27. See Barkey, "State Autonomy and the Crisis of Import Substitution"; and Dietz, "Electoral Politics in Peru."

28. This and the previous quote are taken from *Monthly Review* 41 (10), 1990, p. 11.

29. Barkey, "State Autonomy," On the inefficiencies associated with ISI see also Krueger, *Liberalization Attempts and Consequences.*

30. Haggard, "Newly Industrializing Countries," p. 357; Barkey, "State Autonomy," p. 293.

31. Gill and Law, "Global Hegemony," p. 479.

32. This amounted to a type of bourgeois Keynesianism rather than social-democratic Keynesianism (see Gill and Law, "Global Hegemony").

33. World Bank, *World Development Report,* 1990, p. 15.

34. In an effort to restore its economic health, the core largely succeeded. Following the rise of interest rates, the United States attracted capital from around the globe, enticing its own bourgeoisie to invest in the country and initiating a positive inflow of financial resources from the peripheral states via debt servicing and capital flight. From 1981 to 1987, for example, private foreign investment in the United States increased from $398 billion to $1,253 billion. This massive inflow of capital financed unprecedented U.S. balance of trade and public sector deficits, supplemented domestic consumption, substituted for low domestic savings rate, fed widespread speculative activities, and spawned "the longest post-war economic recovery" in history. See Mack Ott, "Is America Being Sold Out?"

35. World Bank, *World Development Report,* 1988; and 1990, p. 193.

36. Head, "South-North Dangers," p. 261.

37. World Bank, *World Development Report,* 1990, p. 193; Feinberg, "Defunding Latin America."

38. World Bank, *World Development Report,* 1990, p. 181.

39. Dietz, "Electoral Politics in Peru," pp. 142–143.

40. MNCs, for instance, played one government off against another, obtaining important concessions like the elimination of the restrictive policies of the seventies, and even acquiring the state's assets at below cost through extensive privatization and debt equity schemes. The IMF, meanwhile, asserted greater influence over the peripheral state, conditioning loans and the rescheduling of commercial bank debt on structural adjustments, including the scaling back of the state itself (see Manuel Pastor, "Latin America, the Debt Crisis and the International Monetary Fund," for a critical overview of the role of the IMF).

41. This idea comes from Bratton, "Beyond the State," p. 410.

42. *Monthly Review* 41 (11), 1990, p. 8.

43. It is important to emphasize that the analysis here centers mainly on the presence or absence of fundamental political change (breakdown of authoritarian regime) and not what Karl and Schmitter, "Modos de transición en América latina, Europa del Sur y Europa del Este," refer to as the transitionary and consolidation periods following breakdown. Though these are critically important ingredients in the study of reformism, they remain beyond the scope of comparison here because Mexico has yet to reach that stage in the process.

44. According to Munck, "Democratic Transitions in Comparative Perspective," p. 357, the Przeworksi model reflects the O'Donnell-Schmitter model of transitions.

45. Roskin, *The Rebirth of East Europe,* p. 130.

46. Przeworski, *Democracy and the Market,* p. 58.

47. Brazil's liberalization process actually began back in 1974 ,with each step tied to control from above. During the seventies, this process found the regime creating institutional mechanisms for the opposition to participate and express their demands. This period of successful liberalization or reformism was eased along by the favorable international climate and Brazil's record of economic growth. By the 1980s, however, trends shifted in favor of the opposition, guaranteeing a transition to democracy. On the Brazilian case see, for instance, Duncan Baretta and Markoff, "Brazil's Abertura: A Transition from What to What?"

48. Lapidus, "State and Society," p. 139.

49. Sherman, "The Second Soviet Revolution," p. 18.

50. See Preusch and Sims, "Sobre el terreno de suelo extranjero"; and Browne et al., *For Richer, for Poorer.*

51. Russell, *Mexico Under Salinas,* p. 314.

52. The creation of a human rights commission (CNDH) in 1990, for instance, preceded not only the publication of the Americas Watch report, but also the Salinas-Bush meeting to announce intent to negotiate NAFTA (see Aguayo Quezada "The Inevitability of Democracy in Mexico," p. 123).

53. Cited in Russell, Mexico Under Salinas, p. 312. On this Faustian bargain with the United States see Cárdenas, "Misunderstanding Mexico."

54. See Watson, "Perestroika, 1985–1991."

55. MacEwan's review of *Transitions from Authoritarian Rule,* pp. 121–122. Of course, the nature of the pressures differed in each case. In Czechoslovakia and Yugoslavia, for instance, the huge mobilizations of the population forced a multi-lateral negotiation for a political transition, while in Brazil and the Soviet Union, the pressures from below were much less intense, allowing the regime change to be worked out by upper-level negotiations. As a result, the degree of continuity was higher in the latter cases. Though the nature of the transition is crucial in shaping the subsequent period, the point here is simply that regardless of the origins of the pressures or the nature of the transition, these regimes were compelled to change because of the nature and depth of the crisis.

56. Przeworski, *Democracy and the Market,* p. 75. For an excellent analysis of the continued role of the military in Latin America see Loveman, "'Protected Democracies' and Military Guardianship."

57. Chirot, "The East European Revolutions of 1989," p. 165.

58. See *Monthly Review* 41 (10), 1990, p. 12.

59. Chirot, "The East European Revolutions," p. 167.

60. Brown, "Ideology and Political Culture," p. 4.

61. Krasner, "Sovereignty: An Institutional Perspective," pp. 77–80.

3

Conclusion

10

Political Reformism
and the Politics of Mexico

Having survived crises once hailed as fatal and thwarted the pressures of
the 1980s that uprooted a host of authoritarian governments, the Mexican
regime provides an instructive case on the conditions under which reforms
forestall rather than trigger fundamental political change. I have approached the case from a variety of angles, from strategic choice theory
and a case study of the two presidential terms, to regional, historical, and
comparative analyses. Broadly, the study helps focus attention on the nature of political reformism, its characteristics, and the ingredients shaping
it. It also raises questions for further research and provides a framework
for phrasing them. As a case study, the analysis crystallizes the nature of
Mexican politics. Here too it raises important questions about our understanding of the operation of the system and, most intriguingly perhaps, its
future. This chapter addresses these themes.

The Nature of Political Reformism

The Mexican case demonstrates, first of all, the characteristics of a process
of successful reformism. Under a veneer of ambiguity, successful reformism combines change with continuity, positive with negative reform
measures, optimistic and pessimistic signs, and old and new political structures. From a sweeping rhetoric of change and attacks on past political
practices, to experiments in internal party reforms and controlled liberalization, Mexican leaders have constantly supported and promoted political
change without relinquishing control. But despite the many initiatives, and
the tiptoeing of gradual change, the major components of the political system have remained intact, largely resistant to fundamental alteration. Positive reforms provided adaptations, but negative measures consolidated
control, limiting the reach or scope of the reforms.

The results of this seeming duality are many. The reformist dynamic,
above all, casts both optimistic and pessimistic shadows. Riding the wave
of ambiguity, the regime seems to linger without defining itself, making

prediction a difficult game. This provides ammunition to both those choosing to cooperate with the regime to promote change and confrontationalists who seek change through a different route, thereby actually helping to keep the regime's opponents divided. This coexistence of change and continuity also results in a patchwork of political institutions. Rather than eliminating the old to make way for the new, the tendency has been to create new structures, partially marginalizing the old and thereby forcing them to adapt to the logic of the new rules. Hence, institutional remnants of reformism under Calles (revolutionary elite alliance), Cárdenas (corporatism), Alemán (capitalist alliance), Echeverría (state-society clientelism), and López Portillo (multiparty system) exist alongside those crafted by de la Madrid (technocratic takeover) and Salinas (Solidarity alliance and the "new PRI"). Though no single institution functions to maintain what comes to appear as a complicated system, they all contribute to that feat.

More important than the nature of successful reformism though, the Mexican case underscores a series of factors contributing to it: an indication of the importance of "where a country is coming from" in determining the process of regime change.[1] These include, above all, time-restrained presidentialism, a degree of independence between the political and economic spheres, limited pluralism, a strong yet malleable state ideology, and a conducive international environment. Unrestrained presidential power, as shown, provides flexibility, enabling the president to recast political coalitions to accommodate new groups—to coopt supporters, opponents, and the issue of change itself. The six-year *sexenio* sustains this flexibility by ensuring periodic turnover and a rekindling of the hope that political change can come through a peaceful, measured process without confrontation, despite the underlying degrees of political continuity.

The Mexican case also demonstrates the flexibility derived from an institutional arrangement that, on the one hand, allows economic reforms to take place without concomitant political reforms, and, on the other, rules out fundamental political change as an easy option to those in power. Unlike the military in Latin America, the PRI could not simply "return to the barracks" and protect its institutional integrity or its place in the polity; but unlike the communist parties in Eastern Europe, the Mexican regime was able to pursue economic change while delaying political change.

Closely related to this is the role of limited pluralism. The existence of nonmonopolistic organizations in society and measured autonomy projects a variety of institutional means for individuals to express their views and thus provides an important cushion against polarization. Limited pluralism facilitates the use of a divide-and-conquer strategy of cooptation and allows those so inclined (the non-coopted) an outlet for their discontent. At the same time, it grants the regime a critical channel of communication with society that can be used to coopt ideas and key leaders before it is too late. Moreover, by lending credence to the view that pluralism is permitted and that political change is one of degree and not kind, measured pluralism even ensures a degree of cooperation among important actors, thereby limiting the ranks of those adopting a confrontational posture.

The analysis also highlights the role of a strong yet malleable ideology in shaping the reformist process. Such a device weakens the potential for the development of an ideological counterhegemony while at the same time preventing the regime from becoming hemmed in by its own ideology. As a necessary component of political reformism, change must not only have a place in the state's ideology, but the ideology itself must change to accommodate, explain, and justify the political maneuvers needed to survive. Therefore, Mexican presidents have not only employed the "political capital" of the revolution, but have emphasized certain dimensions over others to support the political and reformist imperatives of the moment.

Finally, the analysis touches on the critical role of the United States in contributing to Mexican reformism. Sharing the regime's moderate and optimistic view of change when crisis threatens, the United States has provided critical economic, financial, and political support to the regime, helping it surmount the challenges of the times. While not necessarily downplaying the importance of democratic change in its policy, the U.S. government nonetheless has hailed the regime as either democratic or democratizing, and/or its leaders as willing democrats struggling against the forces of evil. This cooperative posture contributes to the isolation of the confrontationalists and hence the regime's longevity. Given Washington's historic policy of trying to protect stability, it is surely no coincidence that reformism has been so successful in its southern neighbor.

According to de Tocqueville, "The most perilous moment for a bad government is one when it begins to mend its ways."[2] Under such circumstances, the government finds that reforms actually stimulate rather than alleviate the threat, bringing down the regime. Whether the regime has never tried to "mend its ways"—so must "begin" to do so—or it runs up against severe rigidities and is unable to change, the outcome is basically the same. By contrast, the Mexican regime has seemingly been engaged constantly in the process of "mending its ways," escaping rigidities and thereby avoiding this "perilous moment." Whether that makes it a good government or simply enables it to maintain a bad one remains a question of much debate—a debate that is quite typical within an adaptive authoritarian regime.

Despite the effort to provide some comparative focus, a case study is inherently limited. The framework developed here and the case of Mexico hopefully provide some clues that may be useful in the broader endeavor, but important questions about political reformism remain open. Just as the

new regimes of Eastern Europe and Latin America will take years to consolidate and will continue to grapple with serious dilemmas, it will take
time and effort to understand the reasons they have adopted their current
course, the factors shaping their highly uncertain future, and the determinants of the consolidation process. Theoretically, it seems important to
combine the current emphasis on processes with past emphasis on structure and institutions, to discover how the nature of the ancien régime influences the process, and to incorporate a greater concern for the role of
international factors in influencing the process of regime change. Method-
ologically, it is important to expand the comparative scope geographically,
incorporating the Asian and African experiences.[3] It is also important to
further develop the longitudinal dimension by focusing on past periods of
crisis and reform. It is surely no coincidence that the intensity and scope
of the crisis of the 1980s would be such as to undermine the continuity of
many of the institutions and alliances crafted in reformist response to the
global crisis of the 1930s: Stalinism in Eastern Europe, import substitution
in Latin America, and the corporatist model of Mexico's Cárdenas.

The Nature of Mexican Politics

As an analysis of Mexican politics, this book underscores the nature of
Mexico's adaptive authoritarian regime and chronicles recent political
trends. From the "crisis" of the 1980s, to the shocking threat of *cardenismo* in 1988 and the stunning response of *salinismo* in the early 1990s,
to the shocking violence of 1994, Mexico has experienced an incredible
period in its history. Though the government is still racked by corruption—pressured by an array of civil organizations and political parties—
and elections remain questionable, much has changed. The economy has
been drastically restructured, foreign relations have been revamped, and
the polity has become more competitive and participatory than in the past.
    By exploring the adaptive nature of the regime, the analysis has raised
questions about Mexico's past and its future. On the one hand, the contemporary crisis raises doubts about past notions of Mexican politics. It
was once thought, for example, that economic growth was the key to legitimacy and that the nationalistic economic policy (ISI) was critical to
stability; yet the PRI survived despite the economic dip and the policy reversal of the 1980s. It was once thought that apolitical elections kept the
PRI in power and that once the PRI began to cede electorally, a snowball
effect would sweep it from power; yet the PRI has maintained the presidency despite the recent politicization of elections and the rise of opposition parties. It was once accepted that the revolutionary ideology and/or
the division of the left represented the keys to explaining the regime's

longevity; yet under de la Madrid and Salinas, the ideology could hardly be considered revolutionary. Today, even the adage "poor Mexico . . . " seems either irrelevant or just plain wrong. Likewise, the left, which momentarily united in 1988, providing it with a level of support unmatched in the nation's history, not only failed to bring about the end of the PRI-led government, but subsequently divided.[4]

Besides questions about the past and the keys to the regime's legitimacy and stability, the analysis also raises questions about the regime's future. The state, as noted, is now a shadow of its former self; legal changes have chipped away at the role of the PRI and the place for fraud in elections; and internal fissures within the party have become dangerously violent. These will play into the reformism of President Zedillo, who faces both old and new challenges. Like his predecessors, he has taken office promising fundamental political changes. Will he succeed or fall short? Will the regime continue to adapt to crisis, as it has in the past, using reforms to forestall change, or is it near the end of its adaptive life, tinkering ever closer to authoritarian breakdown and/or democratic breakthrough? Change is likely, but if so when? Is Mexico on the threshold of democracy or decades away? The fact that recent Mexican history is littered with signs of positive change, of visions of "things to come," tempers, of course, any projections about the future. How many thought 1968 would bring democracy to Mexico—or 1988? Even so, just because hindsight shows that past feelings were either wrong or premature does not necessarily mean that today's signs or interpretations are equally wrong. Surely it is possible that indications of change accompany both continuity and change, making them difficult to distinguish except after the fact. We are left then with many questions: When will change occur, what might it look like, and will we be able to recognize it when it does occur? Will political change be managed and progressive, marked by continuity, or via political stagnation and rupture? Will it be the product of the political leadership's goodwill or the confrontationalists' ability to corner the leadership and limit its choices? Will the PRI disintegrate, deteriorate, and self-destruct before the opposition is ever able to unite and oust it electorally? Indeed, will the opposition ever unite behind one candidate, forcing a clear choice?

The Mexican saying *"No hay mal que dura cien años, ni tonto que lo aguante"* (There is no evil that can last one hundred years, nor any fool that could stand it) as political graffito reads *"No hay partido que dura cien años, ni pueblo que lo aguante"* (There is no party that can last one hundred years, nor a people that could stand it). But despite serious internal fissures, factional violence, internal reforms, electoral defeats, and variable leadership, both the party and the people so far have done just that. Indeed, history and experience offer mixed signals: that the regime will continue to adapt through piecemeal change, but that limits to the regime's adaptability may exist. Change, they say, is inevitable, but is it any more certain than continuity?

Notes

1. Munck, "Democratic Transitions in Comparative Perspective," p. 371, emphasizes this factor in the development of a theory of regime transition.

2. de Tocqueville, *The Old Regime and the French Revolution*, p. 177.

3. On-going work by Brian Turner on one-party systems is a good example of important comparative work in the area (see, for example, his "Ruling Party Survival in the Breakdown of Single Part Regimes).

4. These hypotheses regarding the regime's stability or legitimacy are composites drawn from a variety of writings and, in a sense, represent part of the accepted wisdom on Mexico.

Epilogue

The First Hundred-Plus
Days Under Zedillo

The first hundred days under President Zedillo were in many ways typical of the contemporary pattern described throughout this book. The period revealed, renewed, and deepened economic and political crises brought on in part by the policies of the prior administration. It featured a bewildering mixture of positive and negative reformist maneuvers, including new efforts at liberalization and frontal attacks on those of the previous administration, anchoring both optimistic and pessimistic interpretations of change and continuity. And it projected an uncertain future, despite the regime's ability to survive such crises in the past.[1]

Enjoying a degree of legitimacy that had been lacking at a similar time under Salinas, Zedillo embraced the need for political change upon taking office. In historic moves, he named independents and even a member of the PAN to his cabinet, opened a political dialogue with members of congress—requesting that they play a larger and more autonomous role in the government, allowed the PRI in the state of Jalisco to select its own electoral candidates, and even initiated a dialogue with the PRD.[2] As Tim Golden of the *New York Times* noted, "With the economy apparently restored to health, Mr. Zedillo proposed finally to risk the power of his long-governing party with 'definitive' steps toward democracy."[3]

In a typical anticorruption move, the government also promoted a major overhaul of the judicial system. The measure, approved in January, forced the resignation of the entire Supreme Court, ostensibly increased the autonomy of the courts, reorganized the police forces, and established the means by which citizens could file complaints against corrupt officials. Enjoying multipartisan support, the measure was seen as a major strike against entrenched corruption and a key feature of Zedillo's reform program.

But the nation's economic health was not good. Three weeks into the term, Zedillo withdrew the Bank of Mexico's official support of the peso, allowing the currency's value to sink. The exchange-rate decision—and its awkward implementation—triggered a severe financial crisis that saw the value of the peso plummet from 3.4 to the dollar to over 7.0 by the end of the period. The peso's free fall and the ensuing financial crisis prompted a series of increasingly painful emergency economic measures, including a $50 billion bailout orchestrated by the Clinton administration, renewed wage and price controls, promises of further privatization of state-owned enterprises, and deep austerity.[4] Despite the emergency measures and the bailout, however, the situation continued to deteriorate, with no end in sight. Forecasts of deep economic recession, high inflation, staggering interest rates, falling wages, and wrenching austerity bolstered the collective sense of déjà vu.

The peso's difficulties reflected in large measure Salinas's pursuit of a policy of least resistance throughout the year 1994. With a slowdown of foreign investments because of the political events of the year—the Chiapas uprising, the assassinations of Colosio and José Francisco Ruíz Massieu, the uncertainty surrounding the elections—coupled with the nation's growing trade deficit, the Salinas government had dipped into the nation's international reserves—to the tune of $20 billion—to shore up the value of the peso. Apparently, adjusting the value of the peso was, at the time, considered both politically dangerous and economically unnecessary. But (unlike his predecessors) Salinas did not devalue after the election and before leaving office, thereby saddling Zedillo with an untenable economic situation. With reserves dipping below $7 billion by mid-December and faced with a debt bill of some $28 billion during 1995, Zedillo could no longer hang on to the exchange rate policy employed by Salinas. With few options, he chose to adjust the value of the peso and confront the political and economic repercussions.[5]

The financial/economic crisis of 1995 reasserted the conjunctural dimension of the crisis that had haunted de la Madrid more than a decade earlier. As occurred then, the economic crisis undermined Zedillo's and the regime's legitimacy, straining the alliances and agreements that had allowed Salinas to muddle through his term, and overshadowing the prospects of political reform.[6] Weary of austerity and feeling betrayed by the economic wizardry of Salinas, thousands turned out to protest the government's economic policy and its seeming capitulation to the demands of the U.S. government.[7] Corporate-based negotiations over the emergency economic plan also proved politically difficult, with labor leader Velázquez actually walking out of the negotiations at one point, again fueling reports in the press that perhaps the labor wing might abandon the PRI.[8]

But the political crisis ran much deeper than the economic troubles. Regionally, the government continued to confront serious problems and setbacks in a number of states. In Chiapas, the Zapatista rebels continued to pose a symbolic threat to the regime nationally and a real threat to regional stability. Though having failed to mount a national movement following the 1994 elections, as they had threatened, the Chiapas rebels nonetheless ended the cease-fire in late December, adding to the pressures exerted by the PRD in protesting the results of the state elections.

As in Chiapas, the government also faced serious political troubles in states such as Tabasco and Jalisco. As had occurred during the Salinas years, the PRI's victory in the November elections in Tabasco triggered massive protests led by the defeated PRD gubernatorial candidate, former *priísta* Andrés Manuel López Obrador. The president's attempt at a negotiated solution in late January, however, ignited protests from with the PRI itself. In the February Jalisco state elections, by contrast, the absence of fraud fostered the PRI's "biggest election defeat in its 65-year history" at the hands of the PAN.[9] The PAN won the governorship and swept the state house.

Beyond such regional conflicts, Zedillo also faced a deepening of the internal crisis ripping the PRI. Much of this stemmed from revelations that the assassinations of the PRI's presidential candidate Colosio in March and Secretary-General Ruíz Massieu in September were part of a "bloody rift between hard-liners and moderates within the party."[10] Indeed by the end of the one hundred day period, the attorney general had arrested more than a dozen PRI officials for the murder of Ruíz Massieu, including Raúl Salinas, the former president's brother. Manuel Muñoz Rocha, a member of the PRI's congressional delegation from Tamaulipas and considered one of the intellectual authors of the assassination, remained at large. At about the same time, the government also altered its version of the Colosio killing, once again claiming a conspiracy. Both cases seemed shrouded in high level cover-ups.

Like the crisis itself, Zedillo's reformist responses to the nation's problems were in many ways typical of those of the past. As part of the anticorruption drive, for instance, the president struck at former officials for wrongdoing. This included not only the numerous arrests tied to the assassinations, but, most spectacularly, the unofficial exiling of former president Salinas himself in March, following his clumsy efforts to escape blame for the nation's economic problems.[11] Such measures, designed to help Zedillo nurture his own reformist credentials, sought to distance the president from those of the past while channeling the public's deep frustrations.

Also typical of the pattern of the recent past, the government juggled a series of positive and negative reform initiatives. In mid-January, for example, the government resorted again to the signing of a new political accord with the major opposition parties, committing to another round of political-electoral reforms. The agreement promised a revision of the electoral law, new limits on campaign spending, and new regulations regarding the media. Meanwhile, in Chiapas, the government wavered between a hard-line military response and a soft-line political approach. After announcing a land reform program for Chiapas in late December and launching new negotiations with the rebels, the Zedillo government unleashed a new offensive in mid-February. The offensive included exposing the identity of the Zapatista rebel leaders, including the popular Subcomandante Marcos, and ordering their arrest. This offensive was followed, however, by a new cease-fire and a call for negotiations, and the issuance of a new amnesty.

Like his predecessors, Zedillo faces an arduous economic and political task. Lacking a solid political base, the president must forge a political coalition to surmount the challenges, but as of the one hundred plus day mark, it remained unclear what type of political coalition he might fashion and what reforms will be needed to foster or maintain it. On the one hand, the president could seek to reestablish and protect the alliance with the old political guard in a bid to surmount the difficult challenges, thereby weakening the early tendency toward reform. This is what he did during the campaign. Indeed, Zedillo may follow the advice and course of his predecessor: political reforms should await better economic conditions. On the other hand, Zedillo could opt to mold a coalition with forces outside the increasingly weakened and divided PRI in an effort to strengthen the presidency itself and the government's resolve to surmount the crisis. Downplaying the PRI during the initial years of the *sexenio* has occurred in the past.

Despite the intense drama of the first hundred days—the intrigues related to the arrest of Raúl Salinas, the travails of Mario Ruíz Massieu, and the exile of the once-popular former president—the parallels with the past are clear.[12] Though the regime is haunted by crisis, the government juggles competing forces and contradictory tendencies, and the future seems as uncertain as at any point in the recent past, Zedillo, like presidents before him, rides a political system equipped and tuned precisely for dealing with such problems. Still, as is so often the case in Mexican politics, the past and the present seem to portend different forecasts regarding Mexico's own future.

Notes

1. A host of newspaper reports and clippings inform this epilogue. Specific news articles are cited only when actually quoted or when just one article highlighted a particular event or interpretation.

2. See, for instance, Michael Wolff, "Zedillo off to a flying start," *Mexico Insight* January 8, 1995, pp. 20–23.

3. *New York Times,* December 25, 1994, p. 8A.

4. The aid package includes $20 billion from the United States, $17.7 billion from the IMF, $10 billion from the Bank of International Settlement, and $3 billion from private banks. See *Mexico NewsPak* 53, 1995, p. 6.

5. On the economic crisis see George Baker, "Salinas, comercio y devaluacion de la moneda mexicana," *Carta Economica Regional* 7 (40), 1995: 6–9.

6. See Laurence Iliff, "Zedillo in free fall," *Mexico Insight* January 22, 1995, p. 7.

7. One poll, for instance, found that 69 percent believed that the previous administration had deceived the public regarding the nation's economic situation (reported in *Los Angeles Times* January 18, 1995, p. 1D).

8. See "The Opposition: Old Guard 'Dinosaurs' Find Something to Roar About," *Washington Post* January 8, 1995, p. 25.

9. "Voters in Jalisco Spurn Ruling Party," *Houston Chronicle* February 14, 1995, p. 1A.

10. The quote is taken from Andres Oppenheimer in the *Miami Herald* October 12, 1994, p. 18A.

11. See Tim Golden, "Salinas, at Successor's Request, Leaves for Virtual Exile in U.S." *New York Times* March 13, 1995, p. 1A.

12. Mario Ruíz Massieu, the brother of the assassinated PRI leader Jose Ruíz Massieu, resigned as deputy attorney general in November after accusing the former attorney general and high officials within the PRI of a cover-up in the assassination of his brother. Later, Mario Ruíz was arrested by U.S. officials for customs violations, prompting reports and charges that he had been involved in a cover-up involving the assassination of his own brother, and that he had channeled an estimated $10 million out of Mexico.

Acronyms

ABM	Asociación de Banqueros Mexicanos (Association of Mexican Bankers)
ACUDE	Acuerdo Nacional para la Democracia (National Accord for Democracy)
ADESE	Asamblea Democrática por el Sufragio Efectivo (Democratic Assembly for Effective Suffrage)
AND	Acuerdo Nacional Democrático (National Democratic Accord)
ANEP	Acuerdo Nacional para Elevar la Productividad y la Calidad (National Accord for the Elevation of Productivity and Quality)
ANOCP	Asamblea Nacional de Obreros y Campesinos Populares (National Assembly of Workers and Peasants)
BANAMEX	Banco Nacional de México (National Bank of Mexico)
CANACINTRA	Cámara Nacional de la Industria de Transformación (National Chamber of Industries of Transformation)
CCE	Consejo Coordinador Empresarial (Entrepreneurial Coordinating Council)
CCI	Central Campesino Independiente (Independent Peasant Central)
CEN	Comité Ejecutivo Nacional (National Executive Committee)
CEPAL	Comisión Económica para América Latina (Economic Commission for Latin America)
CETES	Certificados de la Tesoreira (Treasury Certificates)
CFE	Código Federal Electoral (Federal Electoral Code)
CIDOSA	Compañía Industrial de Orizaba (Industrial Company of Orizaba)
CNAC	Comité Nacional de Auscultación y Consulta (National Reviewing and Consulting Committee)
CNC	Confederación Nacional de Campesinos (National Confederation of Peasants)
CND	Convención Nacional Democrática (National Democratic Convention)

CNDEP	Comité Nacional de Defensa de la Economía Popular (National Committee in Defense of the Economy of the Popular Sector)
CNDH	Comisión Nacional de Derechos Humanos (National Commission for Human Rights)
CNTE	Coordinadora Nacional de los Trabajadores de Educación (National Coordination of Workers of Education)
COCEI	Coalición de Obreros, Campesinos, y Estudiantes del Istmo (Coalition of Workers, Peasants, and Students of the Isthmus)
COFIPE	Código Federal de Instituciones y Procesos Electorales (Federal Code of Electoral Institutions and Procedures)
CONASUPO	Compañía Nacional de Subsistencias Populares (National Company of Subsistence)
CONCAMIN	Confederación de Cámaras de Industria
CONCANACO	Confederación de Cámaras Nacionales de Comercio (Confederation of National Chambers of Commerce)
COPADE	Consejo para la Democracia (Council for Democracy)
COPARMEX	Consejo Patronal de México (Employers Council of Mexico)
COR	Confederación de Obreros Revolucionarios (Confederation of Revolutionary Workers)
CROC	Confederación Revolutionaria de Obreros y Campesinos (Revolutionary Confederation of Workers and Peasants)
CROM	Confederación Revolucionaria de Obreros Mexicanos (Revolutionary Confederation of Mexican Workers)
CT	Congreso de Trabajo (Labor Congress)
CTM	Confederación de Trabajadores Mexicanos (Confederation of Mexican Workers)
CUT	Central Unica de Trabajadores (Workers Central)
DHIAC	Desarrollo Humano Integral Asociación Civil (Integral Human Development Association)
EAP	economically active population
EZLN	Ejército Zapatista de Liberación Nacional (Zapatista Army of National Liberation)
FAD	Frente Amplio por la Democracia (Broad Front for Democracy)
FDN	Frente Democrático Nacional (National Democratic Front)
FEPADE	Fiscalía Especial para la Atención de Delitos Electorales (Special Prosecutor for Electoral Crimes)
FESBES	Federación de Sindicatos de Bienes y Servicios (Federation of Unions of Goods and Services)
FICORA	Fideicomiso para la Cobertura de Riesgo Cambiario (Trust Fund for the Coverage of Exchange Risk)
FNC	Frente Nacional Ciudadano (National Citizen Front)
FNDSCAC	Frente Nacional para la Defensa Salarial y Contra la Austerided y Carestia (National Front in Defense of Salary and Against Austerity and the High Cost of Living)

FONACOT	Fondo Nacional de Cooperación para el Trabajador (National Fund of Cooperation for the Worker)
FPP	Federación de Partidos del Pueblo (Federation of Parties of the People)
FTJ	Frente de Trabajadores de Jalisco (Jalisco Worker's Front)
GATT	General Agreement on Tariffs and Trade
IEPES	Instituto de Estudios Políticos, Economicos y Sociales [of PRI] (Institute of Political, Economic, and Social Studies)
IFE	Instituto Federal Electoral (Federal Electoral Institute)
IMF	International Monetary Fund
IMOP	Instituto Mexicano de Opinión Pública (Mexican Institute of Public Opinion)
INEGI	Instituto Nacional de Estadística, Geografía e Informática (National Institute of Statistics, Geography, and Information)
INESER	Instituto de Estudios Económicos y Regionales (Institute of Economic and Regional Studies [University of Guadalajara])
INFONAVIT	Instituto del Fondo Nacional para la Vivienda de los Trabajadores (Institute of the National Fund for Worker's Housing)
LDC	less developed country
LOPPE	Ley federal de Organizaciónes Politicos y Procesos Electorales (Federal Law of Political Organizations and Electoral Procedures)
MDAP	Movimiento Democrático de Acción Partidista (Democratic Movement of Partisan Action)
MPT	Movimiento Popular Territorial (Territorial People's Movement)
MRM	Movimiento Revolucionario Magisterial (Teachers Revolutionary Movement)
MS	Movimiento Sindical (Union Movement)
NAFINSA	Nacional Financiera (National Finance [Development Bank])
NAFTA	North American Free Trade Agreement
NGO	nongovernmental organization
NIC	newly industrializing country
NIEO	New International Economic Order
OECD	Organization for Economic Cooperation and Development
OPEC	Organization of Petroleum Exporting Countries
PACT	Economic Anti-inflationary Accord
PAN	Partido de Acción Nacional (National Action Party)
PARM	Partido Auténtico de la Revolución Mexicana (Authentic Party of the Mexican Revolution)
PC	People's Congress (Communist Party)
PDM	Partido Democrático Mexicano (Mexican Democratic Party)

PFCRN	Partido de la Frente Cardenista para la Reconstrución Nacional (Cardenist Front Party of National Reconstruction)
PMT	Partido Mexicano de los Trabajadores (Mexican Workers Party)
PNR	Partido Nacional Revolucionario (National Revolutionary Party)
PPS	Partido Popular Socialista (Popular Socialist Party)
PRD	Partido de la Revolución Democrática (Party of the Democratic Revolution)
PRI	Partido Revolucionario (Institutional Revolutionary Party)
PRM	Partido de la Revolución Mexicana (Party of the Mexican Revolution)
PROCAMPO	Progreso para el Camp con Justicia y Bienestar (Progress for the Countryside with Justice and Well-being)
PROFIEX	Programa de Fomento Integral de Exportaciones (Program for Integral Support of Exports)
PRONAFICE	Programa Nacional de Fomento Industrial y Comercio Exterior (National Program of Industrial Support and External Commerce)
PRONASOL	Programa Nacional de Solidaridad (National Program of Solidarity)
PRT	Partido Revolucionario de los Trabajadores (Revolutionary Party of Workers)
PST	Partido Socialista de los Trabajadores (Socialist Party of Workers)
PSUM	Partido Socialista Unificado de México (Unified Socialist Party of Mexico)
SARH	Secretaria de Agricultura y Recursos Hidráulicos (Secretariat of Agriculture and Hydraulic Resources)
SCOP	Sindicato Nacional de Trabajadores de la Secretaría de Comunicaciones y Obras Públicas (Secretariat of Communications and Public Works)
SME	Sindicato Mexicano de Electricistas (Mexican Union of Electricians)
SNTE	Sindicato Nacional de Trabajadores de Educación (National Union of Education Workers)
SRA	Secretaría de la Reforma Agraria (Secretariat of Agrarian Reform)
STFRM	Sindicato de Trabajadores Ferrocarrileros de la República Mexicana (Union of Railroad Workers of the Mexican Republic)
STPRM	Sindicato de Trabajadores Petroleros de la República Mexicana (Union of Petroleum Workers of the Mexican Republic)
UNAM	Universidad Nacional Autónoma de México (National Autonomous University of Mexico)
UNCTAD	UN Conference on Trade and Development
UOI	Unidad Obrera Independiente (Independent Workers Unit)

Bibliography

Acosta, Carlos. "El causante, obligado a justificar lo que gana, lo que gasta, o a la carcel." *Proceso* 807 (April 20, 1992), pp. 6–11.

———. "Gobernadores, funcionarios, empresarios, líderes, caídos ante el poder presidencial." *Proceso* 782 (October 28, 1991), pp. 8–9.

———. "Se acerca 1991 con sus elecciones y no mejora la economía popular." *Proceso* 726 (October 1, 1990), pp. 18–20.

Acosta, Carlos, and Salvador Corro. "Más recursos para el gobierno, más beneficios para la banca, menos poder para los sindicatos." *Proceso* 798 (February 17, 1992), pp. 8–21.

Aguayo Quezada, Sergio. "Casillas Esquizofrénicas." *Siglo 21,* July 20, 1994, p. 2.

———. "Hombres e Instituciones." *Siglo 21,* June 29, 1994, p. 2.

———. "The Inevitability of Democracy in Mexico." In Roett, ed., *Political and Economic Liberalization in Mexico City: A Critical Juncture?* pp. 117–126.

———. "El Primer Tranco." *Siglo 21,* June 22, 1994, p. 2.

Aguilar Camín, Héctor. *Después del milagro.* Mexico City: Cal y Arena, 1990.

Aguirre M., Alberto. "Mago electoral en el estado de México." *Proceso* 910 (April 11, 1994), pp. 10–11.

Alba Vega, Carlos, and Dirk Kruijt. *Los empresarios y la industria de Guadalajara.* Guadalajara: El Colegio de Jalisco, 1988.

Albarrán de Alba, Gerardo. "Análisis con cifras de las auditorías." *Proceso* 924 (July 18, 1994), pp. 18–25.

———. "El PRI acaba la era Salinas derrotado, dividido y empantando en los vicios que se propuso superar." *Proceso* 910 (April 11, 1994), pp. 11–17.

Alcocer V., Jorge. "Fidel, sobreviviente." *Proceso* 800 (March 2, 1992), pp. 34–36.

———. "Salinas y su pronasol." *Proceso* 719 (August 13, 1990), p. 38.

———. "Tres años." *Proceso* 782 (October 28, 1991), pp. 32–36.

Alemán Alemán, Ricardo. "Clase Política." *La Jornada,* August 13, 1994, p. 4.

Almazán, Juán Andrew. *Memórias.* Mexico City: Quintanar Impresores, 1941.

Alonso, Jorge. *Arrollamientos y menoscabos: La elección federal de 1991 en Jalisco.* Monograph, Movimientos Sociales 7, Universidad de Guadalajara, 1992.

———. "Jalisco 88: Auge y desencanto electoral." In Alonso and Gómez Tagle, eds., *Insurgencia democrática: Las elecciones locales,* pp. 85–114.

———. *El rito electoral en Jalisco (1940–1992).* Zapopán: El Colegio de Jalisco, 1993.

———. "Sociedad y gobierno en la coyuntura de las explosiones." In Cristina Padilla and Rosana Reguillo, eds., *Quién nos hubiera dicho: Guadalajara, 22 April.* Mexico City: Iteso, 1993, pp. 173–218.

Alonso, Jorge, and Silvia Gómez Tagle, eds., *Insurgencia democrática: Las elecciones locales.* Universidad de Guadalajara, 1991.

Alvarado, Arturo, ed., *Electoral Patterns and Perspectives in Mexico.* San Diego: Center for U.S.-Mexican Studies, University of California, 1987.

Alvarez Bejar, Alejandro. "Economic Crisis and the Labor Movement in Mexico." In Middlebrook, ed., *Unions, Workers and the State in Mexico,* pp. 27–56.

Americas Watch. *Human Rights in Mexico: A Policy of Impunity.* New York: Americas Watch, 1990.

———. *Unceasing Abuses.* New York: Americas Watch, 1991.

Anders, Cindy. "The Electoral Game." *Mexico Journal,* July 17, 1989.

Anderson, Bo, and James Cockcroft. "Control and Cooptation in Mexican Politics." *International Journal of Comparative Sociology* 7, 1966, pp. 11–28.

"A New Hope for the Hemisphere? Interview with Carlos Salinas." *New Perspective Quarterly* 8 (1) (Winter 1991), p. 8.

Anuario Estadístico de los Estados Unidos Mexicanos. Mexico City: INEGI, 1991.

Arrendondo Ramírez, Pablo. "¿Apocalipsis político o parto democrático?" *Siglo 21,* July 21, 1994, p. 2.

Arroyo Alejandre, Jesús, and Stephen D. Morris. "The Electoral Recovery of the PRI in Guadalajara, Mexico, 1988–1992." *Bulletin of Latin American Research* 12, 1993, pp. 91–102.

Arroyo Alejandre, Jesús, Javier Orozco Alvarado, and Marco A. Casian Márquez. "Opiniones preelectorales de la población económica y politicamente activa de la zona metropolitana de Guadalajara." *Carta Económica Regional* 1 (3), 1988, pp. 1–10.

Ascher, William. *Scheming for the Poor: The Politics of Redistribution in Latin America.* Cambridge: Harvard University Press, 1984.

Aziz Nassif, Alberto. "Chihuahua: La fatiga electoral." In Alonso and Gómez Tagle, eds., *Insurgencia democrática: Las elecciones locales,* pp. 115–128.

———. "Electoral Practices and Democracy in Chihuahua, 1985." In Alvarado, ed., *Electoral Patterns and Perspectives in Mexico,* pp. 181–206.

———. "La fragilidad de la democracia." *Semanal* 113 (August 11, 1991), pp. 20–24.

———. "El movimiento obrero: Tan lejos de Dios." *La Jornada,* March 3, 1992, p. 7.

———. "¿Nuevo padrón electoral?" *La Jornada,* June 24, 1990, p. 4.

———. "Regional Dimensions of Democratization." In Cornelius et al., eds., *Mexico's Alternative Political Futures,* pp. 87–108.

Baer, M. Delal. "Electoral Trends." In Grayson, ed., *Prospects for Mexico,* pp. 35–62.

———. "Mexico's Second Revolution: Pathways to Liberalization." In Roett, ed., *Political and Economic Liberalization in Mexico,* pp. 51–68.

Baez Rodríguez, Francisco. "Elecciones: El fin de los zapatos y los cienpiés." *Nexos* 202 (October 1994), pp. 19–20.

Bailey, John. "Centralism and Political Change in Mexico City: The Case of Solidarity." Manuscript subsequently published in Cornelius et al., eds., *Transforming State-Society Relations in Mexico.*

———. *Governing Mexico: The Statecraft of Crisis Management.* New York: St. Martin's Press, 1988.

Baker, George. "Salinas, comercio y devaluación de la moneda mexicana" *Carta Economica Regional* 7 (40), 1995: 6–9.

Barberán, José, Cuauhtémoc Cárdenas, and Alicia López Montjardín. *Radiografía del fraude: Análisis de los resultados oficiales del 6 de julio*. Mexico City: Nuestro Tiempo, 1988.

Barkey, Henri J. "State Autonomy and the Crisis of Import Substitution." *Comparative Political Studies* 22, 1989, pp. 291–307.

Barkin, David. *Distorted Development: Mexico in the World Economy*. Boulder, Colo.: Westview Press, 1990.

Barta, Roger. "Changes in Political Culture: The Crisis of Nationalism." In Cornelius et al., eds., *Mexico's Alternative Political Futures*, pp. 58–86.

Basañez, Miguel. "Encuesta electoral 1991." *Este País* 5 (August 1991), pp. 2–6.

———. "Is Mexico Headed Towards Its Fifth Crisis?" In Roett, ed., *Political and Economic Liberalization in Mexico*, pp. 95–117.

———. *El pulso de los sexenios: 20 años de crisis en México*. Mexico City: Siglo Veintiuno, 1990.

Basurto, Jorge. *La clase obrera en la historia de México. En el régimen de Echeverría: Rebelión o independencia*. Mexico City: Siglo Veintiuno, 1983.

Bazdresch, Carlos, and Carlos Elizondo. "Privatization: The Mexican Case." Texas University Papers on Latin America, 1992.

Becker, David G., Jeff Frieden, Sayre P. Schatz, and Richard Sklar, eds., *Postimperialism: International Capitalism and Development in the Twentieth Century*. Boulder, Colo.: Lynne Rienner, 1987.

Beltrán del Río, Pascal. "El alcalde perredista de Morelia: Pretenden los del PRI que no logremos gobernar." *Proceso* 697 (March 12, 1990), p. 14.

———. "El centro no va a soltar el poder; la población tendrá que rescatarlo: Ernesto Ruffo." *Proceso* 775 (September 9, 1991), pp. 18–23.

———. "El COFIPE, 'Triunfo de México,' dijo Salinas; el control de los elecciones sigue igual." *Proceso* 716 (July 23, 1990), pp. 18–19.

———. "Con Salinas, cuatro años de una conducción política coyuntural y arbitraria." *Proceso* 834 (October 26, 1992), pp. 6–9.

———. "Desarraigado y desconocido en Puebla, Bartlett se beneficia de la imposición." *Proceso* 814 (June 8, 1992), pp. 6–11.

———. "19 días de protesta, que seguirá hasta enero, por fraudes electorales." *Proceso* 787 (December 2, 1991), pp. 27–28.

———. "División de priístas, que se culpan ya de la derrota en el Estado de México." *Proceso* 731 (November 5, 1990), pp. 10–13.

———. "Las elecciones en Michoacán, reedición de las July 1988." *Proceso* 683 (December 4, 1989), p. 11.

———. "En su estudio, el PRI preveía la perdida de 49 municipios del Estado de México ante el PRD." *Proceso* 732 (November 12, 1990), pp. 16–17.

———. "Mil días bastaron a Salinas para machacar a sus opositores de 1988." *Proceso* 773 (August 26, 1991), p. 6.

———. "El PRI de Colosio pierde la linea y se va de la derrota a la concesión." *Proceso* 781 (October 21, 1991), p. 11.

———. "En Saños, unas 10 propuestas de civilidad y democracia," *Proceso* 888 (November 8, 1993), pp. 30–31.

———. "El repudio a candidates de Neme encona su pugna con Colosio." *Proceso* 777 (September 23, 1991), pp. 28–30.

———. "Si al PRI lo quieren modernizar no van a quedar ni sus siglas: Múñoz Ledo." *Proceso* 719 (August 13, 1990), pp. 18–21.

————. "Solidaridad, oxígeno para el PRI, en el rescate de votos." *Proceso* 718 (August 6, 1990), pp. 8–11.

Benjamin, Thomas. "The Leviathan on the Zocalo: Recent Historiography of the Postrevolutionary Mexican State." *Latin American Research Review* 20 (3), 1985, pp. 195–217.

————. "The Mexican Left Since 1968." Paper presented at the annual meeting of the Rocky Mountain Council of Latin American Studies (RMCLAS), Tucson, Arizona, 1984.

Bennett, D., and K. Sharpe. "The State as Banker and Entrepreneur." *Comparative Politics* 12, 1980, pp. 165–169.

Bergsten, C. Fred., "The Threat from the Third World." *Foreign Policy* 11, 1973.

Bialer, Seweryn, ed., *Politics, Society and Nationality: Inside Gorbachev's Russia.* An East-West Forum Publication. Boulder, Colo: Westview Press, 1989.

Bizberg, Ian. "El México neocorporativo." *Nexos* 144 (December 1989), pp. 47–54.

Brachet-Marquez, Viviane. "Explaining Sociopolitical Change in Latin America: The Case of Mexico." *Latin American Research Review* 27 (3), 1992, pp. 91–122.

Brandenburg, Frank. *The Making of Modern Mexico.* Englewood Cliffs, N.J.: Prentice Hall, 1964.

Bratton, Michael. "Beyond the State: Civil Society and Associational Life in Africa." *World Politics* 41, 1989.

Bravo Mena, Luis Felipe. "COPARMEX and Mexican Politics." In Maxfield and Anzaldua, eds., *Government and Private Sector in Contemporary Mexico,* pp. 89–104.

Brown, Archie. "Ideology and Political Culture." In Bialer, ed., *Politics, Society and Nationality: Inside Gorbachev's Russia,* pp. 1–40.

Browne, Harry, Beth Sims, and Tom Barry. *For Richer, for Poorer.* Albuquerque: Resource Center Press 1994.

Buendía Laredo, J., and Zuckermann Behar, "Escenarios." *Nexos* 164 (August 1991), p. 79.

Bunce, Valerie. "The Empire Strikes Back: The Transformation of the Eastern Bloc from a Soviet Asset to a Soviet Liability." *International Organization* 39 (1), 1985, pp. 1–46.

Calvert, Peter. "The Mexican Revolution: Theory or Fact?" *Journal of Latin American Studies* 1 (1), 1969, pp. 51–68.

Camou, Antonio. "Gobernabilidad y democracia." *Nexos* 170 (February 1992), pp. 55–65.

Camp, Roderic Ai. "The Cabinet and the *Técnico* in Mexico and the United States." *Journal of Comparative Administration* 3, 1971, pp. 188–214.

————. *Generals in the Palacio.* New York: Oxford University Press, 1992.

————, ed. *Mexico's Political Stability: The Next Five Years.* Boulder, Colo.: Westview Press, 1986.

————. "Opposition in Mexico City: A Comparison of Leadership." In Gentleman, ed., *Mexican Politics in Transition,* pp. 235–256.

————. "Political Liberalization: The Last Key to Economic Modernization in Mexico?" In Roett, ed., *Political and Economic Liberalization in Mexico: A Critical Juncture?* pp. 17–34.

Cárdenas, Cuauhtémoc. "Misunderstanding Mexico." *Foreign Policy* 78, 1990, pp. 113–130.

Carpizo, Jorge. "The No Re-election Principle in Mexico." *Mexican Forum* 3 (4), 1983.

Carr, Barry. *Mexican Communism, 1968–1983: Eurocommunism in the Americas?* San Diego: Center for U.S.-Mexican Studies, University of California, 1985.

———. "The Left and Its Potential Role in Political Change." In Cornelius et al., eds., *Mexico's Alternative Political Futures*, pp. 361–390.

———. "The PSUM: The Unification Process on the Mexican Left, 1981–1985." In Gentleman, ed., *Mexican Politics in Transition*, pp. 281–304.

Carr, Barry, and Ricardo Anzaldua Montoya, eds., *The Mexican Left, the Popular Movements, and the Politics of Austerity.* San Diego: Center for U.S.-Mexican Studies, University of California, 1987.

Carrasco Licea, Rasalba, and Francisco Hernández y Puente. "El creciente dinamismo de la inversión extranjera." *La Jornada*, May 4, 1992, p. 29.

———. "Nafin: Micros, pequeñas y medianas." *La Jornada*, June 22, 1992, p. 27.

Castañeda, Jorge. "Cartas marcadas." *Proceso* 770 (August 5, 1991), pp. 36–37.

Centeno, Miguel Angel. *Democracy Within Reason: Technocratic Revolution in Mexico.* University Park: Pennsylvania State University Press, 1994.

Chase-Dunn, Christopher. "Socialist States in the Capitalist World Economy." *Social Problems* 27, 1980.

Chávez, Elías. "Cambio con Zedillo." *Proceso* 910 (April 11, 1994), pp. 12–13.

———. "En medio de exaltaciones al Presidente, Genaro Borrego anuncia la 'refundación' del PRI." *Proceso* 811 (May 18, 1992), pp. 7–11.

———. "Este sexenio, la fiebre reformadora de los líderes priístas se diluyó en el elogio a Salinas." *Proceso* 933 (September 19, 1994), p. 15.

———. "Exhorta la corriente crítica a desconocer dirigentes, incluído Colosio, si es necesario." *Proceso* 695 (February 26, 1990), pp. 6–9.

———. "La lista de candidatos del PRI al Senado, reflejo de la urgencia de Zedillo por afianzar alianzas." *Proceso* 913 (May 2, 1994), pp. 34–37.

———. "Michoacán: Cada voto del PRI costo 239,188 pesos; cada voto del PRD costo 6,916 pesos." *Proceso* 821 (July 27, 1992), pp. 22–26.

———. "Muchos aspirantes en Aguascalientes, pero Otto Granados los aventaja 'por más de diez cuerpos'." *Proceso* 799 (February 24, 1992), pp. 22–25.

———. "La reforma del PRI, que debió hacerse antes, deberá hacerse después." *Proceso* 917 (May 30, 1994), pp. 17–20.

———. "Reunión de emergencia del Consejo Político Nacional del PRI." *Proceso* 912 (April 25, 1994), pp. 20–21.

———. "Totalmente dividio, el PRI espera en Nayarit un 'voto de castigo' en su contra." *Proceso* 869 (June 28, 1993), pp. 17–19.

Chávez, Isidrio. "Liquidados el 89 percent de paraestatales que había en 82." *Novedades*, December 21, 1989, p. 23.

Chirot, Daniel. "The East European Revolutions of 1989." In Jack A. Goldstone, ed., *Revolutions: Theoretical, Comparative and Historical Studies.* 2d ed. Ft. Worth, Tex.: Harcourt Brace, 1994, pp. 165–180.

Clark, Cal, and Donna Bahry. "Dependent Development: A Socialist Variant." *International Studies Quarterly* 27, 1983, pp. 271–293.

Coleman, Kenneth M., and Charles L. Davis. "Preemptive Reform and the Mexican Working Class." *Latin American Research Review* 18, 1983, pp. 3–32.

Collier, David, and Ruth Collier, eds., *The New Authoritarianism in Latin America.* Princeton: Princeton University Press, 1979.

Collier, David, and Deborah L. Norden. "Strategic Choice Models of Political Change in Latin America." *Comparative Politics* 24, 1992, pp. 229–243.

Colosio, Luis Donaldo. "Why the PRI Won the 1991 Elections." In Roett, ed., *Political and Economic Liberalization in Mexico*, pp. 155–158.

Consejo Consultivo del Programa Nacional de Solidaridad, ed., *Solidaridad a debate*. Mexico City: El Nacional, 1991.

Contreras, Ariel José. "Estado y sociedad civil en el proceso electoral de 1940." In Martínez Assad, ed., *La sucesión presidencial en Mexico City: 1928–1988*, pp. 105–122.

Coppedge, Michael. "Democracy: You Can't Get There from Here." In Roett, ed., *Political and Economic Liberalization in Mexico*, pp. 127–142.

Cornelius, Wayne A. "Political Liberalization in an Authoritarian Regime: Mexico, 1976–1985." In Gentleman, ed., *Mexican Politics in Transition*, pp. 15–40.

———. "The Politics and Economics of Reforming the Ejido Sector in Mexico." *LASA Forum* 23 (3), 1992, pp. 3–10.

Cornelius, Wayne A., Ann L. Craig, and Jonathan Fox, eds., *Transforming State-Society Relations in Mexico: The National Solidarity Strategy*. San Diego: Center for U.S.-Mexican Studies, University of California, 1994.

Cornelius, Wayne A., Judith Gentleman, and Peter H. Smith. "Overview: The Dynamics of Political Change in Mexico." In Cornelius et al., eds., *Mexico's Alternative Political Futures*, pp. 1–55.

———, eds. *Mexico's Alternative Political Futures*. San Diego: Center for U.S.-Mexican Studies, University of California, 1989.

Correa, Guillermo. "Documenta el centro 'Bartolomé de las Casas' violaciones de derechos humanos del gobierno de Patrocinio." *Proceso* 807 (April 20, 1992), p. 12.

———. "Manchado de sangre, de principio a fin, el sexenio de Salinas de Gortari." *Proceso* 935 (October 3, 1994), pp. 6–12.

———. "El único cambio en el sindicato petrolero, la entrega a la empresa." *Proceso* 729 (October 22, 1990), pp. 16–18.

Correa, Guillermo, and Salvador Corro. "40 percent de la fuerza de trabajo, en tianguis y otros subempleos; 15 percent en el desempleo total." *Proceso* 781 (October 21, 1991), pp. 20–23.

Corro, Salvador. "Ante las siempre toleradas críticas de Fidel Velázquez, ahora Salinas exhibió enojo." *Proceso* 800 (March 2, 1992), pp. 18–19.

"Cosio, hombre de compadres y compromisos, llegó tarde al cargo con el estilo obsoleto." *Proceso* 808 (April 27, 1992), p. 8.

Couffignal, Georges. "La gran debilidad del syndicalismo mexicano." *Revista Mexicana de Sociología* 52 (3), 1990.

Craig, Ann L. "Institutional Context and Popular Strategies." In Foweraker and Craig, eds., *Popular Movements and Political Change in Mexico*, pp. 271–284.

Crespo, José A. "¿Democracia con el PRI?" *Siglo 21,* July 22, 1994, p. 13.

Cronin, Patrick. "Domestic Versus International Influences on State Behavior: Trade Liberalization in Mexico." Paper presented at the Eighteenth Congress of Latin American Studies Association, Atlanta, Georgia, March 10–12, 1994.

Davis, Diane E. "Divided over Democracy: The Embeddedness of State and Class Conflicts in Contemporary Mexico." *Politics and Society* 17 (3), 1989, pp. 247–280.

———. "Failed Democratic Reform in Contemporary Mexico: From Social Movements to the State and Back Again." *Journal of Latin American Studies* 26 (2), 1994, pp. 375–408.

de Buen, Nestor. "Primero de mayo: Recordando a Haymarket Square." *La Jornada Laboral* 2 (15), 1992, pp. 1–2.

"Declaración del consejo nacional del partido acción nacional." *Proceso* 932 (September 12, 1994), pp. 4–5.

de la Garza Toledo, Enrique. "Independent Trade Unionism in Mexico City: Past Developments and Future Perspectives." In Middlebrook, ed., *Unions, Workers and the State in Mexico*, pp. 153–184.

de Vries, Pieter. "PROCAMPO and the Politics of State Intervention: A Case Study of Direct Subsidies Programme." Paper presented at the Eighteenth International Congress of the Latin American Studies Association, Atlanta, Georgia, March 10–12, 1994.

Dietz, Henry. "Electoral Politics in Peru, 1978–1986." *Journal of Interamerican Studies and World Affairs* 28 (4), 1986–1987, pp. 139–163.

Dresser, Denise. "Bringing the Poor Back In." In Cornelius et al., eds., *Transforming State-Society Relations in Mexico*, pp. 143–166.

———. *Neopopulist Solutions to Neoliberal Problems: Mexico's National Solidarity Program*. Current Issues Brief 3. San Diego: Center for U.S.-Mexican Studies, University of California, 1991.

Duncan Baretta, Silvio R., and John Markoff. "Brazil's Abertura: A Transition from What to What?" In James M. Malloy and Mitchell A. Seligson, eds., *Authoritarians and Democrats: Regime Transition in Latin America*. Pittsburgh: University of Pittsburgh Press, 1987, pp. 43–65.

Durand Ponte, Victor Manuel. "Corporativismo obrero y democracia." *Revista Mexicana de Sociología* 52 (3), 1990, pp. 97–110.

Duvall, Raymond D., and John R. Freeman. "The State and Dependent Capitalism." *International Studies Quarterly* 25 (1), 1981.

Eckstein, Susan. "Formal Versus Substantive Democracy: Poor People's Politics in Mexico City." *Mexican Studies/Estudios Mexicanos* 6 (2), 1990, pp. 213–239.

Eisenberg, Ralph. "The Mexican Election of 1952." Ph.D. diss., University of Illinois, 1953.

Electoral Reform in Mexico. Report of the Council of Freely Elected Heads of Government. Atlanta: Carter Center of Emory University, 1993.

Espinoza Valle, Víctor Alejandro. "Reforma del estado y modernización política en México." Paper presented at the Eighteenth International Congress of the Latin American Studies Association, Atlanta, Georgia, March 10–12, 1994.

Evans, Peter B. *Dependent Development: The Alliance of Multinational, State and Local Capital in Brazil*. Princeton: Princeton University Press, 1979.

———. "Transnational Linkages and the Economic Role of the State: An Analysis of Developing and Industrialized Nations in the Post–World War II Period." In Peter B. Evans, D. Rueschemeyer, and Theda Skocpol, eds., *Bringing the State Back In*. New York: Cambridge University Press, 1985, pp. 192–226.

Feinberg, Richard E. "Defunding Latin America: Reverse Transfers by the Multilateral Lending Agencies." *Third World Quarterly* 11 (3), 1989, pp. 71–84.

Finanzas Públicas Estatales y Municipales de México 1979–1988. Mexico City: INEGI, 1991.

Flores Maldonado, Efraín. *¿Cuál será el destino del PRI?* Mexico City: Costa-Amic, 1989.

Foley, Michael W. "Agenda for Mobilization: The Agrarian Question and Popular Mobilization in Contemporary Mexico." *Latin American Research Review* 26 (2), 1991, pp. 39–74.

Foweraker, Joe. "Popular Movements and Political Change in Mexico." In Foweraker and Craig, eds., *Popular Movements and Political Change in Mexico*, pp. 3–20.

———. "Popular Movements and the Transformation of the System." In Cornelius et al., eds., *Mexico's Alternative Political Futures*, pp. 109–130.

Foweraker, Joe, and Ann Criag, eds., *Popular Movements and Political Change in Mexico*. Boulder, Colo.: Lynne Rienner, 1990.

Franco G. S., J. Fernando. "Labor Law and the Labor Movement in Mexico." In Middlebrook, ed., *Unions, Workers and the State in Mexico*, pp. 105–120.

Fregoso Peralta, Gilberto. *Prensa regional y elecciones*. Guadalajara: Universidad de Guadalajara, 1993.

Fregosos Peralta, Gilberto, and Enrique E. Sánchez Ruíz. *Prensa y poder en Guadalajara*. Guadalajara: Universidad de Guadalajara, 1993.

Frieden, Jeffry. "Third World Indebted Industrialization: International Finance and State Capital in Mexico, Brazil, Algeria and South Korea." *International Organization* 35, 1981, pp. 407–431.

Galarza, Gerardo. "Advertencia a Zapata: Como Florencia Salazar, tendrá que irse." *Proceso* 777 (September 23, 1991), pp. 6–11.

———. "El alcalde panista de SLP: Los golpes del gobierno estatal, por abajo." *Proceso* 697 (March 12, 1990), pp. 18–19.

———. "El Presidente rehusa arriesgar su proyecto económico por la democratización: Federico Reyes Heroles." *Proceso* 721 (August 27, 1990), pp. 16–19.

———. "Sacerdotes, empresarios y ciudadanos de San Luis rechazan el supuesto triunfo de Zapata." *Proceso* 775 (September 9, 1991), pp. 14–17.

Garrido, Luis Javier. *El partido de la revolución institucionalizada*. Mexico City: Siglo Veintiuno, 1987.

———. *La ruptura: La corriente democrática del PRI*. Mexico City: Grijalbo, 1993.

Garrido Noguera, Celso. "Relaciones de enduedamiento, grupos económicos y reestructuración capitalista en México." *Economía: Teoría y Práctica* 12, 1988, pp. 23–59.

Garrido Noguera, Celso, and Enrique Quintana López. "Financial Relations and Economic Power in Mexico." In Maxfield and Anzaldua, eds., *Government and Private Sector in Contemporary Mexico*, pp. 105–126.

Garza, Luis Angel. "En Nuevo León, empresarios contra empresarios; ganaron los del PRI." *Proceso* 785 (November 18, 1991), pp. 26–27.

Garza, Luis Angel, and Fernando Ortega Pizarro. "Monterrey tiene a la mitad de los bancos y el mayor consumo de tortibonos." *Proceso* 812 (May 25, 1992), pp. 12–15.

Gentleman, Judith, ed., *Mexican Politics in Transition*. Boulder, Colo.: Westview Press (Special Studies on Latin America and the Caribbean), 1987.

———. "Mexico After the Oil Boom." In Gentleman, ed., *Mexican Politics in Transition*, pp. 41–62.

Gentleman, Judith, and Voytek Zubek. "Economic Crisis and the Movement Toward Pluralism in Poland and Mexico." *Political Science Quarterly*, 109 (2) 1994: (March 1990): 335–360.

Gil, Carlos B., ed., *Hope and Frustration: Interviews with Leaders of Mexico's Political Opposition*. Wilmington, Del.: Scholarly Resources, 1992.

Gill, Stephen R., and David Law. "Global Hegemony and the Structural Power of Capital." *International Studies Quarterly* 33, 1989, pp. 475–499.

Gilpin, Robert. "Three Models of the Future." *International Organization* 29, 1975, pp. 37–60.

Golden, Tim. "Salinas, at Successor's Request, Leaves for Virtual Exile in U.S." *New York Times* March 13, 1995, p. 1A.

Gómez Tagle, Silvia. "Democracy and Power in Mexico: The Meaning of Conflict in the 1979, 1982 and 1985 Federal Elections." In Gentleman, ed., *Mexican Politics in Transition*, pp. 153–180.

———. "La violencia y la normatividad en las elecciones mexicanas." Paper presented at the Sixteenth Congress of the Latin American Studies Association, Washington, D.C., 1991.

Gonick, Lev S., and Robert M. Roth. "The Structural Location of Third World States Within the International Division of Labor." *Comparative Political Studies* 23, 1990, pp. 355–380.

González, Sergio, and Stephen D. Morris. "Los aspectos políticos de las explosiones del 22 April 1992 en Guadalajara." Paper presented at the Eighteenth International Congress of the Latin American Studies Association, Atlanta, Georgia, March 10–12, 1994.

González Pérez, Lourdes. "De 49 mil 776 mdd, la captación sexenal de capital extranjero." *El Financiero*, August 18, 1994, p. 8.

Gourevitch, Peter. *Politics in Hard Times: Comparative Responses to International Economic Crises*. Ithaca and London: Cornell University Press, 1986.

Granados Chapa, Miguel Angel. *Nava Sí, Zapata No: La hora de San Luis Potosí*. Mexico City: Grijalbo, 1992.

Grayson, George W., ed., *Prospects for Mexico*. Washington, D.C.: Center for the Study of Foreign Affairs, 1990.

———. *The Church in Contemporary Mexico*. Washington, D.C.: Center for Strategic and International Studies, 1992.

Grindle, Merliee S. *State and Countryside: Development Policy and Agrarian Politics in Latin America*. Baltimore: Johns Hopkins University Press, 1986.

Guillén López, Tonatiuh. "Elecciones de 1989 en Baja California." In Alonso and Gómez Tagle, eds., *Insurgencia democrática: Las elecciones locales*, pp. 177–210.

———. "The Social Bases of the PRI." In Cornelius et al., eds., *Mexico's Alternative Political Futures*, pp. 243–264.

Guzmán, Armando. "Nemé Castillo dió 'madruguete' y violó los acuerdos avaldos por Gobernación." *Proceso* 794 (January 20, 1992), p. 31.

Guzmán, Armando, and Ignacio Ramírez. "Deserciones y protestas de priístas de Tabasco, por imposición de candidatos." *Proceso* 781 (October 1, 1991), pp. 8–9.

Haggard, Stephan. "Newly Industrializing Countries in the International System." *World Politics* 33, 1986, pp. 343–370.

"Hank quiere ser el 'padrino': Múñoz Ledo; Signo adverso a la democracia: Castillo Peraza; No es ajeno Salinas: Cuauhtémoc; Que renuncie Hank: Diego Fernández." *Proceso* 912 (April 25, 1994), pp. 14–19.

Hansen, Roger D. *The Politics of Mexican Development*. Baltimore: Johns Hopkins University Press, 1971.

———. "PRI Politics in the 1970s: Crisis or Continuity?" In James W. Wilkie, Michael C. Meyer, and Edna Monzón de Wilkie, eds., *Contemporary Mexico: Papers of the IV International Congress of Mexican History*. Berkeley: University of California Press, 1976, pp. 389–401.

Head, Ivan L. "South-North Dangers." In Steven L. Spiegel, ed., *At Issue: Politics in the World Arena*. 6th ed. New York: St. Martin's Press, 1991.

Hellman, Judith Adler. "Continuity and Change in Mexico." *Latin American Research Review* 23 (2), 1988, pp. 133–156.

Hernández Rodríguez, Rogelio. "La reforma interna y los conflictos en el PRI." *Foro Internacional* 32 (2), 1991, pp. 222–249.

Hinojosa, José. "Televisa priísta." *Proceso* 770 (August 5, 1991), pp. 34–35.

Hirschman, Albert O. *Journeys Toward Progress: Studies of Economic Policymaking in Latin America*. New York: Twentieth Century Fund, 1963.

Howard, Georgina. "Sorpresivo crecimiento reporta SHCP al primer semestre." *El Financiero*, August 17, 1994, p. 24.

Huntington, Samuel P. *Political Order in Changing Societies.* Hartford, Conn.: Yale University Press, 1968.

Ibarra, Manuel, and Salvador Corro. "El PRONASOL, medio de liquidación del federalismo." *Proceso* 732 (November 12, 1990), pp. 11–13.

Iliff, Laurence. "Zedillo in free fall." *Mexico Insight* January 22, 1995, p. 7.

INEGI. *Finanzas Públicas Estatales y Municipales de México 1979–1988.* Mexico City: Instituto Nacional de Estadística, Geographía e Informática, 1991.

Inter-American Development Bank. *Economic and Social Progress in Latin America.* 1990 Report. Washington, D.C., 1990.

"Jalisco ante las urnas." *Siglo 21,* Special Supplement, August 1994.

Jáquez, Antonio. "Comerciantes de la laguna piden que haya reelección presidencial." *Proceso* 772 (August 19, 1991), pp. 10–11.

Johnson, Kenneth F. *Mexican Democracy: A Critical View.* Boston: Allyn and Bacon, 1971.

Kaiser, Robert G. "The End of the Soviet Empire: Failure on an Historic Scale." *Washington Post National Weekly Edition,* January, Nos. 1–7, 1990, pp. 23–24.

Karl, Terry Lynn. "Dilemmas of Democratization in Latin America." *Comparative Politics* 22, 1990, pp. 1–21.

Karl, Terry Lynn, and Philippe C. Schmitter. "Modos de transición en América latina, Europa del Sur y Europa del Este." *RICS* 128 (June) 1991, pp. 283–300.

Katzenstein, Peter. *Between Power and Plenty: Foreign Economic Policies of Advanced Industrial States.* Madison: University of Wisconsin Press, 1978.

Kis, Janos. "Turning Point in Hungary." *Dissent,* Spring 1989, pp. 235–241.

Klesner, Joséph L. "Changing Patterns of Electoral Participation and Official Party Support in Mexico." In Gentleman, ed., *Mexican Politics in Transition,* pp. 95–152.

———. "Modernization, Economic Crisis, and Electoral Alignment in Mexico." *Mexican Studies/Estudios Mexicanos* 9 (2), 1993: 187–224.

———. "Party System Expansion and Electoral Mobilization in Mexico." Paper presented at the Twelfth Congress of the Latin American Studies Association, Albuquerque, New Mexico, 1985.

———. "Realignment or Dealignment? Consequences of Economic Crisis and Economic Restructuring for the Mexican Party System." Paper presented at the workshop Las Dimensiones Políticas del Ajuste Estructural en México, Mexico City, June 1992.

Knight, Alan. "Historical Continuities in Social Movements." In Foweraker and Craig, eds., *Popular Movements,* pp. 78–102.

———. "Solidarity: Historical Continuities and Contemporary Implications." Unpublished manuscript. Rpt in Cornelius et al., eds., *Transforming State-Society Relations in Mexico City: The National Solidarity Strategy,* pp. 29–46.

Korbonski, Adrezej. "The Politics of Economic Reform in Eastern Europe: The Last Thirty Years." *Soviet Studies* 41, 1989, pp. 1–19.

Koslow, Lawrence E., and Stephen P. Mumme. "The Evolution of the Mexican Political System: A Paradigmatic Analysis." In Koslow and Mumme, eds., *The Future of Mexico.* Tempe: Arizona State University Center for Latin American Studies, 1981, pp. 47–98.

Krasner, Stephen D. "Sovereignty: An Institutional Perspective." *Comparative Political Studies* 21, 1988, pp. 66–94.

———. *Structural Conflict: The Third World Against Global Liberalism.* Berkeley: University of California Press, 1985.

Krueger, A. O. *Liberalization Attempts and Consequences.* Cambridge, Mass: Ballinger, 1978.

Lake, David A. "Power and the Third World: Toward a Realist Political Economy of North-South Relations." *International Studies Quarterly* 31, 1987, pp. 217–234.

"La lista de candidatos del PRI al Senado, reflejo de la urgencia de Zedillo por afianzar alianzas." *Proceso* 913 (May 2, 1994), pp. 34–37.

Lapidus, Gail W. "State and Society: Toward the Emergence of Civil Society in the Soviet Union." In Bialer, ed., *Politics, Society and Nationality*, pp. 121–148.

Levy, Daniel, and Gabriel Szekely. *Mexico: Paradoxes of Stability and Change.* Boulder, Colo.: Westview Press, 1983.

Loaeza, Soledad. *Clases medias y política en México.* Mexico City: El Colegio de México, 1988.

———. "The Emergence and Legitimization of the Modern Right, 1970–1988." In Cornelius et al., eds., *Mexico's Alternative Political Futures*, pp. 351–365.

———. "Los partidos y el cambio político." *Nexos* 174 (June 1992), pp. 35–41.

Loaeza, Soledad, and Maria Luisa Tarres. "Middle-Class Associations and Electoral Opposition." In Foweraker and Craig, eds., *Popular Movements*, pp. 137–149.

Loret de Mola, Rafael. *Las entrañas del poder: Secretos de campaña.* Mexico City: Grijalbo, 1991.

Loveman, Brian. "'Protected Democracies' and Military Guardianship: Political Transitions in Latin America, 1979–1993." Paper presented at the Eighteenth International Congress of the Latin American Studies Association, Atlanta, Georgia, March 10–12, 1994.

Loyo, Aurora. "La movilización syndical, factor decisivo en la elección de López Mateos." In Martínez Assad, ed., *La Sucesión presidencial*, pp. 171–186.

Luna, Matilde, Ricardo Tirado, and Francisco Valdés. "Businessmen and Politics in Mexico: 1982–1986." In Maxfield and Anzaldua, eds., *Government and Private Sector*, pp. 13–43.

Lustig, Nora. *Mexico: The Remaking of an Economy.* Washington, D.C.: Brookings Institution, 1992.

———. "Solidarity as a Strategy of Poverty Alleviation." In Cornelius et al., eds., *Transforming State-Society Relations in Mexico*, pp. 79–96.

MacEwan, Arthur. "Review of *Transitions from Authoritarian Rule.*" *Latin American Perspectives* 58 (3), 1988.

MacEwan, Arthur, and William K. Tabb. *Instability and Change in the World Economy.* New York: Monthly Review Press, 1989.

MacLachlan, Colin M., and William H. Beezley. *El Gran Pueblo: A History of Greater Mexico.* Englewood Cliffs, N.J.: Prentice Hall, 1994.

Macotela, Catherine. "El PRI y la elección del primer presidente civil." In Martínez Assad, ed., *La sucesión presidencial en Mexico: 1928–1988*, pp. 123–136.

Martínez Assad, Carlos, ed., *La sucesión presidencial en Mexico: 1928–1988.* 2d ed. Mexico City: Nueva Imagen, 1992.

Marvan, Ignacio, and Aurelio Cuevas. "El movimiento de damnificados en Tlatelolco (Septiembre de 1985–marzo de 1986)." *Revista Mexicana de Sociología* 4, 1987.

Mastanduno, Michael, David A. Lake, and John Ikenberry. "Toward a Realist Theory of State Action." *International Studies Quarterly* 33, 1989, pp. 466–472.

Maxfield, Sylvia. "The International Political Economy of Bank Nationalization: Mexico in Comparative Perspective." *Latin American Research Review* 27 (1), 1992, pp. 75–104.

Maxfield, Sylvia, and Ricardo Anzaldua, eds. *Government and Private Sector in Contemporary Mexico.* Monograph Series 20. San Diego: Center for U.S.-Mexican Studies, University of California, 1987.

Maza, Enrique. "'El Tratado de Libre Comercio es el único medio para satisfacer a los 82 millones de mexicanos." *Proceso* 770, (August 5, 1991), pp. 22–24.

Medina, Luis. *Del cardenismo al avilacamachismo: Historia de la Revolución Mexicana.* Mexico City: El Colegio de México, 1979.

Medina Núñez, Ignacio. "Fuerzas políticas y procesos electorales." In *Jalisco desde la Revolución: Historia política, 1940–1975.* Vol. 9. Gobierno del Estado de Jalisco y Universidad de Guadalajara, 1987.

Meno Brito, Bernardino. *EL PRUN, Almazán y el desastre final.* Mexico City: Botas, 1941.

Meyer, Lorenzo. "Democratization of the PRI: Mission Impossible." In Cornelius et al., eds., *Mexico's Alternative Political Futures,* pp. 325–350.

———. "La encrucijada." In *Historia General de México.* Vol. 2, 3d ed. Mexico City: El Colegio de México, 1981.

———. *La segunda muerte de la Revolución Mexicana.* Mexico City: Cal y Arena, 1992.

Middlebrook, Kevin J. "Dilemmas of Change in Mexican Politics." *World Politics* 41 (1), 1988, pp. 120–141.

———. *Political Liberalization in an Authoritarian Regime: The Case of Mexico.* San Diego: Center for U.S.-Mexican Studies, University of California, 1985.

———. "The Sounds of Silence: Organized Labour's Response to Economic Crisis in Mexico." *Journal of Latin American Studies* 21 (2) 1989, pp. 195–220.

———, ed. *Unions, Workers and the State in Mexico.* San Diego: Center for U.S.-Mexican Studies, University of California, 1991.

Molinar Horcasitas, Juán. "The Future of the Electoral System." In Cornelius et al., eds., *Mexico's Alternative Political Futures,* pp. 265–290.

———. "The 1985 Federal Elections in Mexico: The Product of a System." In Alvarado, ed., *Electoral Patterns and Perspectives in Mexico,* pp. 17–32.

———. *El tiempo de la legitimidad: Elecciones, autoritarismo y democracia en México.* Mexico City: Cal y Arena, 1991.

Molinar Horcasitas, Juan, and Jeffrey A. Weldon. "Electoral Determinants and Consequences of National Solidarity." In Cornelius et. al., eds., *Transforming State-Society Relations in Mexico,* pp. 123–142.

Monge, Raúl. "Balance de Alianza Civica." *Proceso* 933 (September 19, 1994), pp. 8–9.

———. "Observadores, periodistas, ciudadanos y partidos descubren poco a poco el rostro sucio de las elecciones." *Proceso* 931 (September 5, 1994), pp. 20–25.

———. "Testimonio de observadores internacionales sobre los abusos electorales en Oaxaca." *Proceso* 933 (September 19, 1994), p. 7.

———. "Tiempo, recursos, y táctica para recuperar el Distrito Federal." *Proceso* 770 (August 5, 1991), pp. 6–9.

Monsivais, Carlos. "Crónica de una convención (que no lo fué tanto) y de un acontecimiento muy significativo." *Proceso* 928 (August 15, 1994), pp. 24–31.

Montaño, Cristina, and Daniel M. Lund. "Erosion of PRI Support and Credibility: *Los Angeles Times* Mexico Poll." *Interamerican Public Opinion Report,* January 1990, p. 3.

Morones Servín, César Augusto. "Encuesta de opinión preelectoral en la zona metropolitana de Guadalajara." *Carta Económica Regional* 20, 1991, pp. 23–24.

Morones Servín, César Augusto, and Stephen D. Morris. "Análisis de resultados de las encuestas electorales en la zona metropolitana de Guadalajara." *Carta Económica Regional* 24, 1992, pp. 3–7.

Morris, Stephen D. *Corruption and Politics in Contemporary Mexico.* Tuscaloosa: University of Alabama Press, 1991.

————. "Reestructuración económica y la crisis del autoritarismo: Un enfoque global." In Carlos Barba Solano, José Luis Barros Horcasitas, and Javier Hurtado, eds., *Transiciones a la democracia en Europa y América Latina.* Universidad de Guadalajara, Miguel Angel Porrúa, and FLASCO, 1992, pp. 75–99.

————. "Regime Cycles in Latin America." *Review of Latin American Studies* 2 (1–2), 1989, pp. 139–158.

Munck, Gerardo L. "Democratic Transitions in Comparative Perspective." *Comparative Politics* 26, 1994, pp. 355–375.

Needler, Martin C. *Politics and Society in Mexico.* Albuquerque: University of New Mexico Press, 1971.

Nevaer, L. "Mexico's Heartland Hit by Growing Political Turmoil." *Times of the Americas,* April 18–May 2, 1990, p. 35.

Newell, Robert G., and Luis Rubio F. *Mexico's Dilemma: The Political Origins of Economic Crisis.* Boulder, Colo.: Westview Press, 1984.

"New York Times Mexican Poll." *New York Times.* Memeo, 1986.

O'Donnell, Guillermo. *Modernization and Bureaucratic-Authoritarianism: Studies in South American Politics.* Berkeley: University of California Press, 1973.

O'Donnell, Guillermo, and Philip C. Schmitter. *Transitions from Authoritarian Rule: Tentative Conclusions About Uncertain Democracies.* Baltimore: Johns Hopkins University Press, 1986.

Oksenberg, Michael, and Bruce Dickson. "The Origins, Processes and Outcomes of Great Political Reform: A Framework of Analysis." In Dankart A. Rustow and Kenneth Paul Erickson, eds., *Comparative Political Dynamics: Global Research Perspectives.* New York: Harper Collins, 1991, pp. 235–261.

Olson, Mancur. *The Rise and Decline of Nations: Economic Growth, Stagflation and Social Rigidities.* New Haven: Yale University Press, 1982.

"The Opposition: Old Guard 'Dinosaurs' Find Something to Roar About," *Washington Post* January 8, 1995, p. 25.

Ortega, Max. *Estado y movimiento ferrocarrilero 1958–1959.* Mexico City: Ediciones Quinto Sol, 1988.

Ortega, Max, and Ana Alicia Solís de Alba. *Mexico: Estado y sindicatos, 1983–1988.* Mexico City: Mesa Obrero-Sindical MCCLP, 1992.

Ortega Pizarro, Fernando. "Germán Carcoba y Roberto Hernández adelantan públicamente su voto por Zedillo." *Proceso* 924 (July 18, 1994), pp. 37–39.

————. "Inestable, especulativa, peligrosa, La Bolsa de Valores se ha convertido en centro y sosten de la economía." *Proceso* 808 (April 27, 1992), pp. 16–19.

————. "Propuesta de una ley que iguale al fisco a los causantes." *Proceso* 807 (April 20, 1992), pp. 6–9.

————. "Todo en manos privados, por ley, exige la Coparmex." *Proceso* 781 (October 21, 1991), pp. 16–19.

Ortiz Pinchetti, Francisco. "Pruebas del fraude en gestión, aportadas por el propio gobernador." *Proceso* 660 (July 3, 1989), pp. 24–27.

————. "Salinas, en reunión privada con Gutierrez Barrios y Colosio, decidió la caida de Aguirre." *Proceso* 774 (September 2, 1991), pp. 6–11.

————. "La solución para el PRI sería el suicidio pacífico: Enrique Krauze." *Proceso* 721 (August 27, 1990), pp. 13–16.

Ortiz Pinchetti, José Agustín. *La democracia que viene: Ejercicios de imaginación política.* Mexico City: Grijalbo, 1990.

Ott, Mack. "Is America Being Sold Out?" In Jeffry A. Frieden and David A. Lake, eds., *International Political Economy: Perspectives on Global Power and Wealth*. 2d ed. New York: St. Martin's Press, 1991, pp. 220–229.

Pacheco Méndez, Guadalupe. "Voter Abstentionism." In Grayson, ed., *Prospects for Mexico*, pp. 63–74.

Padgett, Vincent L. *The Mexican Political System*. Boston: Houghton Mifflin, 1961.

Palacios, Juán José. *La política regional en México, 1970–1982*. Guadalajara: Universidad de Guadalajara, 1989.

Paré, Luisa. "The Challenges of Rural Democratization in Mexico." *Development Studies* 26 (4), 1990, pp. 79–96.

Pastor, Manuel, Jr. "Latin America, the Debt Crisis and the International Monetary Fund." *Latin American Perspectives* 16, pp. 79–110.

Pastor, Robert. "Post-Revolutionary Mexico: The Salinas Opening." *Journal of Interamerican Studies and World Affairs* 32 (3), 1990, pp. 1–24.

Pellicer, Olga. "La oposición electoral en México, el caso del henriquismo." *Foro Internacional* 17, 1977.

Perey, Allison. "The Revolutionary Potential of Mexico in the 1980s." *Journal of International Affairs* 40 (2), 1987, pp. 373–385.

Pereyra, Carlos. "Estado y movimiento obrero." *Cuadernos Políticos* 28, 1981, pp. 35–42. Rpt. in vol. 54/55, 1988, pp. 61–68.

———. "México: Los límites del reformismo." *Cuadernos Políticos* 1, 1974, pp. 52–65. Rpt. in vol. 54/55, 1988, pp. 31–44.

Peschard, Jacqueline. "PRI: Los desafíos de la recuperación." *Cuaderno de Nexos* 43 (January 1992), pp. i–iii.

Pfister, Ulrich, and Christian Suter. "International Financial Relations as Part of the World-System." *International Studies Quarterly* 31 (3), 1987, pp. 239–272.

Philip, George. *The Presidency in Mexican Politics*. New York: St. Martin's Press, 1992.

Phillips, Paul. "The Debt Crisis and Change in Eastern Europe." *Monthly Review* 41 (9), 1990.

Poitras, Guy, and Raymond Robinson, "The Politics of NAFTA in Mexico." *Journal of Interamerican Studies and World Affairs* 36 (1), 1994, pp. 1–35.

PRD: 1989 informe de la situación nacional. Mexico City, 1989.

Presidencia de la República. *Las razones y las obras. Gobierno de Miguel de la Madrid. Crónica del sexenio 1982–1988, Quinto Año*. Fondo de Cultura Económica, 1987.

Preusch, Debra, and Beth Sims, "Sobre el terreno de suelo extranjero: Los programas del gobierno estadounidense en México." *Carta Económica Regional* 33, 1993, pp. 9–46.

Przeworski, Adam. *Democracy and the Market: Political and Economic Reforms in Eastern Europe and Latin America*. Cambridge: Cambridge University Press, 1991.

Purcell, Susan K. *The Mexican Profit-Sharing Decision: Politics in an Authoritarian Regime*. Berkeley: University of California Press, 1975.

Purcell, Susan K., and John F. H. Purcell. "The Nature of the Mexican State." Washington, D.C.: The Wilson Center, Working Papers No. 1, 1977.

Pye, Lucian. "Political Science and the Crisis of Authoritarianism." *American Political Science Review* 84, 1990, pp. 3–20.

Ramírez de la O., Rogelio. "The Mexican Crisis: A Private Sector Perspective." In Grayson, ed., *Prospects for Mexico*, pp. 173–176.

Ramírez Saiz, Juán Manuel, and Jorge Regalado Santillán. "Guadalajara: La respuesta social a los desastres." *Ciudades* 17, 1993, pp. 9–13.

Reding, Andrew. "Las elecciones en Nuevo León: ¿Parteaguas o excepción?" *Proceso* 770 (August 5, 1991), pp. 16–17.

Reyes del Campillo, Juán. "Candidatos: Hacia una nueva Cámara." *Nexos* 164 (August 1991), pp. 56–59.

Reyes Heroles, Federico. *El poder: La democracia difícil*. Mexico City: Grijalbo, 1991.

Reynolds, Clark W. "Power, Value and Distribution in the NAFTA." In Roett, ed., *Political and Economic Liberalization in Mexico: A Critical Juncture?* pp. 69–94.

Reynoso, Víctor Manuel. "Sonora: Tres piezas para armar." *Cuadernos de Nexos* 40 (October 1991), pp. vii–viii.

Riding, Alan. *Distant Neighbors: A Portrait of the Mexicans*. Rpt. New York: Vintage Books, 1984.

Rivera Velázquez, Jaime. "Comentario a una encuesta." *Cuaderno de Nexos* 48 (June 1992), pp. i, iii–iv.

Robles, Manuel. "Trabajadores de TAMSA torturados, presos y con una deuda de miles de millones." *Proceso* 718 (August 6, 1990), pp. 22–25.

Rodríguez, Victoria E., and Peter M. Ward. *Policymaking, Politics, and Urban Governance in Chihuahua*. U.S.-Mexican Policy Studies Program, Policy Report No. 3, University of Texas at Austin, 1992.

Rodríguez Araujo, Octavio. "La disidencia política organizada del henriquismo y la imposición de Ruiz Cortines." In Martínez Assad, ed., *La sucesión presidencial*, pp. 137–170.

———. "En la hipótesis de la ingeniería electoral." *Este País* 5 (August), 1991, pp. 6–9.

———. "El henriquismo: Ultima disidencia organizada en México." *Estudios Políticos* 1 (3–4).

Rodríguez Castañeda, Rafael. "Atrás de las declaraciones de Zedillo, la línea de intolerancia que está dominando en el PRI: Manuel Camacho." *Proceso* 920 (June 20, 1994), pp. 7–9.

Rodríguez Reyna, José Ignacio. "Nuevo empresariado: La política como inversión." *Este País* 10 (January), 1992, pp. 2–8.

Roett, Riordan. "At the Crossroads: Liberalization in Mexico." In Roett, ed., *Political and Economic Liberalization in Mexico: A Critical Juncture?* pp. 1–16.

———, ed. *Political and Economic Liberalization in Mexico: A Critical Juncture?* Boulder, Colo.: Lynne Rienner, 1993.

Roskin, Michael G. *The Rebirth of East Europe*. Englewood Cliffs, N.J.: Prentice Hall, 1991.

Ross, Stanley R., ed., *Is the Mexican Revolution Dead?* New York: Knopf, 1966.

Rother, Larry. "Mexican Opposition Finding Unity Elusive." *New York Times*, October 22, 1988, p. 2

Rothgeb, John M., Jr. "Compensation or Opportunity: The Effects of International Recessions Upon Direct Foreign Investment and Growth in Third World States, 1970–1978." *International Studies Quarterly* 30 (2), 1986.

Rubin, Jeffrey W. "State Policies, Leftist Oppositions, and Municipal Elections: The Case of the COCEI in Juchitán." In Alvarado, ed., *Electoral Patterns and Perspectives in Mexico*, pp. 127–160.

Rubio, Luis. "La transición administrada." *Nexos* 174 (June 1992), pp. 43–47.

Russell, Philip L. *Mexico Under Salinas*. Austin, Tex.: Mexico Resource Center, 1994.

Salinas de Gortari, Carlos. "Reformando al Estado." *Nexos* 148 (April 1990), pp. 27–32.

Sánchez Susarrey, Jaime. *El debate político e intelectual en México: Desde la represión de 1968 hasta nuestros días de Encuentros y Coloquios*. Mexico City: Grijalbo, 1993.

———. *La transición incierta*. Mexico City: Vuelta, 1991.

Schneider, Ben Ross. "Partly for Sale: Privatization and State Strength in Brazil and Mexico." *Journal of Interamerican Studies and World Affairs* 30, 1988–1989, pp. 89–116.

Sheahan, John. *Conflict and Change in Mexico's Economic Strategy: Implications for Mexico and for Latin America*. Monograph Series, 34. San Diego: Center for U.S.-Mexican Studies, University of California, 1991.

Sherman, Howard J. "The Second Soviet Revolution or the Transition from Statism to Socialism." *Monthly Review* 10, 1990, pp. 14–22.

Skocpol, Theda. *State and Social Revolution: A Comparative Analysis of France, Russia and China*. Cambridge: Cambridge University Press, 1978.

Smith, Peter H. *Labyrinths of Power: Political Recruitment in Twentieth Century Mexico*. Princeton: Princeton University Press, 1979.

Snider, Lewis W. "Political Strength, Economic Structure and the Debt Servicing Potential of Developing Countries." *Comparative Political Studies* 20 (4), 1988, pp. 455–487.

Sodi de la Tijera, Demetrio. "¿Por qué ganó el PRI? *La Jornada,* August 23, 1991, p. 8.

Spalding, Rose. "State Power and Its Limits: Corporatism in Mexico." *Comparative Political Studies* 14, 1981, pp. 139–161.

Stepan, Alfred., *The State and Society: Peru in Comparative Perspective*. Princeton: Princeton University Press, 1978.

Story, Dale. *Industry, the State and Public Policy in Mexico*. Austin: University of Texas Press, 1986.

———. *The Mexican Ruling Party: Stability and Authority*. New York: Praeger, 1986.

Tamayo, Jaime. "Neoliberalism Encounters Neocardenismo." In Foweraker and Craig, eds., *Popular Movements and Political Change in Mexico*, pp. 121–136.

Teichman, Judith A. *Policymaking in Mexico: From Boom to Crisis*. Boston: Allen and Unwin, 1988.

Tocqueville, Alexis de. *The Old Regime and the French Revolution*. Translated by Stuart Gilbert. Garden City, N.Y.: Doubleday Anchor Books, 1955.

Topete, Jesús. *Terror en el Riel*. Mexico City: Cosmonauta, 1961.

Trimberger, Ellen Kay. *Revolution from Above: Military Bureaucrats and Development in Japan, Turkey, Egypt and Peru*. New Brunswick, N.J.: Transaction Books, 1978.

Turner, Brian. "Ruling Party Survival in the Breakdown of Single Part Regimes: A Framework for Analysis." Paper presented at the Seventy-first Meeting of the Southwestern Social Science Association, New Orleans, March 17–20, 1993.

Vargas, Pablo E. "La insurgencia en las elecciones municipales de 1984 y 1987 en el Estado de Hidalgo." In Alonso and Gómez Tagle., eds., *Insurgencia democrática: Las elecciones locales*, pp. 47–62.

Vera, Rodrigo. "Caciques del PRI expulsan a familias chamulas de Chiapas." *Proceso* 807 (April 20, 1992), pp. 10–14.

"Voters in Jalisco Spurn Ruling Party," *Houston Chronicle* February 14, 1995, p. 1A.

Ward, Peter M. "Social Welfare Policy and Political Opening in Mexico." In Cornelius et al., eds., *Transforming State-Society Relations in Mexico: The National Solidarity Strategy*, pp. 47–62.

Watson, Sam. "Perestroika, 1985–1991: Gorbachev's Response to International, State and Societal Stimuli." Unpublished.

Whitehead, Laurence. "Mexico's Economic Prospects: Implications for State-Labor Relations." In Middlebrook, ed., *Unions, Workers and the State in Mexico*, pp. 57–84.

———. "Why Mexico Is Ungovernable—Almost." Working Paper No. 54. Washington, D.C.: Wilson Center, 1979.

Wiarda, Howard J. "Mexico: The Unraveling of a Corporatist Regime?" *Journal of Interamerican Studies and World Affairs* 30 (4), 1988–1989, pp. 1–28.

Wolff, Michael. "Zedillo off to a flying Start" *Mexico Insight* January 8, 1995, pp. 20–23.

World Bank. *World Development Report*. 1987, 1988, 1990. Washington, D.C.: World Bank.

Wyman, Donald, ed. *Mexico's Economic Crisis: Challenges and Opportunities*. San Diego: Center for U.S.-Mexican Studies, University of California, 1983.

Zamora, Gerardo. "La política laboral del estado Mexicano." *Revista Mexicana de Sociología* 52 (3), 1990, pp. 111–138.

Zermeño, Sergio. *México: Una democracia utópica: El movimiento estudiantil del 68*. Mexico City: Siglo Veintiuno, 1978.

Zwick, Peter. "The Perestroika of Soviet Studies." *PS* 24 (30), 1991, pp. 461–467.

Index

About the Book

Do political reforms unleash the forces of fundamental change? Or do they alleviate the pressures for change? Posing these questions, Morris explores the historical ability of Mexico's one-party-dominant, authoritarian regime to weather frequent periods of political and economic crisis, as well as its potential for surviving into the coming century.

Part 1 of the book traces Mexico's contemporary political crisis and the efforts of Presidents Miguel de la Madrid (1982–1988) and Carlos Salinas (1988–1994) to "change the system to save it."

Part 2 then provides three complementary comparative approaches: regional, historical, and cross-national. The regional perspective looks at reformism in Mexico at the state level. The historical perspective compares the periods of crisis/reform through the 1990s. And the cross-national perspective considers how the most recent crisis resulted from changing global conditions that challenged authoritarian regimes throughout the world—and why, in contrast to other countries, Mexico successfully adapted to and overcame these obstacles.

STEPHEN D. MORRIS is assistant professor of political science and director of international studies at the University of South Alabama. He is author of *Corruption and Politics in Contemporary Mexico.*